A father dies unexpectedly an ....s only daughter. Another woman lands a contract to write a completely unconventional Baja California guidebook. But to do it, she needs an RV and three women to travel with her for a month.

Meet Dana—adventure-starved executive chef; Holly—bossy ecotour guide and author; Camille—outspoken deejay and songwriter; and Barb—straight-laced businesswoman with a deeply-rooted fear of dirt.

This unlikely foursome invites you to travel the Baja Peninsula with them. By the time you've finished, you'll know them better than you know most of your real-life friends. You'll be chomping at the bit to take this trip yourself and you'll have the knowledge to do it too....

Set against a backdrop replete with history, scenery, culture and adventure, *Cartwheels in the Sand* is touching, revealing, knee-slapping and engrossing. It's about coming to terms with life at midlife—a true renaissance journey of the soul.

Ann Hazard is a third generation Baja Aficionada. She began traveling the peninsula with her family when she was a child, flying into remote places in old World War II cargo planes and landing on dirt roads. She's camped on deserted beaches and in lush palm oases where her family was the only group of gringos for miles around. And of course, she's traveled Mex 1 and spent time in all the places her characters visit in this novel. A graduate of U.S. International University, Ann lives in Solana Beach, CA with her children, Gayle and Derek and an assortment of pets. She shares a weekend getaway with her sister, Nina and brother-in-law, John in La Bufadora—just a few miles south of Ensenada in Northern Baja.

CARTWHEELS IN THE SAND —
Baja California, Four Women and a Motor Home

A Novel by Ann Hazard
Author of COOKING WITH BAJA MAGIC

Renegade Enterprises
Solana Beach, CA
1999

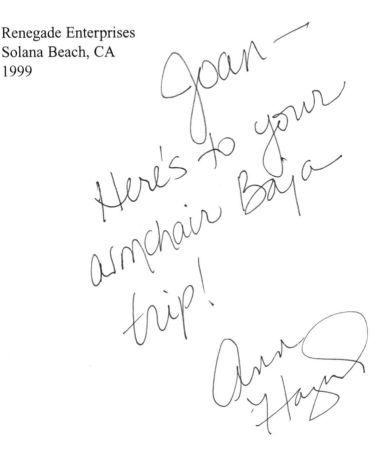

Joan —
Here's to your
armchair Baja
trip!

Ann
Hazard

Library of Congress Cataloguing in Publication Data

Hazard, Ann
Cartwheels in the Sand

A Renegade Enterprises Book
I. Title: Cartwheels in the Sand
        ISBN 0-9653223-2-7
1. Fiction/Literature
2. Travel & Travel Guides
3. Women's Issues

Front Cover Illustration by Valerie Dawn Smith
Book Design by Terri Zumstein
Chapter Illustrations by Mary Damigos
Edited by Nina Hazard Baldwin

See inside last page for ordering information

Other books by Ann Hazard:
Cooking With Baja Magic—Mouth–Watering Meals from the Kitchens and Campfires of Baja

This is a work of fiction. All characters, with the exception of those named in Appendix IV, are fictional. Any resemblances to persons, living or dead, is purely coincidental.

Dedication
This book is dedicated to Nina Hazard Baldwin,
my sister, my best friend
and my unfailing, brilliant business partner.

Acknowledgments

My sincerest thanks go to those closest to me who helped make this dream into a reality: my sister—of course—and her husband, John Baldwin; *mi amor,* Terry Hauswirth; my infinitely patient children, Gayle and Derek Tresize; my supportive parents, Dottie and Togo Hazard. Thanks once again to Terri Zumstein for her incredible sense of book design, along with Valerie Dawn Smith and Mary Damigos—the artists whose work makes this book unique and beautiful. A round of applause to my friends and fellow Baja Aficionados who provided invaluable knowledge and editorial input. Without you this book wouldn't be what it is: Sue and Jim Graham, Gene Kira, Hugh Kramer, Lynn Mitchell, Bob Holt, Mike MacCarthy, Judy Botello, Victor Villaseñor, Graham Mackintosh, Harry Crosby, Roy Baldwin, Bucky and Russ Haley, Christy and Chuck Geiling, Kathy Alward, Emilie Winthrop, Susan and Dennis Monken, John Austin and Wendi Benecke. A special gracias to my fellow Baja traveler, Kit Worthington and his parents: Doris and Netter, and another to Dee Norton of the San Diego National History Museum. Last, but never least, hugs to Mary and John Bragg of Restaurant Pancho's in Cabo San Lucas, Marc Spahr of Caffé Todos Santos, Janet Howey of Tecolote Libros in Todos Santos and Steve Chisolm and Imelda and Chuy Valdez of the Buena Vista Beach Resort.

Mil gracias a ustedes....

Cartwheels in the Sand
Table of Contents

Page

Prologue
       Encinitas, CA.. 1

Chapter One
       Baja California Sur.. 2

Chapter Two
       Los Barriles, BCS.. 9

Chapter Three
       Encinitas, CA...17

Chapter Four
       Encinitas, CA...26

Chapter Five
       San Diego, CA..35

Chapter Six
       Encinitas, CA...45

Chapter Seven
       Encinitas, CA...55

Chapter Eight
       Tijuana to Ensenada, BC...............................64

Chapter Nine
       La Bufadora, BC..75

Chapter Ten
       La Bufadora to San Quintín, BC...................84

Chapter Eleven
       San Quintín, BC...94

Chapter Twelve
San Quintín to Cataviña, BC..................................106

Chapter Thirteen
Bahía de Los Angeles, BC 117

Chapter Fourteen
Guerrero Negro to San Ignacio, BCS.....................129

Chapter Fifteen
San Ignacio, BCS..139

Chapter Sixteen
San Ignacio, BCS..148

Chapter Seventeen
Santa Rosalía, BCS..160

Chapter Eighteen
Mulegé to Bahía Concepción, BCS........................172

Chapter Nineteen
Loreto, BCS...185

Chapter Twenty
Ciudad Constitución to La Paz, BCS......................195

Chapter Twenty-One
La Paz to Los Barriles, BCS...................................205

Chapter Twenty-Two
Los Barriles, BCS...215

Chapter Twenty-Three
Cabo San Lucas, BCS...225

Chapter Twenty-Four
Todos Santos, BCS..235

Epilogue
Todos Santos, BCS..245

Appendix I
    Recipes from *Cooking With Baja Magic*..................... 253

Appendix II
    Where to Get Information on Baja............................ 264

Appendix III
    Baja Restaurants and Hotels.. 266

Appendix IV
    Real People of Baja... 268

Appendix V
    Baja Books Mentioned.. 269

MAP LEGEND

1- Tijuana
2- Rosarito
3- Ensenada
4- La Bufadora
5- Maneadero
6- Santo Tomás
7- San Quintín
8- San Felipe
9- El Rosario
10-Cataviña
11- Bahía de los Angeles
12- Guerrero Negro
13- Laguna Ojos de Liebre
14-San Ignacio
15-Laguna San Ignacio
16-Santa Rosalía
17-Mulegé
18-Bahía Concepción
19-Loreto
20-Ciudad Insurgentes
21-Ciudad Constitución
22-San Carlos
23-Bahía de Magdalena

24- La Paz
25- Los Barriles
26- East Cape
    (includes Buena
    Vista, Punta Arena,
    Cabo Pulmo)
27- San Jose del Cabo
28- Cabo San Lucas
29- Todos Santos
30- Tecate
31- Mexicali

BAJA CALIFORNIA MAP

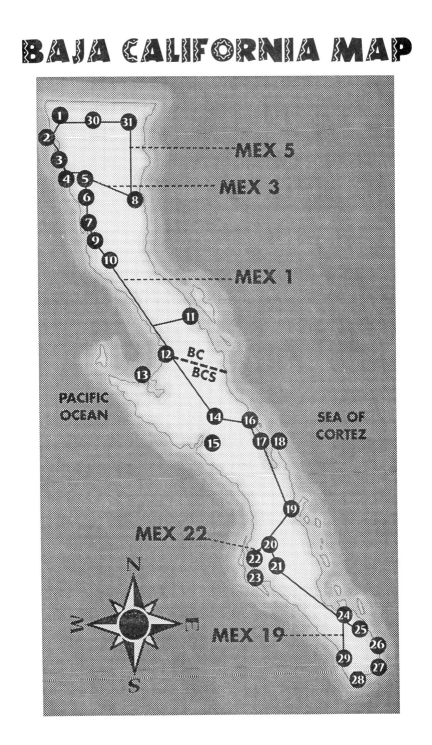

The Mermaid's Dance

A tangled web of heartstrings
        sways in the underwater breeze
        a mermaid backstrokes in slow circles—
        alone in the shadows of a summer night.

Half-open eyes fix on a waning moon
        tail leaves a wake of trembling effervescence
        until she gives it a resolute flip—
        and surrenders her heart to the inky blackness.

All night long she swims on her back
        eyes to the heavens, salty tears dripping into salty sea
        essences mingle with a lover's prayer—
        the one she has lost she craves evermore.

Heartstrings reach past the bounds of the sea
        flow up the cliff to the castle that houses her beloved
        desperately search out his sleeping form—
        aching to wrap him in a tender embrace.

Across the screen of his sleeping brain images flash
        a desire deeper than the sea floods his soul
        he groans alone in the darkness—
        aching with unbearable agony, fear.

Heartstrings turn and flow back to the sea
        powerless to scale the walls of his heart
        love returns to her, pure and increased—
        the terror that binds him holds her no more.

Love's song, burning brighter than the rising sun
        bursts forth from the caverns of her heart
        lifts her right up out of the water—
        and whirls her across the tips of the waves.

PROLOGUE   **Encinitas, California**
                               August 7, 1997

The phone dropped from her hand onto the speckled gray carpet.

She stared at it, her eyes blank, brain whirling. Her ears roared with the sound of waves pounding against the sand.

"He's gone," she whispered to her dog. As the dog, Casey, rubbed her head against her hand, she added, "My dad. He's gone."

She dropped to her knees and rocked backwards in a timeless gesture of feminine grief. A long, low moan erupted from deep inside her. A trail of tears worked its way down her cheeks and dripped, one at a time, onto the bare skin of her thighs.

On the floor next to her, the phone blared. "If you would like to make a call, please hang up and try again. If you need help, hang up and then dial your operator." As it began the endless chant of "Rant, rant, rant, rant, rant" she picked it up and threw it across the room. It slammed against the wall, still ranting, and the dog, who had been licking the palm of her hand, slithered away into the bathroom.

CHAPTER ONE   Baja California Sur
                                   August 10, 1997

"Mom, how much longer 'til our plane lands?" asked 13-year-old Ashley.

Dana Wallace leaned across her daughter and looked out the window of the jet. Below her the Sea of Cortez shimmered in the blazing summer heat. Its color changed from a pale aquamarine in the shallow waters bordering deserted white beaches to an ever-darkening shade of azure blue as the water deepened. Flashes of light sparkled across the moving surface of the sea. She smiled as she remembered the story he'd once told her about the mermaids—how they danced with wild abandon in the refracted sunlight on the tips of the waves.

She counted the bays on the island below her. Twelve on the west-facing side. Recognizing it as Isla Espiritú Santo, she shifted her gaze south, toward the city of La Paz. She felt more than heard the high-pitched whine of the engines as the Alaska Airlines jet cut its power, readying itself to land at Los Cabos International Airport. The "Fasten Seat Belt" sign flashed on and she nudged both of her daughters.

"We should be there in less than ten minutes," she said.

Ashley's twin, Sara piped in. "Will Ellen be here to pick us up?"

Dana smiled in spite of herself. "Who knows?" she said. "She told me this morning she might send Jorge. She said she was going out for a long, long ride on her quad. All the way up to Punta Pescadero, or maybe south to La Ribera. *No lo sé, mijas*—I don't know, babes. We'll have to see who shows up."

Ellen, her father's widow, was 54 years old and borderline eccentric. Her dad had been 71—and definitely eccentric—when he died unexpectedly in his sleep three days before at their beach-front home in Los Barriles. Less than an hour north of the Los Cabos Airport, the East Cape resorts of Los Barriles and Buena Vista were not just places where retired expatriated Americans moved to live their last years in affordable comfort. They were that—yes—but more. So much more.

To Dana, Baja was a place of exquisite, pristine beauty set against a backdrop of near desolation. It was her favorite place on earth—a place of endless cactus-inhabited hills, sunny skies and see-through water that teemed with brightly colored fish. A smiling place of real-life cowboys and surprise oases. A place where hot springs bubbled up to the ocean floor, burning her toes as she played in the waves under the light of the moon. A place where gray whales came each year to give birth to their young. It was a place of boisterous yet achingly beautiful mariachi music. It was a place of paradox—where joy danced hand in hand with sorrow. It was also one of the premier sport fishing and tourist destinations in the world.

Dana had been coming to Baja since she was eight. She felt more at home here among the Mexican people than she did among her own. She'd never understood exactly why, she just knew in her gut that it was so. It only figured that her father, Bud Wallace, would choose to have his ashes scattered off the back of his screaming yellow panga in the Sea of Cortez. It was only fitting that it would be here, off the East Cape of Baja California—the place he too loved most in the world.

Wiping at a tear with the back of her hand, she reached into her purse for a tissue. She blew her nose. Sara took her hand and squeezed it. "It's okay, Mommy," she said. "It's okay to cry. I miss him too." And the three of them, mother and twin daughters—who had been alone together for nearly seven years since Dana's husband left and married first the next door neighbor's wife, then later a dentist he met at a convention in Houston—cried together as the plane screeched to a landing and taxied to the brand new Los Cabos terminal, where it lined up behind a Mexicana jet, an American Airlines jet, two charter jets, an Aero California jet and an America West jet.

Jorge pulled the ancient VW van into the driveway of her father's house. Sweat pouring off of her body, Dana swung the side door open and stepped out into the searing August heat. Taking a deep breath, she pulled her sundress down over her knees and headed through the garage into the house. Before opening the door, she made a quick mental note. Both Ellen's and Bud's quads, those four-wheeled ATVs [all terrain vehicles] they roared up and down the beach on, were there. She smiled, swallowed and blinked as she felt the tears threatening to start up again. She slipped off her shoes and went inside.

The earth-colored Tecate tile floor was cool against her bare feet. The thick block walls, plastered over and painted white, kept the house from overheating. The windows were open to the breeze. The hum of the ceiling fans mingled with the muffled roar of a distant motor as a turquoise panga cruised by offshore. Her eyes traveled around the room, taking in the wheat-colored sofas; thick, fuzzy handmade rugs; colorful folk art paintings; carvings and sculptures. Ellen's own ceramic creations made up the lamp stands. There was a creature that looked to be half-iguana, half-fish that stood, brazen and defiant, in front of the tiled fireplace.

It was a compact house, no more than twelve hundred square feet, yet able to sleep ten people comfortably. Every bit of it was welcoming. It embraced and was at one with its environment. The sea called out from every room. There was a huge cardón cactus and a garden of cirio, ocotillo and other indigenous plants off the ocean-front patio, where cocktails were often served as daylight faded from the sky and pelicans put on air shows, diving for their dinners in the opalescent light. Wooden shutters bordered every window and there were no screens.

"Ellen? You here?" she called out.

From around the corner came her stepmother, wiping wet hands on flowered shorts. Her twin bassett hounds, Jack and Jill, panted behind her, skinny strands of drool wrapped around their muzzles. "Dana! Oh good God in heaven! I'm so glad to see you! Come on over here and hug me right now!" The two women embraced.

"Sit. I made you an *agua fresca* [a refreshing and tasty home-made Mexican drink using fresh juices]. The kind you said tastes even better than an Orange Julius."

"Oh. Yum. I'm dying of thirst. I forget how hot it gets here in the summer."

Ellen cringed at the mention of the word, "dying." She stepped back and looked around. "Where are the girls?"

Just then they came inside, banging the back door behind them. "Ellen!" they screeched in unison and the three of them were laughing and crying and hugging. Dana stood off to the side, watching. Their

relationship with Ellen had always been effortless, so unlike their relationship with her own mother, their blood grandmother. The three of
them got along like peers—forever plotting naughty little pranks to
play on Bud and Dana. She turned away as her eyes filled once again.

"Okay, talk to me," Dana said later as they were sipping orange
drinks on the deck and watching as the girls snorkeled in front of
them. "Was he sick? Did you have any indication that he might, you
know...."

Ellen took a long swallow. "No. Yes. He made that special trip up
to the States last month and did some tinkering on his will. I thought
that was odd. You know how much he hated to make the drive during
the hot months." Dana nodded. He'd stayed with her and the girls for
three days before heading back south. They'd gone fishing on a day
boat off Oceanside and picnicked on the beach afterwards. Their time
together had been, she realized, an incredible gift. "But, other than
that he seemed pretty normal. You know, he still fished like a maniac,
he still rode his quad down every afternoon to Tío Pablo's to play
poker or gin rummy with the guys. He spent a couple of hours a day
online, communing with the outside world. Everything seemed normal."

What she didn't say was that he'd been as attentive and irrepress-
ible a lover in the last few months as he'd been when they'd first met,
back when she was 24 and Dana was in junior high school. Their sex
life had been far more amazing in its second bloom, because of their
understanding and acceptance of each other. She smiled inwardly as
she remembered their long nights together, holding each other as their
bodies rocked and reverberated, as the music they created somehow,
so magically together, rose and fell in crescendos and led them on a
journey of symphonic sensual surrender. In all of her life, she'd never
experienced anything so wonderful, so joyous, so completing.

"I think he knew," she said finally. "I think he knew." She got up
off the chaise lounge and walked to the edge of the patio, looking for
Ashley and Sara. Relaxed as she spotted them bobbing along in the
current about 50 yards offshore.

"Jorge and I went over the will this morning. Bud left most everything to me. He left you and the girls each some money." She named
some figures that brought a look of surprise to Dana's face. "I know,
honey," she added. "Your daddy liked to live nicely, but simply. You
know how much time he spent after *chubasco*—hurricane season

helping people rebuild their homes. You know how devoted he was to stopping the gill net fishing that was ruining the gulf by killing off our fish population. And to fighting the salt mines in San Ignacio Lagoon so the Japanese don't jeopardize the gray whales." She smiled and her eyes crinkled in merriment. "He loved those causes of his and I promise you I'll pick up where he left off." Her breath caught in her throat. Neither spoke for a few long moments.

Ellen smiled mysteriously. "He left you the motor home."

Dana sat up straight and shot her stepmother a puzzled look. "The motor home? Why? I don't get it. Why me? Why not David? He's a man. He has a family...." Her brother David lived in Idaho on a ranch with his three boys and his wife, Wendy. He was an avid outdoorsman. He'd love a motor home. Dana, on the other hand, was a single mom who hadn't had a date in over a year. And hadn't had a boyfriend in over three. What in the world would she do with it?

Ellen stood. "Why don't you go snorkel with the girls? I left some extra gear down by the water. I need a few minutes to myself before everyone else shows up. Do you mind?"

"Of course not."

The older woman got up and walked to the door. Then she turned and looked back. "Dana, I can't answer you about the motor home. You'll have to answer that question for yourself. It is, however, the most perfect gift your father could have ever given you."

Still shaking her head in confusion, Dana walked a hundred yards down the sand to their beach chairs, towels and cooler. She scanned the shallows for her daughters as she sorted through the snorkeling gear. Couldn't find them. Panic rose up in her throat. She searched again. Then she saw them, their hot pink snorkels skimming the sea's surface. She grabbed a pair of fins, a mask and snorkel and dashed across the burning sand.

She waded out into the water. In patches it was scalding. Grains of sand crunched up between her toes, lacing them with gritty fire. She felt the near-boiling water as it escaped from an undersea spring, mingling with the salt water and inflaming it. She put on her fins, shuffled along through the water until she found a cool spot, fastened the mask and snorkel onto her face and dove. She swam out toward her twins.

As she neared them, they saw her and waved. Both squealed through their mouth pieces and raced toward her. She reached out for them and Ashley took her left hand in her right. Sara took her right hand in her left. The three swam together, their fins propelling them across the surface of the Sea of Cortez.

Sara motioned with her free hand. Look!

A lightning-quick needle fish sped by.

They swam on, through schools of yellow and gray-striped tiger-fish, spiny brown-spotted blowfish and rainbow-colored parrotfish. Dana let go of their hands and pointed. They nodded. She took a deep breath and dove 12 feet down to the reef below. Seaweed waved at her. Fish stared and swerved, startled from her path. Her ears crackled. She swam on, searching the cracks between rocks for those devious, dart-ing flashes of fluorescent blue, yellow and turquoise—those tiny, exotic tropical sea creatures that were the most spectacular of all.

Moments before her air ran out, she found two. Turned toward the surface and pointed. She heard Ashley and Sara's water-muffled laughs as the fish burst forth to gleam briefly in the ripples of reflect-ed sunlight. Then she saw an eel, leering at her from between two rocks. She pointed again and surfaced. Dana reconnected with her daughters' hands and steered them to the north. When they ran out of reef to explore, they turned toward the sand. A gentle wave caught them, urged them to shore and beached them simultaneously.

Mother and daughters removed their snorkels and sat together as the waves lapped at their legs. Then the girls moved away and began to dig together in the sand like little kids. A castle began to take shape.

Dana looked around, as if seeing the place for the first time. There was no one else in sight. It was chubasco season. The usually barren landscape was alive with color. The hillsides to her back were covered with wild California red bougainvillea. Flowering shrubs twined themselves seductively around the tall, many-armed cardón cacti. Stocky, over-built elephant trees lounged next to orange-blos-somed, lush-leafed, skinny-armed ocotillos. The desert had been transformed into a tropical thorn forest of jungle greens, perfumed with fragrant crimson, yellow and purple blossoms. Up toward the highway, she saw a pair of cows grazing along the roadside, gorging themselves on the abundant grasses. They ambled across the pave-ment, oblivious to the danger they imposed, both to themselves and to oncoming vehicles.

She turned. The shoreline to her left was disrupted by a washed out, transient river bed. When the rains unloaded on the mountains to her back, water raced to meet the sea, ripping up pieces of vegetation and tossing the debris of the hillsides onto its now tranquil shores. She felt the sun's rays prickling her burning shoulders. She rubbed them.

She'd never been here in August before and marveled at the intensity of the heat, even this late in the afternoon. The air was still. The winds were hiding out now as the sun sank toward the mountains.

"Come on ladies. It's time to head back." She picked up her gear and headed back up the beach. After a couple minutes she looked back. Her daughters were hunting together, trailing their toes in the warm surf, stopping every so often to scoop up the tiny, half-dollar-sized jellyfish that had begun to drift in with the tide. To the untrained eye, they looked like delicate, benign sea treasures. They floated about like transparent, hand-blown glass globes with networks of purple threads trailing behind them. They cried out to be touched, but wherever one of them grazed human skin, it left nasty welts like a cluster of bee stings. Dana watched as her daughters carefully scooped up the creatures with their masks. Then she turned and walked on ahead.

CHAPTER TWO   **Los Barriles, Baja California Sur
August 10, 1997**

Alone with her thoughts, Dana was suddenly transported back in time. Nearly seven years. She saw, she felt, she heard—as though the whole scene was replaying itself in front of her eyes. She was both participant and spectator this time around....

The engine screamed. Tires spun against the sand. She stood motionless, her eyes shifting from his face in the rearview mirror to the tires. Only half of each of the four rear tires was visible now. Still the engine raced. Still the wheels spun. They dug in deeper and deeper.

Her husband opened the driver's door and leaned out. "Bitch, why didn't you tell me the sand was so soft here?! You were supposed to help me guide this ancient piece of shit! You weren't paying attention!"

She wiped at the sweaty crust on her forehead. "You're buried, Brad."

He got out of her father's motor home, slammed the door and walked over to where she was standing. "Brilliant observation. Get the shovel. I'll get the two-by-fours. The least you can do is wake up and help me dig this thing out."

He turned and marched to the back door of the RV. He flung it open, hoisted himself inside, tossed the cushions off the seat at the kitchen table, lifted up a piece of plywood and pulled out four pieces of wood. She blinked. He stood in the doorway and threw them in her direction. They landed within three inches of her toes. Particles of sand sprayed her. She wiped her mouth and chewed, the sand grinding between her teeth. She turned her head and spat.

"Where's the shovel?"

She swallowed. Stared at him. Couldn't move. Couldn't speak. Couldn't think. Rage distorted his features. His eyes blazed. His upper lip curled toward his nose. She didn't recognize him. Didn't know him.

"Dana?! Where's the shovel? Help me, will you?!" His eyes shot to the Rolex on his wrist. "Your dad will be back in 20 minutes and we promised him we'd move this beast back to the house for him."

She swallowed again. Her mouth moved, but no words came out. Her throat was as hot and dry as the desert wind blowing against her bare legs.

"Dana!"

She jumped as a bolt of adrenalin shot through her. She couldn't tolerate his presence. Not for another second. She turned and walked away.

"Dana?! Get back here! Come back here!" he called after her, swearing under his breath. She ignored him and walked toward her dad and Ellen's house.

She opened the door and smiled weakly. It was empty. The tiles cooled her burning feet. She walked through the living room and into the room she and Brad had been sharing with the twins. She sat down on the big bed and sighed.

For the entire three days they'd been here, Brad and Dana had been locked in the prison of their own private hell. She recited the facts to herself one more time. She'd been married for nearly ten years to Brad Leonard an oral surgeon a cold-hearted responsible man whose passion was his work. That and the outward trappings of life. He filled his voids with material assets, fancy vacations, a BMW convertible.

He'd been born on the outskirts of wealth and worshiped it. She, on the other hand, was more comfortable in the blue collar than the white collar world. Their backgrounds skewed their attitudes toward life, toward each other.

She blinked and shifted on the bed. Half-smiled at the decor. She loved this house. The Guatemalan bedspreads, so colorful and so in sync with the carved Mexican furniture, the crude but delightful, whimsical paintings her father had done on the wall. She ran her hand up and down the hand-plastered white walls. Pain streaked through her, twisting like a knife inside her gut. He treated her like an unmanageable child so much of the time. The life she'd always dreamed of husband, children, career all blending together in perfect harmony had proved to be an illusion. A pitiful joke.

Undeniably, Brad's most prized possessions were their identical twin daughters. They had his tall, athletic build, his Nordic coloring and pale blonde hair. They'd inherited Dana's green eyes, dimples and hunger for the outrageous. At his insistence, they'd gone to the right preschool, the "in" kiddie gym, the most expensive private elementary school. They hung out with the offspring of upwardly mobile set who typified their parents' values. Or Brad's rather. The girls had been birthed precisely at the onslaught of the yuppie baby boom, in June of '84. Brad viewed these children as his sole creation, although for the life of Dana, she couldn't ever recall his belly extending to mammoth proportions. She never remembered him grabbing at his ribs, trying to ease the dull, persistent roar of pain as his bones shifted, creaking like an old wooden stairway that's been trounced on for far too many years. He didn't spend six weeks in bed fending off premature labor. In fact, he didn't do labor at all. He just videotaped it.

Her reverie broke as the door opened.

She couldn't look at him.

"Where have you been?!"

"Nowhere," she told the bedspreads.

"Where are the girls?!"

"I don't have a clue."

The door slammed with the force of his expletives. He sat down on the wooden dresser, away from her.

She looked at him. "You swear too much."

"Where the hell are they?! How dare you...."

"Please calm down, Brad. They're with Dad and Ellen. Look out the window, for God's sake."

"I want a divorce, Dana."

Her brain wrenched and spun. There was a hard clenched fist where her heart was supposed to be. She leaned into her suitcase, grabbed a tissue and dabbed at the tears leaking from her eyes. She concentrated on breathing. In. Out. In. Out. She said nothing.

Brad got up and started pacing. Watching him move reminded her that they hadn't had sex in eight months. Hadn't even slept next to each other in almost as long. He moved back to the dresser, leaned against it and glared down at his wife. It was as though he'd read her mind.

"You're a fucking corpse in bed. Hopelessly frigid. You haven't given me enough sex in years. So I've had to get it elsewhere. I've had affairs. Lots of 'em! Do you hear me?" His voice rose to a near bellow. Still she said nothing.

"Damn you, Dana! Did you hear me?!"

"You're yelling."

"I'm leaving you. Do you hear me?! I talked to an attorney before we left. You disgust me. You're weak, you're unattractive, you're stupid. You don't read the newspaper. You think only of the kids and that idiotic fucking job of yours. You're a pathetic excuse for a wife."

"Who is she?"

The answer struck her like a slap across the face. "Laurel Blakely." The next-door neighbor's younger, childless, aerobically inclined wife. Her almost-friend.

She studied him, her heart somehow disconnecting from her mind. He was undeniably handsome. He had hair the color of fresh straw that thinned and receded slightly at the crown, aloof blue eyes and a body honed to perfection. He prided himself on his appearance and chided her regularly for hers. Why, just a year ago he'd given her a gift certificate to get breast implants and liposuction for her birthday. Plus a six month membership at a trendy gym. She'd torn the papers up and flushed them all down the toilet.

As the memory of his anger at her refusal to be bullied into being physically transformed hit Dana, she felt his eyes take their turn and cruise her body. Relieved that she had a t-shirt on over her bathing suit, she nonetheless felt a blush flaming up through the sunburn on her cheeks. She held in her stomach and in spite of herself, willed herself thinner.

She grabbed another tissue from the box beside her. The ball of pain inside of her exploded and spread, cutting off her heartbeats, blocking her airways. She gulped for air. She could practically see tendrils of loathing as they seethed from him, slithering around the room like an upended nest of serpents. No! she screamed silently inside her head. No! This may not be the best marriage in the world, but it can be saved. It has to be! I promised myself I'd never raise my children in a broken home!" She reached for him. "Brad..."

He shoved her away. "Don't touch me!" he yelled. "I'm getting the next plane out of here. I hate this place. I'm sick of you, your dad and his ridiculous fishing stories, his clingy, sappy wife. You make me sick. All of you!" She edged her way to the doorway and nearly left the room. Right before she did, she turned and looked back at him. For a split second, she saw a glimmer of emotion, a hint of vulnerability flicker in his eyes. She'd adored him once, been seduced by the glamorous life she'd envisioned with him. She remembered how he'd looked at her after Ashley and Sara's birth. His face had been bathed in wonder as he'd cradled a tiny five and a half pound baby in each arm. He'd laughed. He'd bought Dom Perignon for the doctor, the *anesthesiologist, the nurses. She choked back a sob and he stiffened, his armor in place once more. She ran out of the house.*

Her father found her sitting alone in his motor home an hour or so later. Her wonderful, irreverent father who had built his dream home on the edge of the Sea of Cortez just three years before. It was October 14, 1990. Her thirty-eighth birthday. Next week was his and Ellen's twenty-second anniversary.

"What are you doing in here?" he asked, bursting into the motor home smelling of suntan lotion and salt water. His large, still-athletic form filled the doorway. A former tight end at USC in the aftermath of World War II, he hadn't gone to fat. He was a rugged, over 60 version of the Marlboro man and a bona fide Baja Rat. "It's a gorgeous day out there. And it's hotter than hell in this shoe box."

Dana tried to arrange her face in an unreadable pose.

"Come on. Let's take a walk down the beach and check out the fishing boats. You want to go for a ride in my Yellow Bird, mija?"

Dana considered it. She loved riding in her dad's panga, a wooden Mexican fishing skiff powered by an oversized outboard motor. He was angling for a private talk, she was sure of it. But did she want her dad to know that Brad was leaving her? For another woman? She wasn't sure she could even force the words out of her mouth, so deep was her pain—so overwhelming her fear. She remembered their last panga ride, just yesterday. The fresh air had cleared her head. The boat's motion had calmed her. The water had been so transparent that they'd been able to see the fish swimming below them. They'd even seen the boat's shadow trailing them on the sandy bottom. They'd watched and commented as sea gulls and pelicans dipped and swooped, snapping up bait fish from the turquoise sea. Her stomach growled.

"I'd rather go to Enrique's for tacos," she said.

"Let's go," he said and turned to leave.

As they walked down the beach toward the slab of concrete poured right onto the sand and sheltered from sun and rain by only a roof of gray, dried-up palm fronds, Dana smiled to herself. In Bud's opinion, no one had lived until they'd eaten at one of these open-air establishments that housed some of the best restaurants in all of Baja. The fish was always the freshest, the salsa the hottest. And, of course the beers were the coldest—crystals of ice clinging to the bottles as the cheerful, chatty waiters deposited them in front of thirsty patrons.

As father and daughter neared Enrique's, he saw them and waved. Dana and Bud waved back. They ran across the sand and threw themselves into two rusted green metal chairs. Within seconds, they were sipping at perfectly chilled Pacifico beers. Dana studied her dad's face. There was a crusty glob of lime green sunscreen covering most of his nose.

"You know, don't you, Dad?" she finally asked.

He smiled sadly. "It'd be pretty hard to miss." He paused and pretended to study the menu Enrique handed him. "Dos tacos de pescado con guacamole," he said.

"Dos tacos de carne para mí," she added, ordering two beef tacos.

"I'm willing to listen to anything you want or need to say," he said as the waiter retreated to the kitchen. He crossed his heart like a kid on the school playground. "And I promise, if you and Brad make up, I'll forget everything you've told me. Deal?"

She told him. Everything.

Bud's brow furrowed. "I want you to know something, Dana."

"What?"

He scratched behind his left ear and took another swig of beer. "Well, your mom and I had problems a lot like yours and Brad's. We probably never should have gotten married, even though," he said as he smiled at her, "I wouldn't have missed watching you and David grow up for the world. But we were too different. Like you and Brad. Mary Ann always wanted the high life. Fancy parties, expensive clothes, trips to Europe and Hawaii. You know me. I like to drink beer, play cards and fish."

She laughed at the contrast. "Total opposites. She was much happier married to Bert, huh?"

"Yeah." Bert Hawkins, her mother's second husband, had been a restaurateur who'd owned a dozen upscale eateries throughout Southern California. He'd died three years before and left his wife the restaurants and a pile of money. She'd sold the restaurants and was enjoying the life the money bought her.

Bud went on. "But you know? I think she's even happier with him gone. After all, she has plenty of cash and no one to answer to. Your mother doesn't really like looking after a man. Always said I was worse than a third child."

Dana nodded. She remembered that recurring line from their fights. Her dad continued. "She's happiest when she can do her charity parties, spend her days golfing or playing bridge."

"How'd you two fall in love, Dad?"

He laughed. "You know the basic story. College football jock meets high school homecoming queen and sweeps her off her feet. She was so gorgeous, and so difficult." He laughed and his eyes sparkled at the memory.

"You liked it that she was difficult?"

He chuckled. "Sure. It made me want her more."

"Makes perfect sense to me." It did. It was one those insipid idiosyncrasies of human nature, Dana thought to herself. People always want most what is the most unattainable. And unmanageable.

He was still talking. "Only trouble was that I didn't let her put me through med or law school like she wanted."

"What?!" Up shot Dana's eyebrows. Open flew her mouth.

"Yup. Had my whole future planned out. I even went to med school for a semester and dropped out. Went back to construction. Like my dad before me. Broke your mother's heart. I don't think she ever forgave me."

"I bet not. She hid it well though." She had too. Until Dana was in junior high.

"We tried. When you kids were little, no one got divorced. There was a real stigma to it. So we made the best of it. Compromised. Or tried to. But it didn't work. I wasn't happy in her world and she certainly didn't like my middle-class attitude."

In spite of herself, Dana laughed at that one. Before he'd retired and moved to Mexico, her dad had owned a franchise for Pacific Western Equipment Rental, where he rented forklifts, dump trucks, backhoes, water trucks and such to local construction companies like Sundance Homes, the builder she worked for. Now he and his second wife, Ellen lived here in Baja with two slobbering basset hounds and traveled in their creaky old motor home during the cooler months of the year.

"Well, I guess I have followed in your footsteps, Papa-san. First I go to work in the construction industry. Then I marry a pretentious man from an almost-rich family who tries to make me over into his image of the ideal wife." She swallowed. "And dumps me when I fail to comply."

"You're a rebel, Dana. Always were. Always will be."

"How do you mean?" she asked as a ghostly image of herself with perpetual acne and teenaged awkwardness chased her for the remainder of her life.

"You rebelled against your mom before she left us. Then you rebelled against me and Ellen when you were in high school. You rebelled against your mother's idea of a career for you by going to work in a construction trailer. Against me and Ellen again when you married Brad. Now you're rebelling against him."

Dana stared at him. He patted her arm. "I've been watching you *and Brad up close these past few days. He's an arrogant son of a bitch. You don't see this right now because you've been rejected and you're in shock, but I promise you—you'll be so much better off without him!" He laughed as his daughter's right eyebrow shot up in a perfect imitation of her mother's.*

Dana laughed then—a huge, liberating outburst of surprised laughter that erupted from the frozen recesses of her soul. They leaned back in their chairs and laughed together until they were gripping their sides and tears were streaming down their cheeks.

CHAPTER THREE   Encinitas, California
                                 August 15, 1997

Dana locked the door to her eight-year-old minivan and walked into work. She was exhausted. It had been so hard saying good-bye to her dad. She still expected to hear his voice on the telephone, telling her he'd just been on an extended fishing trip—that it had all been a big joke. Helping scatter his ashes behind his canary-colored panga, his beloved Yellow Bird, had been the most painful thing she'd ever done. Her chest convulsed with another round of as yet unshed tears. It still hurt. Hurt. Hurt. Hurt. Would she ever stop missing him? Would this pain ever go away? Would losing her father be worse than when Brad left her? Or when she caught Peter cheating on her and they broke up? She sighed. Didn't have a clue at this point. Gotta ride this one out, she said to herself. Gotta ride it out.

She opened the door to Hacienda Gaviota, the trendy southwest restaurant right on the beach in Cardiff, in northern San Diego County, where she'd worked for nearly six years. The restaurant whose menu she'd created mostly by herself. The restaurant where she was now the executive chef. I don't want to be here, she thought. I'm tired. I'm tired of working split shifts and fitting my children in between everything else. I'm tired of having no social life, of being the only adult in my house. I'm sick of sleeping alone. I haven't had sex with anyone except my shower massage in over a year and the last man I had sex with didn't love me—nor I him. I'm almost 45 years old and this isn't how I imagined my life would turn out. This is not the life I want!

Pushing her sadness down and pasting a smile onto her face, she said hello to Juan and Carlos, the bus boys. She said hello to Maya and Merilee, the first two waitresses on duty and to Eduardo, the dishwasher. "Where's Danny?" she asked no one in particular, referring to her assistant. "Is Jeff coming in today?" Jeff was the restaurant's manager. "What time's Jay scheduled?" Jay ran the bar.

"Eleven," answered Maya. "They're due in then all three of them. I just checked the schedule." Cute, perky and petite, Maya looked as exotic as her name implied. She was unsure about the exact racial and geographic origins of her ancestors, but Dana guessed her to be a Creole or something similar. She was 28 and a kick.

"I'm sorry about your dad," Maya said softly. Everyone else murmured in agreement. She touched Dana on the right shoulder. "How was Baja?" she asked. "Did you find any new and exciting dishes to add to the menu?"

"No," said Dana. "It was hard. We pretty much ate in and people brought stuff over. Can you get me a double espresso please? I'm way pooped."

"No problema."

Dana yawned and hoisted herself onto a barstool. She loved this place, she really did. Subtropical plants hung from beams stretching across the ceiling below the roofline. Carved wooden sea gulls, *gaviotas* in Spanish, were suspended at random from the rafters and drifted lazily in circles, powered by slow-moving ceiling fans. The building was constructed of bleached wood and glass and faced the Pacific Ocean. Her eyes wandered to the Mexican and Indian paintings on the walls. Her favorite piece was a richly colored oil, painted on a huge canvas that hung at the back of the bar. Part abstract and part impressionistic, it showed two Indian chiefs, in full tribal regalia, their feathered heads—together as they stood silhouetted in front of a brilliant sunrise high on a hilltop. There was a mystical quality to the painting that never failed to absorb her.

There were other pieces painted by Mexican artists. A pastel of an outdoor marketplace set deep in the tropical mountains by Pescina. A Lepe serigraph where chubby, smiling angels hovered above a coastal village was her kids' favorite.

Scattered about were pieces of Native American folk art from both sides of the border. Her eyes found the shadowboxes made of twigs lashed together with leather tongs. Inside these boxes resided clay and wooden figurines, Mexican peasants in bright local garments, replicas of Aztec and Mayan gods, Navajo Kachina dolls. In others were colorful balsa wood lions, tigers, and coiled, hissing snakes. On the floor, next to the rounded, adobe fireplace constructed in authentic Santa Fe style, a carved larger-than-life coyote howled at an imaginary moon. Another back wall was taken up entirely by a gigantic Guatemalan weaving, its colors blaring, contrasting and dramatic.

The furniture was Mexican. The glassware was hand blown, *Hecho en Mexico*—Made in Mexico, crystal clear but imperfect in texture and symmetry and rimmed in cobalt blue. The plates, bowls, saucers and coffee cups were American stoneware, in complementary shades of turquoise, aquamarine and periwinkle. Long strands of red New Mexico chiles hung next to strings of speckled Indian corn from the doorways and window frames.

She looked out the windows. In today's late summer heat, the beach was already crowded with families, surfers, joggers and the like. Her eyes followed a pair of surfers as they paddled out through the waves, spun, caught one and rode it almost to shore.

Maya handed her a steaming cup of espresso. "You have a whole stack of phone messages back in the office at your desk," she said. "And what's-her-name, that Baja tour guide lady, she's come in about *four* times in the last four days looking for you. We explained about your dad and that we weren't exactly sure when you'd be back, but she just kept showing up!"

"Holly?!" Dana's face brightened as if the sun had just emerged from behind a big, dark cloud. "God, I haven't seen her in eons! And you say she came by here four times?! Did she say what she wanted?"

"No. Just that it was important. Urgent. Maybe you should call her."

Dana jumped up, grabbed her coffee and ran into the back of the restaurant. "Where's my messages?" she called, seconds before she found them, neatly stacked on her neatly organized desk. She grabbed the cordless phone and punched in Holly Malone's number.

"You what?!" she practically screamed, her voice echoing all through the nearly empty restaurant. "You're kidding! This is totally bizarre! We need to talk! Tonight!"

It was 10:45 p.m. and the restaurant was closed. The two women were hunched over a bowl of salsa fresca, loading up as much of the spicy dip as they could onto tortilla chips before they popped them in their mouths. Two nearly full Pacifico bottles stood nearby. Their heads bobbed in unison, one with long, tangled, dishwater blonde hair and the other whose short, curly hair was a pale shade of blonde. Tall and sturdily built, they looked enough alike to be sisters. It was obvious that they were in cahoots with one another in whatever it was they were discussing.

"Okay," said Holly. "I have to leave by mid-October, right after chubasco season's over. I need to be gone at least a month, maybe longer. I have to be back before the holiday rush sets in 'cause I'm booked solid with whale-watching and cave-painting tours. My publisher expects me to have the first draft of my manuscript done before I go south for the winter. I was planning on renting a motor home to do this trip, but if you're up for the adventure and can get away well, then hey! I can rent yours! But I really want you to come along. I need four women total. That's one of the prerequisites."

Dana's head was spinning. "Wow. I dunno. This is so out of character for me! I mean, I haven't gone anywhere since my divorce except up to L.A. to visit my mom and down to Baja to visit Dad and Ellen. I've never been away from the girls for more than a few days. And to be gone a *month?!* Wow," she repeated.

"Well, think about it. Talk to Camille. I'll give you a call in a few days. And I'll e-mail you with all the details in the morning. If you're up for it, and if you two can think of one other woman, or a few to consider, let me know, okay?"

Dana nodded.

"Oh. The fourth. Our idea is to find someone who hasn't traveled much and who's never done any camping."

"Well, Camille hasn't. I know that for a fact."

Holly smiled. "Perfect. I need someone even less adventurous than Camille for the fourth. To make it this guidebook really and truly believable for novices."

Dana nodded a second time. Exhaustion flooded her again, followed almost immediately by a rush of exhilaration. She couldn't stop seeing Ellen's face in her mind, couldn't stop hearing those words about the old motor home being the perfect gift for her. What had she meant, anyway? They'd never discussed it again. David and his family had arrived. The realities of Bud's impending funeral service intruded upon them and their private time evaporated. Now Holly

coming here like this on her first day back and making this offer—
well—it was all just a little too coincidental to ignore. When the puz-
zle pieces of life came together this magically, Dana didn't believe
they should be minimized or blown off. On the contrary....

She closed her eyes and leaned back in her chair, massaging her
temples and neck. She stretched. Yawned. A series of images of herself, Camille and Holly flashed across the movie screen of her mind.
She saw them walking barefoot at dawn on the beach at the edge of
the Sea of Cortez as the sun rose all orange and fuchsia over the water.
She saw them giggling, eating dinner at twilight under a palapa, their
naked toes wiggling in the still-warm sand. She saw them kayaking
and snorkeling in the pristine waters of Bahía Concepción and roast-
ing marshmallows around a campfire under the stars. She saw them
laughing, dancing to Jimmy Buffett tunes. She saw them crying as
they bared their souls to one another driving across the desert at midday.

The last image, the one that made up her mind for her, was of four
women. She wasn't sure who the last one was. But they were four and
they were strolling along the bay in La Paz. The sky was wild with
storm clouds set against the afterglow of a brilliant sunset. Pelicans
were dipping, swooping, diving and slamming into each other as they
churned up the water in a feeding frenzy just offshore. In her imagi-
nation, she inhaled the salty air. Dana absolutely adored La Paz. She
hadn't been there since her parents divorced. It was time. Time to go
back.

Dana checked on her daughters before she called Camille. Sara,
on the top bunk, lay sleeping on her back, mouth wide open, snoring
gently. Her hair was pulled back in a ponytail, and though she longed
to stroke it the way her daughter so loved, she didn't want to wake her.
Instead she planted a kiss on the tip of her freckled nose and stepped
off the ladder.

Underneath, Ashley lay, her blonde hair spread out over her pillow and her face smashed against Ellie, the stuffed gray elephant she
still slept with. Dana kissed her too and she stirred, smiling in her
sleep. She marveled at these two, these identical twins who'd been
born six minutes apart more than thirteen years ago. Where had the
time gone? These girls had spent half their lives being shuttled back
and forth from Mom's house to Dad's house. Brad and his third wife,

Monica, lived twenty minutes away. He had them for six-day stretches every other week. It was hard on her, still. After all this time, she couldn't find it in her heart to forgive him for cheating on her and then describing those liaisons to her in blood-curdling detail. She couldn't forgive him for taking her to court and fighting her for custody of the twins. He'd told countless lies about her to the court-appointed psychologists, trying to prove her an unfit mother. In the end he'd failed and they ended up with court-ordered joint custody. She knew he despised her and wanted her out of the girls' lives. He took pleasure in wounding her and she hated herself for being unable to stop him.

She took a deep breath and regrouped. He loved his daughters, she had to give him that. He was a decent father and his girls adored him. They weren't delighted with Monica, but they tolerated her and vice versa. Brad showered them with gifts and attention. He took them to Sea World, the Zoo, the Wild Animal Park, Disneyland. He'd taught them to surf and to rollerblade. She smiled down at her daughters. They were growing up, their breasts budding, limbs and torsos lengthening and rounding into slender, shapely, delicate young women's bodies. As she studied these creatures that had grown inside of her belly, an ancient, dark sadness welled up within her soul. She felt old. Washed up. Used up. Empty.

Then, abruptly, she remembered. Baja. The motor home. Holly. Camille.

She nearly laughed out loud. You idiot, she chided herself as she closed the bedroom door. You sit here night after night feeling sorry for yourself, playing that same old Poor Pitiful Pearl tape over in your head. Well, guess what, dear heart? You're going to Baja! You are! You are! You are! You can do this! Now get to that phone and call your neighbor. Now!

Camille came right over. Neighbors since the day they'd become single moms, Dana and Camille were closer than sisters. Grinning at her better-than-best friend, Dana saw her as though for the first time. She hadn't really changed a bit over the years. Tall, with unruly burnt auburn hair, she was built like an aging Barbie doll. She had the big boobs, narrow hips and legs that went on forever. She seldom wore makeup, but her face was perfect without it. Almost ethereal. Her eyes were brown and touched somehow with a trace of puppy dog sadness. Her skin was clear and white except for a sprinkling of freckles across her nose. She was slightly overweight, but hid it well inside an array of flowing dresses. A disc jockey, musician and songwriter who dabbled in massage work on the side, Camille was an earth mother without a mate, a consummate artist and a latter-day hippie. She had two boys, Eric, who was nine and Matt, who was the same age as the twins.

Two years older than Dana, she'd been the first female disc jockey back in Fort Lauderdale, Florida back in the early '70s. As Camille told her when they first met, she had the voice. She knew the music. She had the body and she was more than willing to have her photograph plastered all over Southern Florida in a very tight, very wet WYRS t-shirt. She'd been notorious back then and she was still the feistiest woman Dana knew, although she'd been pretty subdued the last year since her second husband Drew had moved out of the house and out of her life. Poor Camille. She'd cried for the better part of six months after he'd left. Her divorce was due to be final in a month or so. Neither she nor Dana could bear the thought of dating anymore.

"So what's the big deal?" she asked as she uncorked a bottle of Chardonnay. "It's midnight for God's sake!"

"Well, who has to get up early?"

"We do! Remember? Eric gets me up at the crack of dawn! I have to do Mommy Duty and be at work by ten. And then...."

"All right, all right! Shut up, will you?! Pour yourself a glass of wine and sit down! I have something completely, unbelievably, incredibly wonderful to tell you."

Camille's eyebrows shot up. Her mouth fell open. For once she said nothing, simply did as she was told. When she was on the couch, she patted the spot next to her and said, "You sit too. I'm all ears."

"I'm not asking, Camille. I'm telling. We are going to Baja. For a whole month. You, me, Holly Malone. We're gonna go in my dad's old motor home, the one he left to me. We'll get it up here somehow and we'll pack it up and we're gonna take off and have ourselves a serious once-in-a-lifetime experience!"

"Hold on. Wait. Back up. I'm not getting this. Would you please start at the beginning? I know about the motor home. But how in the hell am I gonna get a month off work? Why are we doing this? It sounds like too much hassle and too much money and too much time away." She stared hard at her friend. "Are you out of your fucking mind?!"

Dana stood up. Rolled her eyes at Camille. Walked over to her stereo and looked through the CDs. Selected one and put it on. Cranked it up. It was Bud's favorite mariachi song "Rancho Grande" and the rowdy, toe-tapping, whirling, swirling music filled the tiny beach house. "Dance with me!" she demanded and pulled Camille to her feet. They danced through three songs, until they were breathless and panting and fell back again onto the couch, exhausted.

"Holly got a contract to write a guidebook on Baja," she explained. "The publisher wants her to write it from a woman's perspective. For so long only men have had the *tanates*—that's balls in case you're wondering—to travel in Baja. Women can tag along, but the popular belief of the modern American gringo is that there are banditos in Mexico lying in wait, ready to ambush, rape, pillage and plunder all unsuspecting tourists. Especially females. Holly's been traveling in Baja for years. She leads tours all over the peninsula. She drives down to her place in Mulegé alone all the time whenever her husband's away. Which is most of the time."

"Isn't it dangerous?"

"No. It's wonderful. If we're respectful of the people, the culture —if we stay on the beaten track we won't have any problems. You know how long I've been going there...."

Camille nodded. "I trust you. So. This Holly. She's married?"

"Sí. She is. Her husband's a captain in the merchant marines. They're an unusual couple. Independent and adventurous but going in totally separate directions. Her idea for the book is to get together a group of four women and spend a month doing Baja—living the book she's gonna write while she's doing the research."

"Why you? Why me?"

"She's liked you ever since you guys met at that Cinco de Mayo gig the first year you and I were single. Remember?" Camille nodded again. "She knows I traveled a lot in Mexico as a kid. And hey, I'm a chef in a trendy pseudo-Mexican restaurant! You're on the radio! We're both fairly high profile, ya know? Good publicity." Camille nodded. "She says we both came to mind immediately."

Dana had stopped traveling in college and afterwards, when she was focusing on her career and climbing the corporate ladder in the construction industry. She tried to revive the gypsy inside herself when she got married, but Brad had hated Mexico. Couldn't tolerate the beggars in line at the border in Tijuana the one and only time she took him there when they were dating. Said he'd never go back again. She'd talked him into flying to Puerto Vallarta once, and they'd stayed at the Sheraton Bougainvilleas, a five-star American hotel where none of the third-world dirt could possibly rub off on him. They'd also gone to Club Med in Ixtapa, but it was run by the French, and to Dana, it didn't feel like Mexico at all. She'd never stopped missing Baja during the years she'd been married to Brad. Bud and Ellen built their house in Los Barriles when the girls were toddlers, and she took them down a few times without him. That one time he did go, he left two days early to go back to San Diego and file for divorce.

She sighed. She'd been down once or twice a year since then. But this time it had been different. This last trip down for her dad's funeral had awakened something in her. A deep unquenchable aching, an indescribable longing to go not just back to the East Cape, but to travel all over the peninsula. To live on the road and immerse herself in the culture, the geography, the history, the people. To discover what it was that made her feel so much more at peace there, so much more at home in a foreign country than in her own. Dana wanted to be happy again. She wanted to giggle like the teenager she'd once been, kissing that boy and dancing with him in the surf in the moonlight, right about the time she turned 17.

Camille must have read it all in Dana's eyes. She finished her glass of wine and put in on the table. "Darlin', you are right on. We're going. I don't know how the hell we'll pull it off. But we will. This much I know...."

CHAPTER FOUR   **Encinitas, California**
                                 August 24 and 25, 1997

"I've met her several times, actually," Dana said. "She's a businesswoman, clear and simple. A little on the uptight side, but with impeccable integrity. She's worked with Camille for years at the station. Actually, she's the promotions director for all three stations owned by Bonn Communications.

"Yeah. I know. Married. No kids. Not a traveler. Kind of frail. But smart. And interested. Definitely interested. You wanna meet her?" Dana asked into the phone. "Okay. Tomorrow's Monday. I'm off. Camille's working middays. She doesn't get off 'til 2:00 p.m. Can we meet after that? Great. Sure. See ya then, Holly! And don't forget to bring your maps and photo albums, okay?!"

She hung up and hurried back into the kitchen to finish up the brunch orders. It was busy at Hacienda Gaviota the week before Labor Day. The horse races were in full swing at the nearby Del Mar Racetrack and the tourist season was at its peak. The weather was perfect. Absolutely perfect. Made her wish she was out there in the water, boogie boarding.

Barbara Benton walked in with Camille. It was nearly 3:00 p.m. and the place was deserted. Dana came out of the kitchen, wiping her hands on her smudged apron. She took off her chef's hat, untwisted the knot in her hair and shook it out. It fell in a long tangle to the middle of her back. "There was an emergency in the kitchen and they put me to work," she said. "So, how funky is my hair?"

"Way funky," Camille responded.

"Hi Dana."

"Hi Barb. How goes it?"

"Great. I love your messy hair, by the way." She touched the tight bun at the nape of her neck. "It makes you look feminine and sexy. I wish I had the guts to just fling mine loose like that." She shook her head and gave a nervous laugh.

Camille's eyes traveled over her navy blue, pinstriped business suit and prim white blouse. She poked Barb in the ribs. "You? Doing something loose? Isn't that an oxymoron?"

"Hey Cinnamon Girl. Chill, will you? Sit down. I should be safely off duty from this point on. Moral of story. Stay away from work on your day off!"

The three women sat, ordering and then sipping iced tea while they waited for Holly. "So, did you talk to your husband about the trip?" Dana asked Barbara.

Barb nodded. "I did. I talked to Bob about it at length last night. He was concerned—of course—about us driving in Mexico—four women without any men to look out for us. Neither he nor I have ever been any further south than Tijuana and he caught an immediate case of third world paranoia. But I'd anticipated that. I went online and found several informative Baja and Mexico websites. Sent him an e-mail at home with the links included." Her face brightened. "I woke up last night around 3:00 a.m. and there he was, hunched over his laptop, totally engrossed in those websites. I think he'll come around. That is, if Holly decides to include me." She looked from Camille to Dana and back. "How will you ever manage to leave for a month? Who will take care of your kids?"

Camille answered first. "My ex. The boys' dad. He's looking forward to it. He's a computer consultant and works out of the house, so his schedule's flexible."

Dana spoke next. "I haven't got it all worked out yet. Brad won't commit to more than his usual twelve days a month. But I've been talking to Ellen about it and she really wants me to go. I think she's almost talked herself into driving the motor home up here next month and staying at my house. It would be ideal. The girls love her. My dog loves her dogs. Brad would be off the hook and I could leave with a crystal clear conscience!"

"So what's the hang up?" Barb asked.

"My dad died unexpectedly a little over two weeks ago and Ellen's not feeling real grounded. She's not 100 per cent sure she's ready to come stateside. But I know her and I believe she'll pull through for me. I think it would be good for her, actually."

Barbara grimaced and touched Dana's arm lightly. "Oh dear. I'm so sorry. I had no idea..."

A tear glistened in the corner of Dana's eye. "It's okay...."

Camille interrupted. "Hey! I talked to the PD [program director] at the station. I have plenty of vacation time coming. He thinks it's a great opportunity to grab a shit load of press coverage. Get this. He wants me to call in every Friday morning from the road and entice our listeners with tales of our adventures! Then they're gonna throw their first annual 'Bona Fide Baja Bash' for us—and our listeners of course—when we come back."

At the sight of Dana's raised eyebrow, Barbara spoke up. "It's true. Camille and I both lobbied the powers that be at the station. Can't you just see it now? RockSteady's own Cinnamon Girl, Camille Fleming on a road trip in Baja—reporting in via cell phone every week on the Wise Guys Show-Gram! It will be a hot draw, we're all convinced of it!"

"What about you, Barb? Can you get a month off?"

"She nodded. I have ample vacation time coming. And, in a crisis, I can hook up via modem."

Dana shook her head. "I wouldn't count on being able to do that too often," she said.

"No?"

"No. Not likely."

Barb's mouth widened into a grin. "Oh. Too bad," she said. "This is sounding like more fun all the time."

"We won't be able to work too much, will we?" asked Camille.

"Not *too* much," said Dana. "Although I'm under orders to search out some new recipes for the restaurant. Hector wants me to explore Baja cuisine."

"We all know I have a book to write." It was Holly, who'd just come up behind them. She pulled out the fourth chair and sat down. "Hola y'all."

Dana introduced Barbara and Holly. "I've heard so much about you, I feel like I already know you," Holly said. "But I need to ask you some questions, okay?" The interview began. Holly grilled Barb on her background, lifestyle, attitude and travel experience. Barb had spent a summer traveling in Europe after college, so she wasn't an inexperienced traveler by any means. "What makes you want to do this?" Holly finally asked her. "You look like four- or five-star hotel kinda gal. Isn't camping in the dirt somewhat out of character for you?"

Barbara smiled. "Of course it is. I haven't ever camped. I haven't gone barefoot in years. That's why I want to go. To be perfectly honest with you, I turn 40 this coming winter. I don't have kids. I can't. I've been married nearly 15 years and at my job for more than half that time—quite unusual in the radio business, believe me."

Camille nodded. "Ain't that the truth."

"I feel stale. Washed up. Burned out. I have to admit, the idea of traveling in Mexico in a motor home with three women, two of whom I hardly know—well, it terrifies me. But I have the need to do something that stretches me, challenges me—on all levels. Especially physically. I've never been athletic or outdoorsy. It's either go with you women or have an affair—and I love my husband too much to even consider that, thank you very much!"

"Good call," Dana agreed. "Definitely a good call."

"You won't choke on us, will you?" Holly asked.

"What do you mean?"

"What I mean is..." Holly stopped and took a sip of tea. "What I mean is," she repeated, "even though I want this to be a stretch for you, I can't be stuck with someone who's timid and won't take risks."

"You're afraid I'll wimp out on you. Is that it?"

"Exactly."

"No. You have my word. I may be scared out of my mind. I may want to wimp out with all my heart and soul. But I will not."

Holly looked at her in silence for a while. "Okay," she said. "I admire your truthfulness. I'm one of those people who trusts their gut, Barb. And mine tells me that your level-headedness will be a good thing on this trip. We'll make a very interesting foursome—I have no doubt about it."

"No kidding!" laughed Camille. "Two blondes and two brunettes. Two single moms and two married women. A renegade tour guide. An upscale chef. A loud-mouthed deejay and a sophisticated businesswoman. Yee-hah! Are we gonna kick butt or what?!"

Jay, the burly bartender called to them. "Hey. I'm sending over four shots of tequila—on the house. Complete with salt and limes. Mexican limes. There is no way you girls can sign on to make a trip like this without sealing the bargain in tequila."

Dana smiled. "He's right you know. It's the Mexican way."

"Has been since the Spaniards discovered the mystical, medicinal purposes of the blue agave," added Holly.

"But I don't drink. At least hardly ever...." interjected Barbara.

Holly poked her in the ribs. "Here comes the tequila, Barb. It's time for your first lesson in Baja Adventuring 101. How to drink tequila correctly. Like a real Mexican." Jay set the drinks down in front of them along with a plate of quartered limes and a shaker of salt. Holly put up her hand. "Watch me. It's follow-the-leader time."

She licked the fleshy pad between the thumb and forefinger on her left hand, then poured a small amount of salt on it. She picked up a piece of lime. "Put the lime in your mouth and just barely taste it." The other three copied her. "Okay. Now you're gonna shoot the tequila—at least half of it. Then you'll lick the salt off your hand and pop the lime into your mouth, chomping down on it good and hard. When you're done, breathe out like this." She exhaled loudly. "Let me go first."

She shot the tequila, licked the salt and sucked the juice out of the lime, finishing off the ritual by blowing out hard. She shook her head. "Whoo! Now you do it."

Dana and Camille picked up their shot glasses. Barb shrugged her shoulders and followed their lead. When all three had finished, Dana and Camille looked at each other and gave the wild Mexican yell, in unison. "Brrrrrrr-eeeeeeeeeee-hah! Ay! Ay! Ay!" Holly laughed out loud and clapped her hands. Jay cheered from behind the bar.

"Oh dear," moaned Barb when she could catch her breath again. "What in the world have I signed on for?"

Holly snorted with laughter. "You said it yourself. We are the antidote to your burnout. We will not bore you or disappoint you, Barb. Have faith!"

Camille took off her shoes and tossed them onto the floor next to the couch. She looked around, loving this house as much as she had the first day she'd set eyes on it, so many years ago. It was a poorly insulated beach cottage that got too hot in the summer and wouldn't stay warm in the winter, but she'd never felt more at home anywhere. It was at once unique and comfortable. Way out and artsy.

A three-piece threadbare couch curved in a smooth arc across the living room. Covered in a turquoise, pale yellow and flashing black art deco pattern, this sectional sofa was a treasure she and Drew, her most recent [almost] ex-husband had found at an estate sale. It was a classic from the early '60s. The tiered black Formica end tables were from a garage sale. They went perfectly with bright yellow lamps he'd given her their first and only Christmas together as husband and wife. There was a stereo, a TV perched atop a chest that looked like it could have once held buried treasure and a few abstract pieces of art on the walls. The overall effect was one of pure, vintage funk.

Camille went into the kitchen to get a glass of water. In an alcove off to her left was an upright piano, an acoustic guitar and a set of keyboards. The kitchen table was antique oak. She sat down at it and pulled a half-smoked joint out of the cigarette pack in her purse. She lit it and took three quick hits. Then she stubbed it out, slid it back into the pack and lit a cigarette.

She remembered the first time Dana had come over here and seen her go through this routine. Camille was a closet toker and a closet smoker. Denying her tandem habits to the outside world, she hid out, lighting up only here, behind closed doors and when the boys were gone. Afterwards, she'd open the windows and burn incense to mask the telltale smells. She had the drill down. She'd brush her teeth, spray perfume on her body, lather her hands with lotion and put spray in her hair before allowing herself within 20 feet of a non-smoker.

Camille laughed to herself. She'd quit smoking cigarettes altogether when Drew moved in—God was it nearly three years ago? And started up again when he left nearly two years later. She'd never given up the pot—she just pretended to. As she sucked the tobacco smoke into her lungs, she couldn't help but wonder how he was. It had been too much for him, taking on a woman with two sons. He'd been 52 when they got married. Too old, too set in his ways—or something. Camille could still picture him in her mind, standing barefoot under a canopy of trees that December as the two of them recited their vows. Did she love him still? She'd thought she'd die when he left, it had hurt so much. Kaleidescoping images raced through her mind as the memories assaulted her one more time. No, she told herself when they stopped. I'm pretty close to being over him. I have to be....

She'd met Drew when she was married to Craig. He was a musician, a mentor, a friend. He still was. Always would be. Back then, when Eric was a newborn, Craig had convinced her to quit the radio business and be a stay-at-home mom. He made enough money. He wanted her to support him in his career the way his mother had always supported his dad. Camille complied but her postpartum depression never left. It worsened and soon her doctor put her on Prozac.

During this bleak period of her life, she discovered Drew at a coffee house in Encinitas, near where she lived. Instantly enthralled with him, she'd sit in the back of the room with Eric on her lap and drink coffee, listening to him play his guitar and sing in the late afternoons before her husband came home from work. She loved his music. It touched her heart and stirred her up inside. But they weren't friends

back then. She didn't have the nerve to even speak to him. Craig did
not believe that, however. He followed her there one Saturday. He was
positive Camille was cheating on him with this older, long-haired hippie guy. His temper became more volatile and he became increasing-
ly abusive. Especially in public. And even more so after he'd been
drinking. Nothing she did was right.

Living with Craig got to be like wearing a corset that was two
sizes too small—24 hours a day, seven days a week. Knowing that she
would suffocate and die if she didn't make some major changes,
Camille did. In November of 1990 she landed a job at RockSteady
102.9. Less than a week later she left her husband. She moved into
this house, exactly one day after Dana moved in across the street.
They'd been each other's sole unflinching support and lifeline to san-
ity ever since. She crushed out the cigarette and leaned back in her
chair, closing her eyes. As she felt herself relax, it all came back to
her. It was the day they met and she was seeing it now through Dana's
eyes, as it had been replayed to her so many times before....

*The sound of a door slamming, followed by a woman's screaming
awoke Dana at 7:00 in the morning. The roar of a car engine filled
her ears and she bolted upright. Still fogged in with sleep, she stumbled to the front door and looked out onto the street. The "For Rent"
sign was gone from the house across the street. There was a shiny red
300 ZX Nissan in the driveway, poised as if ready to make a quick getaway.*

*Her new neighbor stood in front of the driver's door of the sports
car, clad in a ratty pale green bathrobe that was gaping open in front,
revealing half a boob. She was arguing with the guy inside. Then, suddenly, the car ground into reverse and backed out of her driveway.
She chased after it, her fists pounding at the car window.*

*"I hate you, Craig!" she shouted. "Open up the fucking window!
Come back here! You can't leave like this!"*

*She aimed her right foot at the driver's door, kicking and kicking
at it. The guy inside rolled his window down halfway and screamed
curses at her. "Get out of my way, Camille! Can't you see this is a new
car?!"*

*"You can't refuse to pay child support, you bastard! They won't
let me take the boys back to day care until I pay the bill! How am I
supposed to work?!" She was choking on her words, gulping for air.
"You arrogant asshole! You're just punishing me because I couldn't
put up with being your 'Stepford Wife' another minute!"*

*He hit the power button on the window and it closed silently,
shutting her out. Camille's face contorted with rage as she kicked at*

the car, the impressions of her feet leaving a cluster of dents on the driver's door. Craig shifted into first, let out the clutch and laid rubber on the pavement as he screeched off down the street, away from her.

She ran after him, yelling, "Come back here! You can't do this to me! Come back here.... you...."

She chased him to the end of the block, her bathrobe flapping open, flashing her boobs at anyone who happened to be watching. She was oblivious to her own screeching hysteria, to the futility of her pursuit. Right before he turned the corner onto Highway 101, he stopped and rolled down the window. He looked at her, leered actually and yelled out, "You cunt! You'll get yours! Your karma's gonna suck—big time!" Then, tires screeching, he took off.

Panting, she threw herself down onto the curb and sobbed, her head pushed into her knees.

Moments later, Dana was there, sitting on the curb next to her, handing her a tissue. "Hi. I'm your new neighbor," she said.

Camille opened her eyes, sighed and stretched. Yeah, things had changed since then. She and Craig had made peace. He was remarried and had a new baby—a baby he took care of during the day while his wife worked outside the home. Go figure! But at least he paid her the child support on time. At least he was consistently there for Matt and Eric. He took the boys every other weekend. He was looking forward to spending that chunk of time with them from mid-October to mid-November. He had a big house up in one of the subdivisions of Pacifica Heights, near where Brad and Monica lived.

Her thoughts drifted back to Drew. She still missed him—a lot. If she was completely honest with herself, she had to admit that she was more crazy about him now than when they'd been together as a couple. She'd always expected to spend the rest of her life with him, but their marriage hadn't been easy from the get-go. It was like once the vows were said and the reality sank in that they were really and truly married, some switch inside of each of them had clicked into the "off" position and they had ceased to nurture each other. She complained that he treated her like chattel property. He complained that she never initiated lovemaking anymore and that she put the boys above him in all ways.

She sighed again. Had their commitment been so shallow—a big mistake like he'd told her over and over again after they split up? Had he really only married her because he'd wanted to make their affair legitimate and not because he loved her? Had she really loved him or was it just that the sex between them was so fucking great? Had she been so desperate for a mate that she seduced him and kept on seducing him until he married her like that therapist said? Had he ever loved her or was he telling the truth when he said he'd done it out of guilt—to get the church folks off their backs?

She rolled her eyes up toward the ceiling. When, she wondered, would these feelings stop? When was she ever gonna get over this man? Sometimes she'd go a week or even longer without missing him, but then—sure enough—the feelings would resurface—and she'd be flooded with a longing so intense, so sexual that she would feel like she was gonna lose her mind. She did a quick internal inventory. How long had it been since she'd wanted him like this? Oh yeah. The last time they played music together. Well, no wonder. She couldn't help smiling to herself. That had been *some* night! Like Drew always told her, it was the music that had gotten them in trouble in the first place. It was the music that lit them on fire, forcing open their reluctant hearts, loosening their tight, unwilling bodies and demanding that they surrender and dance. That they give in and allow themselves to flow in time with the tides of life—in and out—in and out—in and out.

Ah, the rhythm, she thought. Gotta love that rhythm. No, she told herself. Not tonight. You are not allowing yourself to go see him tonight.

She got up and went into the alcove where her piano was, sat down and began to play. Her fingers pounded the keys and she sang at the top of her lungs, expelling the pent up passion and frustration trapped inside her.

CHAPTER FIVE

San Diego, California
September 8, 1997

Holly Malone glanced at her watch as she pulled into the parking lot of the office complex that housed RockSteady 102.9. 1:47 p.m. Slightly early. She pulled her 11-year-old Toyota Land Cruiser into a cramped, narrow space marked "Compact," grabbed her bag of books, maps and lists and got out of the car. Locked it. Headed toward the elevators.

Five minutes later she was in the conference room waiting. She was the first one there. She wandered around the room, peering at the dozen or so posters lined up on the walls. Station events. Framed news articles about the Wise Guys, San Diego's second most notorious morning team. The duo, Johnny Gaines and Mark Hendricks, had bounced back and forth between radio stations over the last ten years, moving each time their contract came up for renewal. Holly had the inside scoop since she knew Camille. Like the number one team they seemed to follow around, these guys kept getting better and better deals every time they changed positions on the radio dial. Holly tuned them in whenever she was in town. She found their irreverent, naughty banter to be adolescent but hilarious. You just can't help but crack up at these guys, she thought to herself. There were plenty of times she'd been driving down the freeway in the early morning laughing out loud at their antics and then glancing over at nearby cars in consternation, only to see that the other drivers were laughing too.

She scratched her head and took a sip of water. How long had they been at RockSteady? A year? She checked the dates on several clippings. Yeah. She'd guessed right.

"Can I help you?" boomed a voice behind her. She jumped. Turned. Gaped. She'd known he was a big guy, but up close he was *huge.* Larger than life.

"Oh! You scared me."

He let out a Santa Claus chuckle and put out his hand. "I'm Mark Hendricks," he boomed again.

Holly laughed. "I could tell. Holly Malone. I'm here for a meeting with Camille Fleming and Barbara Benton and your station manager, Carl Emory."

The bear of a man smiled down at her. "Ah. You're the Boss Banana of the Bodacious Baja Babes, am I right?"

She laughed again. "You are. I am."

"I'll be sitting in on the meeting to coordinate Camille's call-ins on our morning Show-Gram." He pulled out a chair and motioned for her to sit. "So tell me," he said as he squeezed himself into the chair next to her, "How much luck will she have with a cell phone way down there in the outer recesses of Baja?"

Holly smiled. "Good question. I just spent the morning down in Tijuana getting the latest info on that very thing. From what they tell me—and you have to understand that in Mexico you never really know until you get there—we shouldn't have any problems at all. They've got microwave relay stations all up and down the peninsula. We shouldn't be out of service range too often, because we're not about to go off-roading in Dana's old motor home! When we're in towns, there are pay phones, *Ladatels*—everywhere that are way cheaper than cell phones."

"Cool. What about the computer? Where will Barb be able to go online?"

"Unfortunately not in too many places. Yet. Mulegé, Loreto, Los Barriles, Cabo. Maybe Todos Santos. Believe it or not, the Mexican government's spent the last two years installing a state-of-the-art fiber optic cable line down the length of Baja. It runs from Guaymas on the mainland across the Sea of Cortez to Santa Rosalía about halfway down and then follows Mex 1, the transpeninsular highway all the way to Cabo at the tip. It won't be done in time to benefit us, but from what I heard today, it should be operational next year sometime."

"Is your information reliable?"

Holly chuckled. *"¿Quién sabe?*—Who knows? I hope so. I've seen the crews and equipment working on the cable. It looks nearly done. The big question now is whether it will work or not. If it does—

when it does—Baja will have better, faster Internet access than we do up here."

"Whoa."

Just then the door banged open and in walked Dana, Barbara, Carl Emory. "Where's my Cinnamon Girl?" asked Carl.

Mark Hendricks glanced at the wall clock. "She should be off the air by now. I'll go get her. Wanna come, Holly? I'll give you the nickel tour."

They walked down the hall and came up to the glass-encased deejay booth. In spite of herself, Holly gaped. The room was a lot, lot smaller than she would have expected. A control panel the size of a large drafting table extended in front of Camille, taking up almost half the space. She was gesturing and explaining something to the guy next to her, the afternoon drive jock. A million colored switches and lights blinked on the sound board. There were three mikes and three stools, with as many sets of headphones hanging on hooks next to them. Off to Camille's right was a telephone switchboard, three CD players and rows upon rows upon rows of cassette-encased CDs. On the wall behind her was a chalk board and a bulletin board overflowing with snapshots of station events. In the middle of the board was a six-year-old photo of Dana and Camille dancing together on Cinco de Mayo—the day Holly'd met them both.

She watched, fascinated as Camille cleared her throat, donned her headphones and adjusted the levers on the board. Before she went on mike, she cued up the next song. Then she was talking. "It's 2:02 on Thursday afternoon here at RockSteady 102.9, where you can always count on 50-minute, commercial-free music sets, day and night. I *am* Camille Fleming, your Cinnamon Girl, signing off for today. Next up is Peter Mays, who will continue to burn up these airways as he brings you the very best in classic rock."

She hit another button and Jethro Tull's song "Locomotive Breath" filled the hallway. She yanked off her headphones and swiveled to face Holly and Mark. She waved, said her goodbyes to Peter and left the booth, hugging herself and rubbing at goose bumps on her bare arms.

"Damn. It's cold in there! Can you get maintenance to turn the AC down a little?" she asked the receptionist as they walked past her desk and turned left into the conference room.

Two AAA maps were taped together and spread out, covering almost the entire table. A red line zigged and zagged down the peninsula, from the border separating San Diego and Tijuana all the way to

Cabo San Lucas at the tip, a journey of 1,059 miles on Mex 1. There was a blue star at every location Holly had designated as a campsite. She gestured, pointed and began to explain the itinerary.

"We're set to spend Monday, October 13th packing up and getting up to snuff on the motor home. We'll leave early Tuesday morning, on the 14th."

"That's Dana's birthday," interrupted Camille.

"Cool," said Mark. "We'll have to do something with that. How old, Dana?"

"Half-way to 90."

"Oooh. You look pretty damned good for such an old broad."

"Shut up, Mark," chided Camille. "For once!"

"Come on you guys. Settle down," said Carl. "Go on, Holly."

She looked at her notes and picked up a stack of itineraries. "Here's what my publisher and I came up with." She kept one and handed the rest off to Camille, who was on her left. " We want to do a bona fide tour of the peninsula, hitting as many of the great spots as we can, but we won't be going off the beaten track. We want this book to have a broad appeal, to adventurous women—and men. To first-timers like Barb, who want to expand their horizons. If we make it too off-roady or too rugged, we'll scare people off. And we'll lose credibility. This has to be very do-able, ya know?"

Everyone nodded. "I'm relieved," said Barb. "I'm sure my husband will be too. He's been having second thoughts lately."

"Wuss," accused Mark under his breath.

"Okay. Quiet everyone. Back to our trip. If everything goes smoothly, we'll be gone exactly a month. Thirty days. We're scheduled to return on Wednesday, November 12th. Now, here's the itinerary. It's still fairly hot in October and even into November," she said. "We won't be spending all that much time in Northern Baja. One night in Ensenada at the Estero Beach Resort and another at La Bufadora, just south of there. Another night in San Quintín.

"Then we'll go to Cataviña and spend two nights there. I have to show you guys the Indian cave paintings. And take you hiking. It's up in the mountains, midway between the Pacific and the Sea of Cortez. The rock formations and the cardón, cirio and elephant tree forests up there are spectacular." She looked around the table. "Cataviña is a sacred place for me. In a lot of ways, it's nothing more than a truck stop. The only things there are a Hotel La Pinta, a fairly primitive campground, a junkyard and mechanic's shop, an occasionally open Pemex station and a restaurant. I prefer to stay down the road apiece at Rancho Santa Inez when I'm camping. It's only about four bucks a night and it's right in the Natural Park. Oh," she smiled. "And they serve absolutely killer tacos and enchiladas there."

Everyone laughed. "What are all those funny plants you just rattled off?" asked Mark.

"There are 100 types of cactus in the Central Desert of Baja, 80 of which grow nowhere else on earth. This is some serious scenery, folks! A cirio is also known as a boojum tree. It's a gangly cactus built on a stocky trunk. It has this long body that wiggles and woggles all over the place like some kind of wild dancer. When it rains these guys get all dressed up in green and sprout crowns of white and gold flowers on their heads. I love 'em. They're practically human. Cardón are huge, multi-armed cactus that stand guard over the Baja like an indigenous army. Elephant trees are squatty and almost aboriginal in appearance. These three are the most prolific of all we'll see in Baja. And they're wonderful, magical...."

Dana sighed. "I'm ready to go. Can we leave tomorrow?"

"Nope. From there we'll hit Bay of L.A., known as Bahía de Los Angeles in Spanish. And do a little exploring." She pointed it out on the map. It's a side trip off Mex 1, but worth it. It'll be our first glimpse of the Sea of Cortez. We'll be able to do some serious kayaking and beach-walking there. It's an other-worldly kind of place. So stark it's almost lunar. Tons of sea life and the bluest water surrounded by desolate mountains and islands. I love it there. Then it will be off to Guerrero Negro—salt capital of the western world."

The station manager interrupted her. "I went all the way down Baja back in '75, right after the highway opened. Went down in an old Ford van with a bunch of guys, in search of secret surf spots. It was great. One of the best times in my life. Will you be focusing on mainly the tourist spots, or will you be visiting some of those out of the way places?"

Holly blinked. Smiled inwardly. Common ground. "This book will be geared to women, but my publisher thinks men will read it too. People in the 30 to 50 age group, Baby Boomers and Gen Xers. Folks who have a serious craving to experience nature up close and personal, but want to do it safely. And somewhat conservatively. People who love sports," she added with a grin. "Kayakers. Wind surfers. Quad riders. Jet skiers. And, of course fishermen and women too. Just not the snowbirds."

"The who?" asked Mark.

"Snowbirds. The senior citizens who cruise Baja in these monster

motor home caravans. They come from the colder states and Canada
and they descend on Baja in flocks from about November through
May. It's nuts if you get behind 'em on the road. Takes forever to pass
'em. They'll descend on a Pemex station—that's a government owned
gas station—and they're all government owned—and run it right out
of gas in one fell swoop. That's one reason why we always take at *least*
10 gallons of extra gas when I go down there. You never know...."

"So you're hitting the Xers and the Boomers," repeated Carl.
"That's our audience."

"Exactly. Most of the Baja books out have been written by the
old-timers. The trailblazers—mostly men—who pioneered this peninsula in the days before the highway was paved—when the best you
could hope for was a washboard road. One of my favorite authors is
Erle Stanley Gardner, the guy who created the Perry Mason TV
show."

"He was a Baja traveler?" asked Barb.

"Oh yeah. He wrote five books that I know of about his travels in
Baja, back in the '60s. He was old then too—in his 80s. He had the
audacity—and the *dinero*—money to hire helicopters to explore
Baja's mountains, deserts and coasts. He discovered lots of the Indian
cave paintings. He and his buddies started out in old World War II
jeeps and built the first three-wheelers themselves. One of my favorite
stories was when he and his friends were building a runway, so that
Francisco Muñoz, the most famous pilot in all of Baja, could land his
plane in a remote village. You know what they did to make a runway?"

Everyone around the table shook their heads, no. "Well, they got
hold of some old Mexican *troques*—trucks—and drove them up and
down, up and down, up and down a piece of land until they'd cleared
off a strip large enough to land Muñoz' plane."

"Is this Muñoz fellow still alive?" asked Carl.

Holly nodded. "He..."

Dana interrupted. " I know him! I flew with him as a kid—back
when he ran Baja Airlines! He and my dad were really good friends!"

"You know him?! You flew with him? Where?"

"Um. Let me think.... Bay of L.A. Mulegé. La Paz. Puerto
Vallarta. Loreto. The Meling Ranch."

"Wow," said Holly. "I've met him a couple of times. He's an
amazing man. People have started calling him The Forest Gump of
Baja. He's been everywhere—I mean everywhere! Anytime something major happened from the end of World War II until the late '70s,
it seemed like Francisco Muñoz was always there! When was the last
time you saw him?"

Dana scratched her head. "I don't know. Right after my parents got divorced I think. We went to La Paz. No wait. We went to Puerto Vallarta after that, I think. I forget. He and my dad stayed friends. Do you know where he is these days?"

Holly nodded. "He has a place down in Bay of L.A. where he spends about half the year now. The rest of the time he lives near here. I called him the other day and left a message for him about my book. I was hoping to get together with him when we're down there."

"If you hear back from him, would you mind telling him about my dad?"

"Not at all."

Carl looked at Camille. "I want you to tape an interview with him if at all possible, okay? Then we can Fed Ex it up here. Or, wait a minute, do they have Fed Ex in Baja?"

Holly laughed. "No. But they have several shipping companies that make the run between Cabo and Tijuana every couple of days. And there are buses too. I'm still researching that part of it, but so far I'm leaning toward DHL."

"Good."

"I checked out some books from Discover Baja Travel Club." She opened her bag and carefully placed eight books on the table. I want all of you, ladies, to read them before we go." At the chorus of groans, she added, "Well, at least read one or two each. We still have three weeks. You can read the rest—or we can read them together out loud when we're on the road."

"I'll take *Off the Beaten Track in Baja,*" said Dana. "I was a Perry Mason addict growing up. I'm dying to read about Erle Stanley Gardner's trips."

"Take this one you bimbo!" Camille said, pushing *Cooking With Baja Magic* by Ann Hazard too across the table to Dana. "You're supposed to be researching the new Baja cuisine, right?"

"Bimbo?! I beg your pardon. For your information, Cinnamon Breath, Bimbo is the largest bread manufacturer in Mexico. It's the equivalent of Weber's Bread up here. And, contrary to what you may think, its logo is not a dumb blonde but a cuddly little white bear with a 'B' on his chef's hat."

"Good God in heaven," said Camille, shaking her head. "Bimbo Bread?! You're kidding, right?"

"No. She's not," said Holly. Camille groaned and put her head in her hands.

"One more thing, girlfriend," added Dana. "I bought *Baja Magic* last week. So you take this copy. The travel stories in it are as good as the recipes, trust me. I want to read up on fishing. Give me *The Baja Catch* by Gene Kira and Neil Kelly."

"Okay. Okay. I relent. I'll take it." She took the book from Dana.

"Take two each. Dana, take Ginger Potter's *Baja Book IV* or Walt Peterson's *Baja Adventure Book.* Camille, you take either *Hovering Over Baja* or *The Hidden Heart of Baja* too," said Holly. "Those are both by Gardner. Both will give you a feel for Señor Muñoz. And you, Barbara, how about taking the Auto Club's book on Baja and Fred and Gloria Jones' *Baja Camping.* That should give y'all a good start."

She passed out the books. Carl stood. "I have another meeting to get to. You only got as far south as Guerrero Negro. Run Mark through the rest of the itinerary and set up some call-in times. Figure out some other on-the-road interviews. I want Camille to introduce each one of you women every week. If you run into some amusing, unusual characters, I want you to tape interviews with them too. We'll run those at different intervals during the week."

Camille nodded. "Will do," she said. He left.

Holly pointed at the map again. "Okay. Next place we go is San Ignacio. It's a beautiful oasis with a huge palm grove, a lake and an old Spanish mission right in the center of town." She paused. "We'll spend the night and hook up early the next morning with some more guys I know to do a day trip to see a couple of the best cave painting sites. I'd love to take you out to San Ignacio Lagoon, but there won't be any whales so early in the season, so there's no point in it."

"We'll just have to book a tour this winter," Barb said.

"Right. From there it's Santa Rosalía. That's a copper mining town that was built and run by the French up until fairly recently. It's great. It's also the street food capital of all of Baja."

"Street food?" asked Barb, obviously alarmed. "You mean we eat food right off the streets? Won't we get *sick?!*"

Holly and Dana laughed in unison. "No!" exclaimed Holly.

"I don't have to eat it, do I?" Barb asked. "I can't. I mean, I need to know that my food is sanitary. What if it's been washed in contaminated water? Or not washed at all? What about the flies and the dust and the dirt and the germs and...."

"Whoa. Chill out, wimp woman!" bellowed Mark. "If you are going to get all weak at the knees and turn to chicken shit on my Baja Babes you're gonna have to excuse yourself from the trip. Holly here is the Boss Banana and if she says you're gonna eat off the streets in Santa, what was it?"

"Rosalía."

"Santa Rosalía. If she says you eat off the streets, you eat off the streets. You trust her. It's called Follow the Leader. Without whining. Got it?"

Barbara chuckled in spite of herself. "Cut me some slack, wise ass. I'm a Third World Neophyte, remember? They'll have to be patient with me."

"Or just leave her in the motor home to eat tuna or Campbell's Soup or some other canned delight while we go out exploring!" said Camille under her breath.

"Good idea," said Dana.

"All right, all right. Let's finish up here," said Holly. "We're only on day 12 and barely halfway down the longest peninsula in the world." She went on to show them the rest of the route. Down to Mulegé. Along the edge of the mind-bogglingly beautiful Bahía de Concepción, to Loreto, up and over the spine of Baja to Ciudad Constitución and down into La Paz. Around the "Loop," from La Paz down to the East Cape where Dana's dad had lived, south to San Jose del Cabo and Cabo San Lucas—the two towns that comprise the celebrated resort area known the world over as "Los Cabos." From the tip of the peninsula at Land's End, they would head north on Highway 19, back along on the Pacific side toward the expatriate artist colony of Todos Santos. After three days there, they'd drive back to La Paz to begin the journey back up Mex 1.

"Any questions?" she asked.

"Puh-lease! My head is spinning." said Camille. "I have some major homework to do before we go. Basic Baja Geography 101 for starters. I can't be calling in from the road as ignorant as I feel today or our ratings will go way down!"

"Don't worry, in five weeks time you'll be able to speak intelligently. In two months you'll be an expert. Our next meeting will be here, same time next week. Dana, when's your stepmom coming up north with the motor home?"

"I'm not sure. Sometime before the 13th. Knowing her, she'll show up Sunday night, so we'll have barely one day to learn how to drive the thing, figure out what to do if something breaks, how to dump the holding tank, load the kayaks on and off the roof—all that stuff men usually do!"

"How big is this rig anyway?" asked Mark.

"Twenty-eight feet. It's supposed to sleep five—so we'll have enough room."

"Sounds pretty cozy to me. Like four farts in a skillet. Pop, pop, pop, pop—kapow! I want to know how long it is before you lovely ladies start biting each other's heads off. I wonder which one of you will freak first and head for the nearest airport...."

Camille leaned over and punched him. "You disgusting dick wad!" she said. "I bet you'd love it if we all got PMS simultaneously and killed each other off in a hormone-induced frenzy!"

"Ooh. Yeah! You said it, Cinnamon Candy Ass. I'm outa here. See you Bodacious Baja Babes next week."

"Wise ass!" Barbara and Camille called after him.

CHAPTER SIX　　　　　　　　　Encinitas, California
October 12, 1997

"Mom! She's here!" Ashley screamed. An air horn squawked, even more loudly, "Arooooogah! Arooooogah! Arooooogah!"

Dana folded the pair of blue jeans and topped off the pile. She said into the phone, "She's here. Did you hear? Yeah.... I don't know how you could've failed to hear it either. About ruptured my eardrums too. Yeah.... Peek out your window, Gladys Kravitz, and see for yourself. Then get over here ASAP!" She hung up and ran outside.

"Ellen! How are you?! It's so good see you!" exclaimed Dana as she threw her arms around her stepmother. The basset hounds, Jack and Jill, jumped up on Dana as they hugged. "Get outta here, you slobbering goof balls," Dana said, shoving them away. They ran into the house. "God." She stepped back and took a long look. "You look great. Fantastic."

Ellen's face relaxed into an easy smile. Dana couldn't help but notice that she looked better than ever. Her wavy gray hair was long and braided. It hung down her back. She wore a faded patchwork skirt and a denim blouse, rolled up at the sleeves. Silver earrings hung from her ears. At least a dozen silver bracelets circled her left wrist. She wore no rings. On her feet were a dusty old pair of flip-flops. Her skin, as always, was the color of pale copper. But it was her eyes that surprised Dana. Somehow she'd expected Ellen to exude pain. But that wasn't what she saw. Not at all. As she gazed into her father's widow's eyes, the only thing she could think of was slow-dancing. Yeah, that was it. Ellen had a certain deep peacefulness slow-dancing through every atom of her being. Anger flared up like a flash of lightening inside Dana and caught in her throat. Then it receded, just as quickly. *Cálmate*—calm down, she reminded herself. Don't get mad at her just because she's not suffering like you are....

Her stepmother seemed oblivious to the storm going on inside Dana. "I loved the drive up here. Jorge came with me as far as Ensenada. He's visiting relatives. The terrain was so beautiful. You'll love it. Everything down south is lush as a jungle. Up north it starts getting brown and dry, but it's beautiful just the same. Oh," she said as she gave a leisurely stretch, looking like a cat who'd just awakened from a late afternoon nap, "it's good to be here. Where are those exquisite daughters of yours?" And she was gone.

Shaking her head to clear it, Dana walked up to her motor home, this 1978 Jamboree that her dad had bought back when he retired 12 years ago. She poked around the exterior. Ran her finger along the turquoise and sky blue stripes that had been recently applied. Hmm, she noted. Nice paint job. It looked practically new. Amazing. Her dad had always kept it in meticulous shape mechanically, but the interior had been rust and brown earth tones, and he'd never repainted the outside. Boy oh boy oh boy, but it had been really tricked out since the last time she'd bothered to notice.

She opened the door, stepped inside and looked around. No more '70s color scheme. Ellen had painted the interior for her. Sewed new curtains too. And the seat and bed cushions had been reupholstered. Everything was immaculate and done up in shades of turquoise, periwinkle and aquamarine, accented with the hues of the desert sandstone, ochre, fuchsia. She sat down at the dinette and looked out the window, up to the twilight sky. Looked back at the quote written in flowing calligraphy and decoupaged onto the refrigerator. Her father's favorite quote. She read it out loud:

"The very air here is miraculous, and outlines of reality change with the moment. The sky sucks up the land and disgorges it. A dream hangs over the whole region, a brooding kind of hallucination."
.   *John Steinbeck—Log of the Sea of Cortez*

"Oh Dad," she moaned. "Daddy. I miss you! I need you. I hate it that you're gone! I do!" And the tears came then, the tears that had eluded her for the last eight weeks. "Oh Daddy, I've been so busy with my life, with planning this trip that I forgot to miss you. I'm so sorry. Please forgive me. God. Oh God. Please, God," she prayed out loud. "Please send my daddy down as an angel to guide us on this trip. Please help me to feel his presence. Oh God, I miss him so much!" And she put her head in her hands and sobbed.

A few minutes later she heard and felt the weight of footsteps swinging up into the doorway. "Dana?"

It was Camille. "C'mon in," she said, sniffling and wiping her eyes with the back of her hand. "I'm just in here falling apart."

Her friend walked in. "I was wondering when it would hit you," she said. She came up behind Dana and began to massage her shoulders.

"Mmmmm. Thanks. Boy am I knotted up. You were?"

"Yup. We all were. I know this trip will be painful for you, Dana. It's gonna bring up a lot of stuff. But you'll get through it. You know, your dad had something in mind when he left you this motor home. Obviously he intended for you to go on an adventure or 12. You have to know that he's up in heaven, smiling down at you, loving you non-stop and urging you to go on, to get out of your rut, to grab life by the balls and live it for a change! Don't you think?"

"Huh?" She turned and stared up at Camille for a long moment. "You're right," she said slowly. "He would've said that. Only he would've used tanates! God, he loved that word! He is saying that. I can hear him. I swear I can!" She jumped up. "Look. Let me show you what he and Ellen did. It not only looks like brand new, but it's already mostly outfitted! Come outside! There's a bike rack on the back. We can bring our mountain bikes! There's a kayak rack on top with two kayaks on it. There are four boogie boards and four beach chairs and a big folding table, lanterns, four gas cans, a barbecue and let me tell you what Ellen did to make this thing beautiful for us...."

"Thanks for driving the motor home up here. And fixing it up. It's perfect."

"You're welcome honey. I'm so glad you like the new color scheme. Jorge, María Pilar and I worked like fiends to get it done before we left. María said to be sure and tell you that she's expecting you for dinner when you get to the East Cape. And of course, you have to stay at the house." At the look on Dana's face, she chuckled. "Oh—trust me. You'll all be more than ready to spend some time in a real house. That motor home can get pretty claustrophobic."

"I doubt it'll bother us much," Dana said. "I don't feel like we'll really be inside at the same time at all, except to drive and to sleep. I plan to be outdoors as much as possible." She got up off the couch and headed in the direction of the girls' room. "Let me make sure that no one is on the phone and no one is online. You have to be careful with these two, Ellen. If you don't watch them like a hawk, they'll spend their entire lives doing conference calls on the phone and having buddy chats with their friends online. Even with two phone lines, it's almost impossible for me to get near the phone."

She came back a few minutes later. Ellen had poured her a steaming cup of coffee. She sat down and inhaled the aroma. Took a sip. "Mmmm. Delicious. So how are you doing anyway? You about blew me away when you got here. I've never seen you look so—well—serene. Me, it feels I've always got this knot in my stomach, this tangled up mess of tears always wanting to explode out of me. Sometimes I get so damn pissed at Dad for having a heart attack and dying like that. I mean, I can't help but wonder whether he'd still be alive if he'd come up here and gotten regular checkups like I wanted him to. Don't you think someone would've seen it coming and been able to save him?"

Ellen smiled that slow, easy smile of hers again. "I understand what you're saying. I've had moments when I felt that way too, Dana. You know, I never told you the whole story before. Let me tell you now." She adjusted her long skirt and tucked it underneath her feet on the couch. "I got up before dawn the day he died, like I do sometimes. I took the dogs and hiked to the top of the hill, you know, the one with the monument on it." Dana nodded. "You'll have to do that when you're there. The sunrise over the ocean is breathtakingly beautiful. Anyway, I was gone about an hour or so. When I came back, your dad wasn't up, which was strange. I went into the bedroom and he looked asleep, so I didn't bother him. Instead, I made coffee, squeezed some orange juice, went out on the deck and read for a while.

"When it got to be about 9:00 a.m. or so, I started getting a little concerned. I went into the bedroom again. He hadn't moved. All of a sudden my heart went completely still. And I knew, Dana. I just knew. Before I even touched him and felt that he was cold as ice."

Dana stared at her stepmother and swallowed hard.

Ellen took a sip of coffee and looked off into space. When she spoke again, her voice was quiet, almost a whisper. "I didn't go for Jorge and María Pilar right away. I dropped to my knees on the tile next to him. I took his hand in both of mine. And I prayed, Dana. I talked to God for the longest time with tears streaming down my face like a waterfall. I asked him to take care of this man I loved more than life itself. This man I met when I was only 24 years old—this kind, gentle man who was so rough around the edges. This man who taught me all about love and sex and who treated me like I was his most cherished treasure. I was so blessed, honey. Few women in the world have been loved as well as I have. I will be forever grateful for the 30 years I had with your dad. Truly, down-on-my-knees grateful." She wiped tears from her eyes. "It was his time to go, Dana. Pure and simple. It was between him and God. I saw it so clearly. And I know he was ready. I'm so glad he went quickly. Peacefully. When my parents died, both of them suffered horribly. For too long. It was awful. I'm so glad Bud didn't have to go through anything like they did."

Dana sat unmoving on the couch, tears rolling down her cheeks. Her body convulsed with silent sobs. Finally, when she could speak, she asked, "Why does Mom still hate him so?"

Ellen sighed deeply. "Because she doesn't didn't ever understand him. She never forgave him for being who he was. She wanted to create him in the image of her ideal man. I guess looks-wise he was 'it' for her. But, on the inside, he wasn't at all what she wanted. She couldn't change him, couldn't control him. And it infuriated her."

"Do you know why she left, Ellen? I mean, I hate to ask you this but I've always wondered and I really need to know. Were you and Dad having an affair? Is that why she left? Is that the reason she can't get past being angry with him?"

"Haven't you ever asked your mother?"

Dana shook her head. "No. She and I don't talk about *uncomfortable* things. We tap dance around on the surface of life, sticking to nice, safe, sterile, *appropriate* subjects. My mom doesn't like the sticky, icky, messy, *real* world of feelings."

Ellen laughed. "You're right there. She sure doesn't. But, to answer your question—she left *before* Bud and I became romantically involved."

"Why'd she go?"

Ellen shifted on the couch, untucked her feet and stretched them out in front of her. "I wish she'd tell you herself, but I know she never will. It would be too humiliating for her.

"Do you remember, back when you were about the twins' age, the summer your mom moved to L.A.?"

Dana nodded, her eyes wary, her arms and legs drawn inward.

"Yeah. I was 14. I got caught shoplifting that summer. My mom found out I'd been to an unchaperoned party and put me on restriction for a month. Wouldn't let me out of the house. Did he tell you about it?"

Ellen nodded, silent.

"Mom changed that summer. She raged at me non-stop, hit me with a hair brush on several occasions, told me she wished I'd never been born. She called me a slut and told me she just knew what I was letting the boys do to me. She accused me of smoking pot, taking LSD—things I couldn't even conceive of doing. She was crazy, Ellen. I see that now. I remember finding her in her bathroom one morning that summer. On the floor. In a corner. Crying. I tried to come near her, to touch her arm, but she threw my hand away like I had leprosy. She snarled at me like a wild animal or something."

Dana locked eyes with Ellen. "Go on," said the older woman.

"Well, I left. I came back a while later and she was still there, crouched on the floor. I asked her what was wrong—why she was crying. She beat on the floor and shrieked at me that nothing was wrong, that she was not crying. That I was a disgrace, that I made her sick and should leave her the hell alone. She left right after that, Ellen. The next day, I think. What happened to her?" Dana sat up straight. "Where did she go?!"

Ellen spoke in that near-whisper voice of hers. "This is how your dad explained it to me, honey. By the time your mom got to be about 40, she and your father were barely speaking. They slept in twin beds, remember?" Dana nodded. "She felt like you kids were growing up and didn't need her anymore. She got depressed, I think, and was most likely in peri-menopause. She began to gain weight. That really flipped her out."

"I bet," Dana agreed. Her mother was svelte. Gorgeous. Still. At nearly 70, she had the best body that money could buy and looked at least 20 years younger than she really was.

"She started taking diet pills, but they made her extremely volatile. So she went to a different doctor and got some Valium. At night she'd get into the booze. Then she'd drink coffee and take a sleeping pill or two to get to sleep. She was strung out, Dana."

"My mother?! My always-in-control mother?! I can't believe this!"

"That's why she left. She lost it and she didn't want you to know. Or anyone else for that matter."

"Wow. No wonder the violent mood swings...."

"Exactly."

"Your dad finally sent her away to get better. To a clinic in L.A. A place we'd now call a drug abuse treatment facility. No one knew though. Everything was very hush-hush back then. I don't think Mary Ann ever forgave your dad for sending her away. The shame of it was more than she could bear. She got herself a fancy L.A. lawyer as soon as she was released from the program and filed for divorce."

"How awful," Dana said.

"It was. Your dad was devastated. It wasn't often, especially back then, that a woman walked out on her husband and children. But, of course, she blamed your father completely. And you."

"Wow," was all Dana could say.

"I told Bud that he should tell you the whole story, but your mom had made him promise not to. He didn't want to hurt you even more than he didn't want to betray her confidence. He felt responsible. He'd let her down, and he'd let you down too."

Dana nodded. "Oh no. My poor Daddy. I was so mean to him after she left."

"I remember," Ellen said, nodding. "I was there for the whole ride. My heart went out to him. I'd had a secret crush on him all along. I encouraged him to confide in me. He did, and one thing led to another." Ellen smiled. "Thank God."

Dana reached for her stepmother's hand. "Thank you for telling me, finally. It makes everything else so much easier to understand."

"I'm sorry you had to live for 30 years not knowing. I think it was a mistake. I think one of them should've told you."

Dana squeezed her hand. "I can see why they didn't. Anyway, it doesn't really matter now. What I am grateful for is you. I'm so happy that Dad found you. That he finally got to live life on his own terms. With someone who adored him and who enjoyed the outdoors. Who wouldn't put him down for wanting to go fishing at every opportune moment. Who loved Baja as much as he did. Who had a blast roaring up and down the beach next to him on a four-wheeler."

"We had a great life together. I doubt I will ever remarry. You understand that, don't you?"

Dana nodded and let go of Ellen's hand. "I think so. I think you probably only love like that once in a lifetime. To try to find someone else to measure up to Dad would be pretty difficult! But you never know...."

Ellen laughed. "I spent nearly my entire adult life with Bud. You know I'd never diminish or minimize our years together in any way, but I'm still young. I'm only 54 years old. I want to travel. To go to Europe. South America. Africa. India. China. Everywhere! I have enough money to do it and I'm actually looking forward to doing it on my own. I'll have so much more fun that way."

"Cool," said Dana. "You know what's so weird, Ellen?"

"What?"

"Here you are, widowed and overflowing with gratitude, yet excitement too. It's like you're just opening up your arms to embrace your future. To welcome the rest of your life like it's one huge adventure."

Her stepmother smiled. Nodded. "It is. But you know, Dana your father is still with me, here, in my heart. I can feel his presence—his love inside of me, every minute of the day. I catch myself talking to him in my head all the time." She smiled. "Let me tell you a secret. Death doesn't destroy love. Love is indestructible—everlasting. It doesn't end when someone dies. It just changes form. When you truly love someone, they never really leave you. Bud will always be with me. Always."

They enjoyed a few moments of silence, each of them alone with their thoughts of Bud Wallace.

Dana sighed. "Oh, how I envy you. I want a love like that more than anything on this earth. But I don't know if I'll ever find it. I've been alone seven years and I hate it. My one stab at a relationship, I botched totally. Well, so did Peter. We were both your typical walking wounded paranoid freaks. There was no way we could trust each other. We just kept spinning out on fear. Every time one of us would start to get a little too close or be the tiniest bit vulnerable, the other one would panic, give a giant shove and push the other away. Our game was, 'Advance, retreat. Duck, hit, miss.' It was awful. And he cheated on me...."

"You see him anymore?"

"I just did. He still 'burns up the airways' with Camille. I saw him for the first time in almost three years at our meeting at the station. We were both extremely awkward could barely acknowledge each other. I can't seem to find a way to love my life, to enjoy being single. I keep wanting a man to come in and fill those empty slippers under my bed. To fill all the holes in my life. In the twins' lives. But yet, when anyone tries to get close to me, I totally sabotage the relationship. Or I run."

"That's why he wanted you to have the motor home, Dana."

Dana shot her a shocked look. "What?!"

Ellen smiled that all-knowing smile of hers again. "You'll see. You'll be 45 the day after tomorrow. There's something that happens to a woman as she gets close to 50. You make some choices at a deep level in mid-life. You either face all those 'uncomfortable feelings' that are keeping you in bondage—preventing you from really grabbing life and living it to the fullest or you cop out like your mother did. Like lots of people do. And end up living lives of quiet desperation. You see, Dana, when you face your fear and your disappointment and your rage, when you bring them out into the open and feel them fully, they lose their power over you. If you keep running from them and hiding from them, they will control you. Always."

"What happens if I face these uncomfortable feelings? Will I end up on the floor, screaming in a corner like my mom?"

"Maybe. But if you do, I bet you'll have the guts to take the hand that reaches out to you—even if it's a child's and let people help you, without despising them for it. Am I right?"

Dana nodded, very slowly. Ellen continued. "It's like the Bible says. 'You will know the truth and the truth will set you free.' With every act of courage you get a little more confident, a little stronger. You learn, one day at a time, to embrace the paradoxes, the mysteries of life—the things you cannot know and will not ever know as long as you're on this planet. When you do that, you're able to love more, because you fear less. Fear eats love alive. Look what it did to you and Peter."

"No kidding."

"And finally, dear, you'll be able to trust more. As the fear recedes from your life, you'll see things more clearly. And judge them less. Life will cease to be quite so black and white, and you'll be able to see the beauty in all the shades of gray. You won't be seduced by people like Brad, or by a lifestyle that won't be good for you. Instead, you'll build a life that really works for you—with or without a man. The man part will take care of itself, I think, if you quit searching for one so desperately and shine your flashlight on yourself for awhile. Watch yourself, but without beating yourself up. Find out what pushes your buttons and makes you crazy-fighting-mad or scares you so badly you want to run for the hills. Bring those things into the light of day. Examine them. Don't judge them. Just feel them, think about them and learn from them."

"Wow," said Dana. "You're amazing."

Ellen yawned. "Not really. You ladies have a lot of packing to do and even more information to absorb tomorrow. Plus the twins and I are throwing you a birthday party later on. But there's one last thought I want to leave with you, and then we better get to bed. "

"What?"

"It's this. We all lose our innocence as we go through life. Every time someone hurts us, rejects us, betrays us—every time that happens, or every time we even *believe* it happens, we lose a piece of our innocence—of our souls. And we become smaller—more closed off and fearful. The final step in the growth process, the way we regain that innocence is through forgiveness. Every time we forgive, truly forgive someone who has injured us in some way—even accidentally we regain a piece of our lost innocence. But we have to relive the wounding, to feel it fully before we can forgive it. And once we can forgive it, we learn the lesson we were meant to learn. Then we can go on—as a wiser, kinder, more loving soul."

"How can I ever forgive Brad?"

"You will. You have to. You have to forgive yourself too."

"Does that mean I have to trust him again?!"

"No! Last thought of the night. To forgive is not to reinstate. You can forgive someone without letting them back into the inner sanctum of your life."

"How?!"

"You'll have to ponder that one on your trip. You're gonna have an incredible time. I just know it."

CHAPTER SEVEN   Encinitas, California
                                     October 13, 1997

Holly was there the next morning before Dana and Ellen had finished their coffee. She came dancing in the front door, clipboard in hand, singing Willy Nelson's "On the Road Again." She hurried them all through breakfast and herded Ellen out to the motor home while Dana showered and finished packing. Holly handed Ellen her clipboard. The two women began taking an inventory of everything that was already in the motor home.

"Okay, Ellen. Check these off: Plastic dishes and cups. Paper plates. Napkins. Silverware. Knives. Can opener. Serving plates, spoons, spatula. Bottle opener. Corkscrew. Scissors. Ice pick. Sponges. Dish soap. Mixing bowls. Pots and pans. Casserole dishes. Cleaning supplies. Salt. Pepper. A basic array of spices. Sugar. Flour. Sweet and Low. Coffee Mate. Pancake mix. Canned salsa, frijoles and jalapeños. Green beans. Soup. Tuna. Brownie mix. Instant pudding. Saltine crackers. Chips. Spam. *Spam*?! Do we have to?! I refuse to have this disgusting potted meat product along on my camping trip!"

Ellen laughed out loud. "Bud loved it. Leave it in there so Dana can find it. If it doesn't make her cry, it'll certainly make her laugh."

"Oh. I'm sorry." Holly's cheeks flushed red. She turned away. "I definitely won't throw it away, then. Well, that's everything in here. Make a note. We need more garbage bags and Ziploc bags too. Oh. And paper towels. Toilet paper. Matches."

"The matches are in the third drawer. Under the sink."

"Oh. I found them. Do you have a first aid kit?"

"In the drawer under the bathroom sink. I have a couple of pocket knives and a snake bite kit in there too. And a list of remedies for things like jellyfish, stingray and scorpion stings."

Holly looked up from under the kitchen sink and smiled. "You've made this way too easy!"

"Not true. You have your lists. You did a good, thorough job. I just saved you a little running around, that's all. You have what you need for your book. You don't have to totally reinvent this wheel, you know."

"Yeah. Well, I sure am grateful." She looked at Ellen and nodded her head. "I sure am." Then, back to business once more, she added, "Do you have an ice chest in here somewhere, or do I need to bring mine?"

Ellen pointed. "It's right there under the dining room table. You do know this table folds down into a bed, right?"

Holly nodded. "It's a double bed isn't it?"

Ellen nodded. "Yes it is. Almost." She gave Holly a serious look. "Let me ask you something. Have you ladies discussed sleeping arrangements?"

"Yes, but we haven't finalized anything. Do you have any suggestions? It's kind of a touchy subject."

Ellen nodded her head. "Oh it can be, believe me. Let's sit down for a minute." The two women sat at the dinette table across from each other. Holly's clipboard lay on the smooth Formica surface between them. "I've given your journey a lot of thought. You ladies need to start right out communicating in an up-front, straightforward way with one other. You have to be straight, but you have to be kind and considerate too. Be alert for each other's weak or vulnerable spots and try not to hurt each other. But at the same time, you can't allow someone to be abusive or to engage in damaging behavior."

"What do you mean?"

"Let me tell you a story. A while ago—gosh, it must've been at least ten years ago—Bud and I took the ferry across from La Paz to Mazatlán and drove down mainland Mexico all the way to Yucatán to see the Mayan ruins. We went with two other couples, each of us in our own rigs. We were gone two months. Well, one of these women had a real queen bee syndrome."

"A what?"

"She was what I call a queen bee. She had to be in the spotlight—the center of male attention. She was older than me, but very attractive. Boy, did she ever pull rank on me. I was sure the men would never see it, but in every little gesture, in every conversation, she talked down to me. She let me know, in no uncertain terms, that she thought I was an idiot—nothing more than Bud's young 'trophy wife.' The third woman, Bobbie, was pushing 60 and quite heavy. Our queen bee ever-so-subtly made jokes about her appearance. Constantly. Again, it was in those little ways that men don't catch onto.

"She *ruined* the trip. She ruined it for me. She ruined it for Bobbie. We complained occasionally to each other behind her back, but mostly we cowered like whipped dogs. I was too intimidated by her and too afraid of being labeled a bitch to speak up. The irony of the whole thing, Holly, is that when we got back to Los Barriles, I spilled the beans to Bud. And guess what? *He knew.* He'd known the whole time. He'd been waiting for me or Bobbie to stand up to her. To bring it up to our husbands. To do something! My trip was ruined because I was too insecure to call this horrible woman on her stuff!"

"And the lesson is...."

"Speak up. Not behind someone's back but to her face. If you have a problem, call a meeting. Give everyone a chance to speak. Do not allow name-calling. In fact, do not allow abuse in any way, shape or form. Got it?"

Holly turned and looked out the window. After a bit she gave a slow nod. "Got it," she finally said.

"Good. One last thing."

Holly looked at Ellen and smiled. "Of course."

"They're expecting you to lead the way, and the only way to lead women is by example. Dana, Camille and Barb are all competent, intelligent women. Let them have plenty of input in setting the rules. You're the tour guide—not the queen bee. It's Dana's RV and she's been traveling in Baja longer than you have. So you'll have to defer to her sometimes, if just for the sake of diplomacy." At Holly's frown, she added, "Trust me. There's no way you'll get through this trip without tromping on each other's feelings. It'll take a lot of gracious maneuvering, a lot of counting to ten before losing your tempers and a lot of patience to get through it. Expect to be challenged, but also know that you can and will work things through. Remind them that quitting is not an option. As long as everyone is honest and fights fair and you don't gang up on one another, you'll do fine."

Holly looked down at her fingernails and then looked up. "Okay. Thanks. Now about this table that makes into a bed. What do you have to say about it?"

"Well, this bed, the table, is roomy and comfortable. The only drawback is that whoever takes it probably can't use it except to sleep in at night. So she has comfort going for her and inconvenience going against her."

Ellen walked back to the twin bunks in the back of the motor home, next to the bathroom, vanity and closets. "These are narrow. I've never slept here, but I've heard that they're okay. Whichever two of you end up back here will be awakened by anyone needing to pee in the night. And if the holding tank gets full and starts to stink, they may get gripy about that too."

"I've never dumped a holding tank...."

"Well, I hadn't either until this trip. I had Jorge teach me how. It's very simple, actually. Not nearly as awful as I'd expected. It's easier with two people—one to hold the hose in place over the dump station and the other to pull the chute. As long as you attach the hose properly, you won't have any excrement exploding out at you. Oh, and in case you're wondering, a dump station is just a hole in the ground that leads to a sewer or a septic tank or some such shit hole." She chuckled.

"Do you think we should assign beds or rotate?"

"I took a poll on this very such thing during my mah-jongg game at Tío's last Tuesday. The ladies all decided that you should use the lottery approach."

"Excuse me?"

"Get four pieces of paper. Write top bunk on one, bottom bunk on another, kitchen table on the third and cabover bed on the fourth."

"You don't think Dana will mind? I mean, it's *her* motor home. Shouldn't she have the cabover bed? I mean, it's the best one by far."

"If I know Dana, she'd feel too guilty to enjoy it if you automatically assigned her the best bed."

Holly laughed. "You obviously know her better than I do. So I'll take your advice on this. We'll do the lottery thing." She made a note on her pad.

"Okay. Next item. Where are the paddles and seat backs for the kayaks? And life jackets? Do we have life jackets?"

"On top in the storage pod. Here, let me show you what's up there." They went outside and Ellen followed Holly up the ladder on the rear of the motor home and onto its roof. On top, off to the left and strapped to the roof rack, were two yellow plastic ocean kayaks. On the right was a bubble-like white storage pod and four red five-gallon gas cans. Ellen crawled over and popped the top of the pod. "In here are four folding beach chairs. Four boogie boards, two spare tires with a lug wrench and a jack."

Ellen opened a wooden box. "Here's your emergency road kit, Holly. Check this out. You have some nylon rope, some heavy rope and a long enough length of chain to get you towed out of the sand."

"Hopefully we won't get stuck. I really don't want to."

"I don't blame you. But you need it just in case. And here's some flares; a reflector triangle; motor oil; brake, power steering and transmission fluid; extra oil and fuel filters. Here's some stuff that's supposed to stop radiator leaks. And here are jumper cables and all sorts of spare belts and hoses. You ladies are obviously not mechanics, so if anything goes wrong with this beast, I'm sure you'll have to signal for help and wait for either the Green Angels or some other Good Samaritans to come by."

Holly laughed. "No kidding. That's the trickiest part of this whole entire venture. Admitting that we are not and cannot be men. That every single one of the four of us is clueless as to what goes on in an internal combustion engine, not to mention how to change a flat. And finally, that we'll be at the mercy of Mexico should we suffer mechanical difficulties!"

Ellen laughed back at her. "Just remind your group that the rule of the road in Baja is that people help each other. That should keep the fear factor at bay. Next item. Here's the bike pump, some plugs and some extra tubes for the bike tires. How many bikes will you be taking?"

"Just Dana's and Camille's. They both have mountain bikes. I do too, but mine's too expensive to take. And Barb doesn't have one."

"Two will be enough. I think the spare fuses and bulbs are down below, in the storage bin underneath. Let's climb back down and see." She shut the pod and crawled backwards after Holly down the ladder.

"Grill. Charcoal. Lighter fluid. Siphon. Wood blocks. Folding shovel. Machete. Pry bar. Tool box, complete with socket set, wrenches, pliers, screwdriver, hammer and so on and so on and so on. It's all there. PVC. Duct tape. Wire. White glue. Super glue. Goop. Corona soap, which Jorge claims can plug any leak you might have until you can get to the next town. Here are the fuses and bulbs, right in this box with the WD-40 and the tire patch kit. Bud had this other box here full of miscellaneous small parts. Odds and ends. I don't know half of what's in here, but I'm sure if you have a problem, any Mexican mechanic you run into will be able to work miracles with this stuff."

Holly shook her head in amazement.

"We have a whole pack of bungee cords around here somewhere too." She went around to the driver's side of the vehicle and looked in the other storage bin. "Here it is. And here's the sun shower, snorkeling gear, Coleman lantern with extra mantles and fuel. Camping table for dining al fresco. And, of course," she said, leading Holly around to the front of the motor home, "two five-gallon water jugs with spigots here. Use those for purified water. To drink and to wash your veggies and fruit before you eat them."

"You're amazing. I wish you were coming along, Ellen."

"No. You don't. And before you ask your next question no, I won't miss this rig. Bud and I had it 12 years. I want Dana to have it as much as he did." Her eyes sought Holly's. "Tell me something. This is your first motor home trip, isn't it?"

The younger woman's eyes narrowed. She looked away and hesitated for a long moment before answering, as if considering whether or not to tell the truth. Finally she nodded. "I've backpacked all over the Rockies. I've been a ski instructor, led white water rafting tours. I've climbed every *fourteener*—14,000 foot peak—in Colorado. I can tent camp with the best of 'em. I have a stationary trailer down in Mulegé. But no. I've never traveled in an RV."

Ellen looked straight into her eyes. "It'll be better that way. Your writing will be fresher and more exciting than if you were an old hand at this like me. You are extremely well-prepared. You've done your homework and this is a good, solid, dependable old rig."

"It seems like it. Have you ever broken down in this?"

"In a dozen years?! Of course! But nothing major. Nothing that wasn't pretty readily fixable. Just remember the rules of the road in Baja."

"I know. *Drive slow and never, never drive at night!*"

Ellen smiled. "Bud taught me a couple other ones too. You know how the speedometer has the miles and kilometers next to each other?"

"Uh huh."

"He always said we should drive kilometers per hour in Mexico the way we drive miles per hour on our U.S. freeways. That way we avoid things like losing a hubcap in a pothole. We avoid getting caught off-guard when something hairy happens to be coming at us around the next curve. Which happens, you know."

"I know. I've been driving two-lane mountain roads since my early twenties. I've just never driven a motor home. Is it hard?"

"No. It's nothing more than a big van. Let's take it for a spin. But before we go, let me share Bud's other trick. He always admonished me to use the side mirrors when I was driving. Actually, he put it this way: 'They're not just for combing your hair, hon.'" She gave a small chuckle and tossed Holly the keys. "Hop in. I'll check off the things that are in the glove compartment while you chauffeur us to the store for garbage bags, Ziploc bags, paper towels and more toilet paper. Let me check inside with Dana and see if she needs me to get anything else."

She came back a moment later, to find Holly sitting in the driver's seat, a faraway look in her eyes. "She said tampons. Film. A camera battery. And Diet Coke. She's addicted to it. How about the rest of you?"

"Dr. Pepper for me. Camille said Diet Coke. I don't believe Barb drinks that stuff. I think she's into some sort of decaffeinated, healthy iced tea of something. She's a health nut and a clean freak. I have no doubt she'll insist on disinfecting everything she puts in her mouth."

Ellen blinked hard and looked at her straight on again. "Be gentle with her, Holly. I understand from what Dana told me that you picked Barb *specifically* because she's never done anything like this before. She's a critical player in this game. Think of her as your target audience."

Holly swallowed. She didn't respond.

"Okay. Now, hit it! Drive, girl, drive!"

On the way to the grocery store, Ellen pulled the spare keys, vehicle registration, an Auto Club Baja book, a Spanish-English dictionary along with a pair of binoculars, all kinds of maps and three guidebooks one for Western birds, one for tropical fish and one for plant life in Baja out of the glove compartment. "This is easy," said Holly. "It's easier to drive than my husband's old van."

"It is, isn't it? I love to drive it myself. Makes me feel very powerful. Grown up. And free. You know?!"

Holly nodded her head and smiled hugely. "Yes," she said, "Yes, I do. Yes, I can! Yes, I will! Yes!" she half-shouted, half-sang.

"I want Dana to drive this thing too today. And the other two. She and I are going to the DMV this afternoon to register it in her name. On our way do you want us to stop by Discover Baja Travel Club and pick up the tourist cards?"

Holly looked at her. "Yes. And don't forget the insurance. Do you have U.S. insurance on the motor home?

"Yes we do. And Mexican too. All we need to do is change the names on both policies so they match up with the certificate of ownership. We don't want to confuse and upset the Mexican government officials now do we?"

"No way, José!"

"What about fishing licenses?"

"Nope. If we go fishing, we'll just do a day trip out of Los Barriles or something. That way, they'll provide the licenses, poles, tackle and everything else for us."

"Good call."

"Any other words of wisdom you care to impart?"

Ellen thought a moment. "Let me see. Don't let them spend too much time out in the sun. Even with sunscreen, make sure they start with about a half hour and increase each day by about another half hour until they have a solid base tan. Of course you don't have to worry about Dana. She's tan as an Indian already with all the swimming she does. But Camille and Barb are both pretty fair."

"True."

"The usual. Remind them that they're guests in Mexico and to treat the people there with dignity and respect. To obey all laws and to be as responsible there as they are here."

"Would you note those two things on my pad, por favor?"

"Of course." She scribbled away. "One more thing. Teach them the Mexican 'no paper in the toilet' routine. That goes for the motor home too. You'll have to dump the holding tank a lot less frequently if you use a plastic bag for T.P. And, remember to burn the toilet trash along with all your paper trash."

"Right. I know of course about the 'bring out what you bring in' rule. We won't be trashing up any campsites."

"Good girl. You'll do fine."

"Do you have everything on your list?" Holly asked Barb, who'd driven up a few minutes previously.

"I do, Boss Banana."

"Cool. Come inside. Dana and I divided up the drawer and closet space. We don't have a lot of room, so you may have to leave some things in your duffel bag. But that's okay cause we figured we can rotate the clothes around and use the duffels to hold dirty laundry." Holly led Barbara inside and showed her where to stow her gear.

"Let's unload your car and put everything on the sidewalk next to the motor home. You can put your stuff away," she went on, "as soon as I verify that you brought the *right stuff.*"

Once everything was out of the car, Holly picked up her clipboard, flipped to the page marked, "Barb" and began checking off items from the list. "Okay. Personal stuff first: Beach towel. Bath towel. A week's worth of underwear. Swimsuit. Three pairs shorts. T-shirts. Three sundresses. Sweats. Jeans. Jacket. Hat. Flip-flops. Walking shoes. Sunscreen. Toiletries. Flashlight with spare batteries. Bug repellant. Sleeping bag. Pillow. Looks like everything's in order,

Barb. Load her up!"

"Yes, boss."

"Oh, wait a minute. I forgot. Laptop. Cell phone. Sun glasses, birth certificate or passport, camera, lots of film. Notebook. Pens. Any fancy food or beverage items. You have all that stuff in here somewhere?"

"Yes, boss."

"Make that, Sí, Patrón."

"Sí, Patrón."

"Excelente." She watched Barb unloading food into the kitchen cupboard and grimaced. "Jesus Christ. Did you have to bring so much stuff?!"

Barb turned. Looked at her. "Yes."

Holly was silent a moment, then dropped the subject. "Did you see Camille at the station? Do you know when she'll be here?"

"I did. She said to tell you by 3:00 at the latest. She's having one last meeting with dear old Mark." Holly groaned. "What time is Ellen having the big birthday dinner tonight? Can we bring our husbands?"

Holly half-turned. Her eyes flashed with an almost imperceptible sadness. Her mouth flattened into a tight, straight line. "You can. Mine's at sea right now. He'll be meeting us in Mulegé, however on the 25th."

CHAPTER EIGHT   Tijuana to Ensenada, Baja California
                         October 14, 1997

"Stay in the far right lane. They're for sure gonna send us into Secondary. And even if they don't, we have to stop in at Immigration and get our tourist cards stamped."

Dana followed directions. As she eased through the gate at the world's busiest border between San Diego, California, USA and Tijuana, Baja California, Mexico, the light on the indicator in front of her flashed from a green "Pase" to a red "Revisión." The guard waved the motor home into Secondary.

"What's going on?" asked Barbara from her seat at the dinette. "Why are they pulling us over? Are we okay? Will they search us?"

"Quiet. Relax. Smile, nod and let us do the talking. *Buenos días*—Good morning," Holly greeted the Mexican officials.

"Buenos días, señora. ¿Hablas español?—Good morning, ma'am. Do you speak Spanish?" the nearest one asked through the passenger window.

"Sí. Yo hablo. Y también, ella habla—Yes. I speak. And she also speaks." She pointed at Dana. *"Las otras, no*—The others, no."

After a rapid-fire exchange, the guards ascertained the purpose and length of their trip. They made a quick, cursory inspection of the vehicle and waved the four women over to Immigration to have their tourist cards stamped.

"That wasn't so bad," Barb commented as they climbed back into the RV. "I sure am glad you two speak the language. Otherwise, I'd be scared to death."

"Just remember what Ellen and I told you, Barb. Be courteous. Remember that you're a guest in this country. Live by the Golden Rule and we'll all be fine. Contrary to rumor, there is no more crime here than in our country. As long as we're not drug smugglers, gun runners or political dissidents, and as long as we use good common sense, we're as safe here as we'd be traveling in our own country. The Mexican people are more kind and helpful than Americans any day. You'll see...."

Dana stuck her head out the window. Inhaled deeply. "Ah yes. I love the smell of Mexico," she said. "Okay, now remember to get in the third lane from the left to catch the toll road."

"What?" asked Barb.

"Oops. Sorry. I was talking to myself. I always think I should be in the second lane over and end up in downtown Tijuana. I'm reminding myself to ignore my instincts so I can avoid getting lost."

A taxi honked and cut in front of them. "Hey!" yelled Camille from the back. "What a jerk! Why'd he do that?"

Holly and Dana looked at each other and chuckled. "Number one rule of the road when driving in a Mexican city," Dana told her friend. "Whoever gets there first wins."

"Huh? Isn't that dangerous?"

"Not if you're careful," added Holly. "Most of the time, I'm right in there with them, dodging and cutting and honking. It's a blast. But, trust me, this is not a vehicle I'd use to hone my Mexican driving skills. This is a big, ungainly beast."

"This is Boris," said Dana. "My twins named it last night right before they went to bed. Boris the Baja Beast. Our trusty home away from home for the next four weeks."

Dana got into the lane for Ensenada, followed the road around a tight curve and drove along the fence that separated Mexico from the U.S. for about a mile. She urged Boris up a steep hill, then followed the road as it veered off sharply to the southwest, towards Playas de Tijuana. Soon they'd crossed through the first toll gate and were heading down the coast, along the road to Ensenada, 76 miles to the south.

As she drove, she couldn't help but marvel at the day. Her forty-fifth birthday had dawned as hot as any summer day. The air was clear. There were no clouds. The road looked to have been carved right out of the sandstone cliffs. It snaked along, following the shore-line. The Coronado Islands loomed large, brown and barren against the horizon. They passed by the famed party town of Rosarito Beach and the movie studio at Popótla, where the movie *Titanic* had just been filmed.

As they headed further south, Dana was stunned by the increase of American housing projects. She half-turned her head towards Holly. "How many gringos do you think live here, along this stretch between Tijuana and Ensenada?"

"A lot," she said. "More and more all the time. And you can bet most of them are illegal."

"Weird, isn't it, that we make such a stink about the Mexcians who cross the border to work in the U.S. while we have so many retirees living down here. My dad would go on and on about that. It really ticked him off that our media and government treat the Mexicans like criminals when there's well over 150,000 American citizens living illegally in this country."

"Was he legal?"

Dana nodded. "You bet he was. He could never have been politically active otherwise." She rounded a bend and guided the motor home along a precarious piece of roadway that hung over the edge of the bluffs. Suddenly the terrain was empty. No buildings. No billboards. Just the road, cliffs, sea and sky. Dana sat up straight in her seat and said a quick prayer as she realized in that instant that she was a very privileged guest in this world. Things here in Baja were still so much the same as they'd always been—untouched, untainted and untamed. This was truly a place where man's creations were dwarfed by God's.

Dana glanced down the face of the cliffs and watched as waves crashed onto the deserted beach to her west. The winds were blowing, Santa Ana style, from the east instead of the west. White froth was picked up in the fingers of the breeze and tossed backwards, out to sea. The foam looked like delicately crafted lace as it fluttered behind the breaking waves, only to disappear into the atmosphere within seconds. Her face broke into an ear-to-ear grin.

Perched a hundred feet above a rugged sandy beach, the pink stucco buildings and red tile roofs of the La Fonda Hotel emerged as they pulled off the highway at La Misión. The slightly dilapidated 35-year-old bungalows were strewn across the craggy bluffs and practically hidden by a wall of cherry, violet and salmon colored bougainvillea.

"Is that where we're headed?" Barb asked Dana from behind.

"Yes. Lunch on the patio overlooking the Pacific. It's guaranteed to put you in the mood. You know what Jimmy Buffett says. A change in latitude always triggers a change in attitude. As we head further south, we will get mellower and mellower. It's the old latitude-attitude thing. Give me those little latitudes any day, ladies! Give me hot, sultry days, palm trees, year-round flowers and deserted beaches with snorkelable seas and I will be happy forever and ever!" She sneaked a peek over her right shoulder. "C'mon you guys. Open the damned window. Inhale some of that delicious salt air!"

Dana heard the window and screen slide open and laughed as she looked in her rear view mirror. There were Camille and Barb, eyes closed, heads sticking out the window, mouths open wide as they sucked the air deep into their lungs.

She pulled off the toll road and onto the narrow cobblestone road that led to La Fonda. Boris bounced over the rocks until she parked him in front of the hotel's restaurant. She checked the clock on the dashboard. Ten minutes to noon. The group walked into the dark building, blinking their eyes. They followed Holly outside, onto the patio.

The restaurant was perched high atop the cliffs. Dana felt her breath catch in her throat as she took in the panoramic view. The beach went on nearly forever, bordered to the north and south by dramatic rock formations. The ocean was a pale turquoise in the shallow waters, deepening in hue to a darker and darker turquoise and finally becoming an inky blue where it met up with the sky. Waves swelled up rhythmically, cresting, breaking and pounding towards the sand in perfect, symmetrical explosions of back-flying frosty white foam. They found a table and ordered lunch.

Afterward they hiked down the long stairway to the beach. Camille, Holly and Barb all took off their shoes and waded in the shallow water. Dana ripped off her sundress, ran for the shore, dove through a wave, emerged and dove again through the next one. She swam out beyond the breakers, turned to the south and paralleled the shore for a few minutes.

As she got into the rhythm of her swim, her body and mind relaxed in tandem. Breathing in deeply, she dove down as far as she could, then came up, bursting through the surface of the water like a dolphin. She did this again and again—playing—imagining herself a creature of the sea. The water was see-through and she opened her eyes. She could see the blurry outline of several leopard sharks cruising along the ocean floor beneath her. She felt the inevitable surge of adrenaline. Her blood tingled as it rushed down her arms and legs, fortifying them with the strength to make a run for it. She chided herself. It was always such a treat to see these creatures. She knew logically that they meant her no harm, but the sight of their lurking, angular shark shapes always set off the theme to *Jaws* in her head.

She flipped over and began to backstroke, her eyes squinting against the glare of the sun overhead. She flipped again, turned and began to breaststroke back. The ocean was warm for this late in the year. About 68 degrees, she guessed. Her friends looked small against the huge expanse of sand. She waved at them and all three waved back. She came up behind a trio of surfers and chatted with them for a few moments. Then, seeing them turn as they eyed a set of swells coming towards them from the horizon, she raced with them to catch a wave.

She caught it and ducked her head as it lifted her skyward for a heartbeat and then hurled her down its face as it roared with her towards the shore. The top of her bathing suit was thrust up over her breasts and the bottom was yanked down to her knees. What a ride, she thought to herself as she pictured what she must look like to one of the birds flying overhead. As she neared the shore, she tugged her suit back into place. Then she saw the nearly annihilated ruins of a monstrous castle. Built by a group of Mexican children while she and the others were eating lunch, it had been surrounded by a moat and had, at the time, seemed far enough away from the incoming tide to ensure its survival. Not anymore.

The wave carrying Dana washed over it, depositing her on the sand nearby. The white foam receded and the sand was smooth. The castle had melted away entirely. She ran back out, dove under another wave to wash the sand off her body and returned to her friends, wringing her hair out with both hands.

"Will you teach me to bodysurf?" Barb asked as they headed back towards La Fonda.

"Not here. I'll teach you somewhere with easier waves. These can be dangerous, especially when there are rips."

"How'd you get to be so fearless?"

Dana chuckled. "My dad took me and David to the beach all the time when we were little. We knew how to bodysurf before we started kindergarten."

"I wish someone had taught me. Course," she turned towards Dana, "I don't recall that there was much bodysurfing to be found in southern Illinois."

"No. I imagine there was a slight shortage of surfable waves. Anyway, we'll start you out on a boogie board. In Southern Baja where the water's about 85 degrees, the waves are small and there aren't any sea creatures like leopard sharks or stingrays to wig you out."

"A trip to Ensenada would never be complete without a stop at Hussong's, a bar that was founded by the Hussong family, a bunch of German immigrants, back in 1898," explained Holly as she pulled the motor home into a lot behind the world-famous bar. The foursome entered through the rear door and found themselves in a large room with cartoons and other odd pieces of artwork and memorabilia on the walls, sawdust on the old wooden floor and several tables full of Mexicans and gringos alike, drinking and carrying on. A band of mariachis came in the swinging front door and began to circulate, looking to sell a song or two.

Holly led them to four empty stools at the bar. *"Cuatro Margaritas, por favor*—Four margaritas, please," she ordered. "Wait 'til you're served. There's a wonderful story I want to have Roberto, the bartender tell you."

The drinks arrived, with an extra for Roberto. They all raised their glasses. "What toast do we use here?" asked Barb.

Dana raised her other hand. "I know. Teacher, let me!"

"Okay. Go for it."

"This is an old Spanish toast. I'll teach you so we can all do it together. *¡Salud, pesetas y amor y el tiempo para gustarlos!* It means, health, money and love and the time to enjoy them!"

"¡Olé!" they called out in unison.

"The story. Roberto. Por favor, señor."

The gray-haired, circumspect gentleman leaned across the bar towards them. His dark eyes lit up and the years fell away from his face. He began his story in clear, barely accented English. "Back during the early part of this century, during your country's Depression, a young man named Antonio Hussong lived in a small coastal town down Mexico way. He spent his mornings driving his new 1932 Ford pickup down the dirt streets of Ensenada. In the evenings he worked at his father's bar on the north end of town."

The bar grew silent as he told his story.

"As luck would have it, there was a girl. Margarita was young and lovely and just passing through on her way with her family to work in the fields and farms of the rich, fertile lands north of the border. At 13 years of age she was old enough to join in the seasonal picking of oranges and avocados with her father, mother and brother, Juan Castillo. Their stopping in front of Hussong's Cantina was just as much fate that sunny afternoon as was the 1932 Ford truck that pulled up next to them on the well-traveled corner of downtown Ensenada.

"Offering the weary travelers a drink of water and a flyer for his father's bar, Antonio was just passing his day as he usually did. He was unaware of the young girl standing just behind her father. When Antonio did notice the girl, he was immediately overtaken by her beauty.

"In the days and months that followed, Antonio found himself often driving that Ford pickup over the 100 miles of dirt road that skirted the ocean to visit the Castillo family. His love for Margarita was deep and he would often bring her flowers and sweets in order to win her heart. One day, Antonio, using the tools at hand in his father's bar, created a drink in honor of his love for the sweet Margarita.

"First he used tequila, the liquor of his country. He added lime for the spice of his love. A hint of orange for the groves in which Margarita worked with her family. Then he rimmed the glass with salt for the ocean that he drove along to visit her.

"Margarita was overjoyed at his thoughtfulness and accepted his hand in marriage. Soon afterward, Mexico designated the Margarita as its national drink. The Margarita is named for the girl, and one should always remember the love of Antonio Hussong when enjoying this very special libation."

Everyone in the place clapped.

A few minutes later, they thanked Roberto, paid their *cuenta*—tab, and exited the bar. Holly drove by the port and showed them where the cruise ships docked. She drove down the main tourist street of Ensenada and pointed out the various shops.

"Can we please stop?" begged Barb. "Please! I'll die if I don't get to do a little shopping...."

"Yeah, come on. Let us check this out," Camille added.

Holly shook her head. "No. We'll get plenty of shopping in later on in the trip. Not today." A tiny alarm went off in Dana's head as Holly ignored their protests and continued on with her narrative. "One of the miracles of modern Mexico is the supermarket," she explained 10 minutes later as she eased Boris into parking space at what looked to be a brand new Calimax store. "Follow me. This is an adventure in and of itself."

She grabbed a shopping cart and wheeled it up the first aisle. On her left were cans of all sorts of different chiles, salsas, tomato and spaghetti sauces. Next were the bottled salsas—more kinds than Dana had ever seen in one place before. Salsa Huichol, Amor, Extra Hot Amor, Habañero and more than a dozen other brands she'd never heard of. All prices were in pesos. She knew the current exchange rate was eight to one. After doing a quick mental calculation, she figured that a small bottle of Amor sauce priced at four pesos cost about 50 cents. She tossed it in the basket.

Holly led them to the deli case. In it were at least 20 different types of cheeses, three different kinds of bacon, bulk hot dogs, hams and other meats. There were several flavors of fresh yogurt and two types of sour cream sauce. Holly ordered three different cheeses: a *queso fresco*—fresh cheese, a crumbly, salty white cheese to go on top of beans and tacos; a slab of Monterey, the tasty Mexican version of Jack cheese and a bag of string cheese, which she explained was similar to mozzarella. She got a half kilo of bacon, some sliced ham and a half liter of strawberry yogurt.

She led the women up and down every aisle, translating wherever necessary. At the fish counter they bought fresh *huachinango*—red snapper, *cabrilla*—sea bass and *camarones*—shrimp. Then a smiling butcher sold them four beautiful *filetes*—filet mignons, for 40 pesos a kilo. They bought *pecho de pollo*—chicken breasts, freshly made corn and flour tortillas, frosted Mexican cookies, a small pewter press to use for squeezing the juice out of tiny, tasty *limónes*—Mexican limes, *leche*—milk and a half a flat of *huevos*—eggs.

"Here's where we get our pesos," Holly advised as they rounded the corner toward the produce section. "Just put your ATM card into the machine and select how many pesos you want. Don't get more than $200 worth of pesos to start with. We'll stash our money in different places around the motor home, just to be on the safe side. We may not see another ATM until we get to La Paz. And while they deal in dollars from here up the border, once we get further down, we'll be much better off using pesos."

They took their turns at the machine. They loaded up on fresh produce next. Bright red *tomates*—tomatoes that looked to be much tastier than their American counterparts. Avocados that cost about 15 cents apiece. *Lechuga*—lettuce. Cilantro. *Cebollas*—onions. *Ajo*—garlic. *Papas*—potatoes. *Calabacitas*—zucchini. Chiles. *Peras*—pears, papayas, mangos, *plátanos*—bananas, *piña*—pineapple, *naranjas*—oranges and a *sandía*—watermelon. The last stop was the liquor aisle. As they discussed the merits of the different tequilas, a tiny Mexican girl who couldn't have been over 19 tapped Holly on the shoulder.

"¿*Quieres probar una copa de tequila*—Do you want to try a cup of tequila? *Es la especial hoy*—It's on special today." She handed Holly a tiny plastic cup of reposado tequila.

Holly drank it down. "*Muchas gracias*—Many thanks. *Es deliciosa*—It's delicious. ¡*Ahora estoy segura que estoy en Mexico*—Now I know I'm in Mexico! *Unas copas más para mis amigas, por favor*—Some more for my friends, please." The girl poured four more shots.

The total for the overflowing cart of groceries, including liquor, came to 736 pesos, or about $92. "We are set, ladies. We will dine well on this trip. Do you not all agree?"

"Boy I feel like I just got away with highway robbery," commented Barb as they crammed the food into the refrigerator and cupboards. "That's barely more than half the price we'd pay stateside. And it's all really safe to eat?"

Dana and Holly shook their heads. "There's Spam, Barb," said Holly.

"And tuna."

"And canned beans and soup and..."

Barb put her hands together in a T. "Time out. Time out. I'm sorry for asking. Okay?!"

"No problem. In fact, Dana, could you run back inside and grab a package of Lomotil from the *farmácia*—pharmacy? Just in case?" Dana nodded and took off. While the other three put away groceries, Holly explained. "Lomotil will take care of most cases of diarrhea. But you know, the folks that run the tour company I work for have always told our guests that the most frequent cause of quote-unquote Montezuma's Revenge is not unfriendly bacteria."

"No?" Barb's eyebrows shot up.

"Nope. My boss Shirley maintains that it's caused by too much sun, too much booze and too much spicy food."

"I caught that," said Dana as she came back and tossed a paper sack with Lomotil in it on the table. "But don't forget about the lard...."

Holly groaned. "God, I always want to forget the lard."

"They use *lard?!*" asked Camille.

"Didn't you see those yummy-looking big white blocks of pure, saturated animal fat in the Calimax?" Dana asked. "That stuff'll totally harden your arteries!"

Camille grabbed at her heart. "Eeew. I can already feel my cholesterol count rising. And my arteries solidifying into tubes of fat. Not to mention my thighs spreading. You mean we're gonna have to eat that *shit* for an entire month?!"

"Nope. You won't be *eating any shit.* Just load up on sun, liquor and lots of hot sauce, my dear and you will be full of it. Shit I mean. You won't *need* the lard!" Dana said, poking her in the ribs. "Although," she added, her eyes widening with the phony innocence of a scheming 10-year-old, "a little lump of melted animal fat may really add to the dramatic effect of the explosive—ahem—how do I say this daintily? Bowel movements...."

Laughter blocked out her voice.

"Stop!" Camille shrieked, grabbing her sides. "I can't take it! You're worse than Eric! I'm laughing so hard I'm about to pee my pants! Get outta my way! I gotta get to the head!"

Camille pushed by her and rushed into the bathroom. Dana's eyes widened some more. As the laughter died down, she put up her hand. "Excuse me. I was describing the rather raucous bowel movements associated with what is technically known as 'Traveler's Diarrhea.' Camille's son Eric, who is in the outhouse humor stage of life, calls it 'Explosive Diarrhea.' You may know it as...."

"Stop!" Barb shouted at her.

"Okay. You obviously know what I'm talking about. No matter what you want to call it, the bodily eruptions associated with Montezuma's Revenge wouldn't be nearly as dramatic without the lard! In fact, my daddy always maintained that lard was the catalytic ingredient in Montezuma's Revenge. You know, it really speeds up the whole evacuation process. Just think...."

"Dana! Shut up!" Holly yelled.

"What a hasty exit the tequila, salsa and lard'll all make together. Of course the sunburn is strictly for fever enhancement." Camille opened the bathroom door. Dana turned to her. "As far as your thighs go, Camille, if you do this right and get yourself sick enough, you won't have to worry a bit about gaining weight. Your thighs'll be shrinking on this trip, not spreading. So, hey! Let's break out the tequila, salsa and chips! Let's party!"

"Get a soapy rag, Barb. We're washing this girl's mouth out with soap!"

Holly shook her head and started the motor. "I feel like an old school marm on a field trip. Knock it off with the potty talk, children and strap yourselves in. We're burning daylight."

After gassing up at the Pemex station, they stopped at a brand-new drive-through Corona and Pacifico beer store. Holly drove up and bought a case of Pacificos. A tall Mexican gentleman carried it out to the motor home for her. Opening the side door, he placed it on the floor by Camille's feet. "Gracias," Holly said, thanking him. She looked at Barb. "Here. Put some of these on ice. And don't anyone throw away the bottles. The beer costs about half price if we return the bottles."

She ducked down and slid into the driver's seat, put the RV back into gear and pulled out into traffic. A few blocks away she made a right turn and Boris bounced down the rutted road toward the Estero

Beach Hotel. They pulled through the guard station at the hotel entrance and followed directions toward the camp ground. It was off to the left of the hotel, past a gringo colony of trailers and the Baja interpretation of beach houses—rooms, decks and bedrooms built onto, around and on top of the innards of trailers.

The campground was on a small spit of land surrounded on both sides by marshes. While Dana read out loud from the brochure, they drove through. There were 70 sites for motor homes all with sewer, water and electrical hookups. They picked a spot next to the water. "This is the *Estero de Punta Banda*—the Punta Banda Estuary," Dana read. "Where's the bird book? It says here that we should be able to see loons, gulls, pelicans, cormorants, herons, egrets, hawks and even a few coots." She got out of the motor home and looked around. "I have one teeny tiny question to ask you all."

"Now what?" Camille asked.

"Who knows how to kayak?"

Holly laughed out loud. She raised her hand. "I do." The other two were silent. Dana and Holly's eyes met. "Which one do you want?" Holly asked.

Dana thought for a moment. "I'll take Camille. I can't wait to tip her over just to hear her squeal about how I messed up her lovely hair!"

Camille punched her. "I don't want to kayaking with you! I hate you!" she joked. "You think you are such hot shit, just because you know how to bodysurf and kayak and speak Spanish and you own a motor home and and you're in Baja!"

Dana was already climbing up the ladder. "I'm gonna roll these babies on down to you, Cinnamon Breath. One at a time. I know you have teeny little Olive Oyl muscles in your arms, but do me a favor and try not to drop 'em, okay? Then just to spite you I'm gonna force you to pour yourself into a swimsuit and take you out onto this scenic, tranquil and most magnificent lagoon, where I will personally teach you how to fall out of and climb back into your kayak. A safety lesson, you understand. Routine."

"Do I have to, boss?" Camille asked Holly.

"Yes. You know you do. Barb, come with me. Let's figure out how to hook up the water and sewer lines. Then I'll take you for a bike ride. You can ride a bike, can't you?"

Barb looked at her through squinted eyes and smiled sweetly. "Surprise, boss. I can."

CHAPTER NINE　　　　　**La Bufadora, Baja California**
　　　　　　　　　　　　　October 15, 1997

"As much as I liked the Estero, this is much more my style," said Camille as she and Dana paddled out in Papalote Bay toward the world-famous Blow Hole—La Bufadora, around the corner from Ensenada on the southern end of Punta Banda. "It's so beautiful. It feels isolated and disconnected from civilization. You know—it excites me—but at the same time I feel safe and secure, like I've been here before or something. Does this make any sense to you?"

Dana nodded. "I feel it too. I think this is our first real taste of Baja. We've finally escaped from the beaten track and landed in the outback!" She pointed to the ocean and then to the surrounding mountains that seemed to go on forever. "I could hike and swim and paddle around here for an awfully long time without getting bored. Just reveling in the naked splendor of it all!"

"Naked would be good. This looks to be a good place for naked. I bet we could find a million places to go skinny-dipping!"

"The Mexicans frown on skinny-dipping. But I'm surprised at you, Cinnamon Girl. For a city slicker you're taking to this back-woodsy stuff awfully well. How come?"

"I dunno. It's easy, this kayaking. I paddle, I get tired, I stop. I rest and zone out on Mother Nature. She leaned over the edge and looked down into the water. "I can't believe how clear it is down there! Why is that?"

"Holly told me earlier. She said it's cause the cool northern current meets up with the warm southern current here." She pointed toward rock formations at the mouth of the tiny bay. "We're sticking pretty far out to the west. The water's deep and the visibility's excellent. That's why there's a dive shop right here. This is one of the best spots for diving around."

"Here?! But it's so deserted."

Dana spun her boat around so that she was facing the shore. There were close to a hundred brightly colored structures dotting the steep hillside with a network of dirt roads leading from one to the other, all the way up to the top. "Look, Camille. How many houses do you think there are here?"

"I don't know. A lot. But most of them are empty."

"Holly said the ranch is owned by a Mexican family, the León's. They rent lots to gringos, who put trailers on them. Or build houses. Most of 'em are weekenders, I'd bet. That's why there's hardly anyone around now. I like this much better than the trailer park yesterday, even though we have to camp in the dirt and there aren't any hookups. It's so quiet. I love the way it's all craggy and the hillsides run right down to the ocean. It's like Greece. Or Big Sur without the trees. Oh. Look."

She pointed to a big truck lumbering up through the campground where they were the only ones camping. It had a white cab with some lettering on it and a black cylindrical tank on the back. Water or some other liquid kept sloshing out behind it and dripping down into the cloud of dust that followed it as it ground its way up the steep roadway. "Can I see the binoculars?"

Camille paddled over to her and handed them across. Dana put them up to her eyes and read, "Tony Sanchez Water something. I can't tell." They both watched as the truck pulled up next to a large playhouse-sized square box made of concrete block. The guy in the cab got out and climbed on top of the box. He lifted a piece of plywood and peered inside, then got down, unhooked a large hose from the back of the truck and began to pump water into the box.

"I think we've just witnessed how people get their water in these out-of-the-way places in Baja," she told Camille.

"Wow. How do they get lights? Phones? Gas?"

"I know the answer to that one, 'cause my dad had a trailer down the coast from here, just south of La Bocana, at kilometer 181, back when I was a kid." She felt her eyes mist up at the memory. She did not tell Camille that he'd bought it the summer before her mom left and that they'd only managed to take one trip down there before the family fell apart. She choked back the memory. "People who live in these remote areas use solar panels to run their lights. They run them off 12 volt I think, like our motor home. They have these old funky

Servel refrigerators. You remember the ones like they had back in the '50s?" Camille nodded. "They paint them all kinds of wacky colors and rework them so they run on propane. Water heaters and stoves run on propane too. There aren't any phones."

"No phones?! How do these people communicate with each other?"

"How would you?"

She laughed and considered the question for a moment. "I guess I'd spy on them with my binoculars and if they looked to be awake, and had all their clothes on—well—then I'd guess it would be okay to cruise on over for a visit!"

They laughed, then were silent as they paddled together in the direction of the Blow Hole. Each lost in her own thoughts, they both found themselves hypnotized by the sun as it began its daily descent into the sea.

Ever so slowly it sank, until it seemed to run smack into the horizon. Then, in a refracted mass of angular chunks, it slid into the backlit sea. Immediately the sky blazed up pink and tangerine, the colors brightening so quickly that both women gasped. Within two minutes brilliant, darkly resonant hues painted the heavens in painted in streaks of red, magenta, purple and a fiery orange that reminded Dana of the neon crayons her twins used to color with. Dusk began to fall as they paddled beyond the spewing sea fountain of La Bufadora and onward toward the white-tipped rock outcroppings known as the Pinnacles. The colors faded ever so slowly until the sky and sea were interlocking shades of lavender, touched with pink. They turned and began to paddle back to shore.

Losing herself in the rhythm of the dipping paddles and the gentle motion of the sea, Dana slipped back in time. She was at the trailer at kilometer 181, a couple hours south of La Bufadora. It was 1966 and she was 13. Her twins' age. Her whole family was there: Mom, Dad, David and Rango the Labrador Retriever.

She and her mom stood side by side in front of their trailer. It was a dirty, smudged shade of white on the outside and cramped, primitive and Spartan inside. She, David and their dad had been sleeping on cots outdoors, under the stars. Her mom got the double bed inside. No one minded, as David, Bud and Dana loved to snuggle down in their sleeping bags and call out constellations to each other night after night.

Their trailer was parked on a lonely bluff overlooking the Pacific. For three days now they'd had this stretch of beach almost to themselves. There were two other families camped to the south, and she and David had bodysurfed with the kids in the nearest site that morning. To the north was a massive reef, exposed and reaching a quarter mile out to sea at low tide.

Mother and daughter shielded their eyes against the sun with their hands as they watched Bud, David and two Mexicans— Domingo and Manuel work their way across the rocks. The tide was on its way out, past the midpoint. Abruptly, Manuel shouted and dove off the rocks, into the chilly water. Moments later he surfaced, holding a huge red, flailing lobster in his right hand.

David dove next. It took him three tries before he brought up his prize. Domingo cried out, dove in and emerged with a lobster in each hand. All four were deposited in buckets. By the time they returned to the trailer, they had a dozen of the crustaceans. Everyone piled into the back of Domingo's pickup and drove off to his ranchito, several miles up the valley behind them.

His wife Lucía was cooking inside their shack built of odd-sized pieces of weathered plywood and roofed over with corrugated sheet metal. Smoke poured out of the skinny metal chimney on top of it. The men and David popped beers and stood outside sipping at them and communicating in "Spanglish," a curious mixture of pidgin English and Spanish. If Bud didn't know the word for something in Spanish, he'd take the English word and tack an "o" on the end. El sacko, for sack. When he topped it off with his improvised south of the border accent, he assumed everyone would understand him. Dana wondered if they did. What she did know is that they all smiled a lot and said, "Sí, sí."

She hung off to the side by herself, watching. "Come here, Dana. Lucía's making tortillas. Want to try your hand at it?" her mom asked, motioning her to come indoors.

Dana went into the tiny house.

"Hola mija," the rotund little woman said, grinning a partially toothless grin.

"Hola. ¿Cómo está?"

"Bien. Gracias. ¿Quieres ayudarme con la preparación de la comida, mija?" She was asking Dana if she'd like to help prepare the food.

Dana nodded, but her feet stayed rooted in the doorway. She watched, fascinated as Lucía cooked. Her stove consisted of an oil drum, split in half and covered with an iron mesh grill. Inside it was fueled by the red hot coals of a never-ending fire. Skinny, flattened corn pancakes flew onto the "griddle," a piece of flattened metal on one corner of the grill. With deft fingers, Lucía flipped each one after *only a few seconds. Then she tossed it onto a steaming stack on a plate sitting on her miniature, square checkered-covered table. A pot of refried beans sizzled off to one side of the grill. Another pot filled with stewing beef, peppers and tomatoes seemed to call out to Dana. Moving around Lucía, she leaned into the pot and inhaled its spicy, fragrant aroma.*

Lucía grabbed her arm and handed her a ball of maza. Dana pounded it and flipped it onto the grill. They all laughed as the tortilla came out lopsided and lumpy.

"Cómelo," Lucía ordered and Dana popped the steaming tortilla into her mouth.

"Deliciosa, señora. Muchas gracias."

"Es mejor cuando pones un poco de carne y frijoles en una tortilla," Lucía added as she spooned meat and beans onto another tortilla and handed it to Dana. She made a second burrito for Dana's mother and built up a heaping platter for the men outside.

Those were just the appetizers. They stayed for dinner and Domingo cooked the halved lobsters in a vat of sizzling lard over an open fire outside. Everyone ate heaping burritos filled with lobster and beans and smothered with fresh salsa.

Kayaking back to shore in the opalescent twilight, Dana blinked and shook her head. They'd had such a wonderful trip. Two entire weeks of peaceful, unrushed days and starry, clear nights where the moon hung white over the water. Domingo had loaned them two horses and she and David rode deep into the valleys, up the hillsides and across dry grass mesas.

She wiped at the tear with the back of her hand and the boat lurched. Damn, but she was sick of crying. She couldn't help it, though. She missed David. They hadn't been close in years—not since her mother left, really.

Camille too was lost inside her own head. Her thoughts drifted, as they usually did when she was alone, to Drew, her almost ex-husband. Their divorce was due to be final soon—she forgot exactly when. For perhaps the thousandth time since he'd left her, she raised her eyes to the heavens and silently appealed to God to ease her pain. Would it never end, this awful tearing so deep down inside her heart? Would she ever stop yearning for him—reaching out for him in the night aching for his touch, his kiss, willing to give up nearly anything to see his eyes smiling down into hers as they danced together up the stairway to the stars.

Why had she loved too much too soon, not enough when they were together, and then too much again when it was too late? "Oh Lord," she prayed softly, "I finally understand what it means to love a husband. I know something was broken inside of me because of all my years of meaningless sex, drugs, the abortions, the other divorce. I know I didn't think things through. I know I made bad choices. I know I ran when the going got tough instead of toughing things out—*but why can't he see that I've changed?!* How can he divorce me when he says he doesn't even believe in divorce?!" She pounded the side of her kayak with her fist.

"God, it just doesn't make sense! Did I really hurt him so badly he'll never be able to trust me again?! I admit it—I didn't know how to be vulnerable, how to love him. How to receive his love. I know I pushed him away. But why won't he give me another chance?!" She closed her eyes. Opened them. Looked up again. Swallowed. "Lord, when I tried, when I was finally ready—he was gone. It was too late! And that's not fair!"

But, she reminded herself, he isn't all the way gone now, is he? Even though he regrets it and says we shouldn't—he still can't resist me sexually. Maybe one day he will realize that I am truly the woman of his dreams and he will come back for good.

She slipped into her favorite fantasy. In it she would see them standing together, in front of the congregation at their church. The pastor would hand Drew the mike and, with his arm around Camille, he would tell the story of how they reconciled of how they'd both finally come to see the sacredness of the commitment they'd made to each other of the true significance of the covenant of marriage. He'd explain how he'd been healed of his fear of being rejected again and his inability to love some other man's children as his own and how grateful he was to God for keeping this woman safe for him through their trials.

He would turn to Camille then and kiss her in front of everyone. Everyone would cheer as the band began to play a rousing praise song. A blazing sensation rose up between her thighs and instantly, she craved him. Their lovemaking had been so incredible—when was it? Had it been nearly two months ago? She nodded to herself. Yup. It had. It was after they'd played music together that last time.

She'd sneaked over to his house—the house he'd lived in when she met him and left to move in with her. Oh no. She'd been trying not to think about it, because she got so crazed with lust that no amount of masturbation would satisfy her. She ended up screaming into her pillow at night begging God to bring Drew back to her. Now, in spite of her willing it away—it all came back in a blinding flash and she remembered their last time together—all of it.

She pulled over onto the thin patch of dirt at the side of the street. There was no sidewalk, curb or gutter just overgrown vegetation practically up to the asphalt line. She could see the top story of the house and pieces of its roofline peeking out from gaps in the green-ery. She opened the gate, headed up the path through the huge front yard, passed several avocado trees, their branches sagging with fruit. There were lemon trees, a few orange trees, a gigantic magnolia tree. Ferns, ivy and hibiscus grew at random between the trees. At the north edge of the property was an area separated from the rest by two-by-fours and chicken wire where he grew his vegetable garden. Wondering if he'd replanted it since they'd split up, she peeked through the fence. There were rows of romaine lettuce, cucumbers, tomato plants, eggplant, zucchini, radishes and corn. All the vegeta-bles were tiny, and Camille could tell they'd only been recently plant-ed. A huge compost pile was behind the enclosure. In back of it was a greenhouse made of wood and visqueen.

She turned and studied the house. It was built of unstained, weather-beaten redwood. The door had a colorful handmade stained glass panel in it that was designed in an abstract image of a swan, swooping down toward a lake. Patches of rainbow showed behind the bird, the colored glass reflecting the refracted light from the street-light. There was a wooden front porch with an old-fashioned wooden swing.

She looked inside and saw him sitting in a pile of pillows on his futon, in his bathrobe, reading glasses dipped low on his nose, lost in a book. It was the Bible. Drew looked like a hippie but was a devout Christian. He had dark brown hair streaked with gray that had reced-ed a little on top, equally dark, intense eyes and a beard. His face was at once old and young, wise and innocent.

She stood there for the longest time, watching him.

Suddenly he seemed to sense her presence and looked up over his glasses.

"Camille?"

She walked inside and stood with her back to the door. It felt like she was still outside. Plants were everywhere. Tall umbrella trees, cacti, hanging pots of variegated Charlies, Wandering Jews, ferns. On the walls were unframed posters of musicians in action that spanned at least three decades. Oriental paper lamps hung from the ceiling, softly illuminating everything.

They stared at each other across the room, still except for the silent rhythm of their chests rising and falling with each shallow breath.

"Hey you," she said, her voice barely a whisper.

She moved toward him, stopped inches in front of him and looked down at him. Her eyes darted to his mouth and a flood of memories assaulted her. She gulped, then locked into him again. Neither of them moved for a long minute.

Slowly his mouth relaxed into a half-smile. She picked up his hand and brought it to her mouth, ran her tongue across his finger-tips, down the side of his palm and across the fleshy pads at the base of each finger. She slipped his index finger into her mouth and sucked on it. Lick. Suck. Lick. Her breathing was loud in her ears.

His finger played back now, exploring her mouth, stroking her tongue.

In slow motion, her hands moved to her blouse. One by one she unfastened her buttons and shrugged the fabric off her shoulders. The finger moved in and out of her mouth. Faster and faster now. Sweat beaded on her upper lip.

He groaned as she unsnapped her bra and stood before him in the near dark. Then his hands were at her waist, unbuttoning her jeans. He pulled them down and she lifted her feet, one at a time as he helped her step out of them. His tongue traced a long slow trail across her breasts and down her belly. He buried his face between her legs.

She grabbed his shoulders and whimpered into his hair as she shuddered against him coming in explosions of seemingly endless delight....

"Oh Camille, you know I can't resist you," he whispered up to her when she'd finished. "But this will never work."

"Shut up," she said as she pulled him to his feet and tugged his sweat pants off his hips. He sank back against the pillows and she knelt beside him. She looked up at him. Their eyes met. She saw the hunger there and she smiled. "Your turn...."

"Hey!" Dana shouted as a wave came up behind Camille and launched her toward the shore. "Backpaddle! Backpaddle! Be careful!"

The wave caught the back of Camille's kayak, tipped it high into the air and flipped it. She flew through the air and landed face first in the sand with the kayak on top of her. Dana beached her kayak, jumped out of it and rushed up to Camille. She lifted the kayak off her, grabbed the paddle from the surf and dragged the boat up onto the beach. "Are you okay?!" she hollered.

Camille stood up, shook herself off and gave herself a quick once-over. No blood. Nothing broken. Nothing hurt too much. Just a little shook up was all. But, hey, she told herself, that knocked some sense into you, you horny bitch! Hells bells, but that beat a cold shower any day! She flung her head back and laughed out loud.

"Let's go skinny-dipping," she said and ripped her clothes off, dropped them onto the sand and raced out toward the waves. She dove under the first wave that came toward her and stroked out to the middle of the bay. "C'mon Dana! Don't be a candy ass!" she yelled. "Get out here!"

CHAPTER TEN

**La Bufadora to San Quintín, BC
October 16, 1997**

The morning dawned clear and unseasonably warm in La Bufadora. A huge flock of pelicans began to congregate to the right of their campsite, in front of the dive shop. The water churned up and the birds began to dive. Within minutes it was a full-on feeding frenzy as the pelicans swooped, lunged, splashed down hard into the ocean and smashed into one other in their excitement.

"What's going on?" Camille asked. "Look!" She pointed, nearly dropping her coffee cup. Four fishermen had materialized on shore and were casting their lines out into the boiling madness, pulling up two-foot-long yellowtail as fast as they could fling their fishing poles. "Let's go down there!"

Holly ran for her camera. Quickly refilling their cups, the four women hurried down the boat ramp toward the beach. By the time they got there, ten men were out, casting their lines off the rocks and hauling in fish like crazy. Still the pelicans swooped, dove and continued to beat each other up in their hurry to scoop up as many bait fish as they could into their long, pouch-like beaks. One was wiped out by a wave and washed onto shore at Holly's feet. She photographed it as it struggled to its feet and shook itself. It staggered around in circles for a full minute, then, regaining its equilibrium, spread its wings to the sky and flew off again to rejoin the orgy off-shore.

"What's this all about?" Holly asked a crusty old guy who looked as though he'd just crawled out of bed.

"Yellowtail. Brought in by this El Niño thing. The water's a whole helluva lot warmer than it's supposed to be this time of year. We only see these fish in mid to late summer, out a coupla miles off shore. They never come in this close and never this late neither." The pole jumped in his hand and the line raced off his reel in a high-pitched whine as the fish fled away from shore, toward deeper waters. The man waited, then began to crank the line back in. "Fourth one I've caught so far. Fan-fuckin'-tastic!"

Dana put her toes into the water. "The water must be five or six degrees warmer than yesterday. How weird."

"Yup," he agreed. "It's weird all right. What are y'all doin' here in the middle of the week? Saw you makin' camp over there on the cliffs yesterday, just before sunset."

Dana and Camille shared a private grin. "Binoculars," Camille mouthed. Dana nodded and her cheeks flushed red. Camille turned away. Holly, meanwhile, was giving the man and his companions a detailed explanation of their itinerary and the purpose of their trip. The other three women wandered away and headed back to the motor home to finish cleaning up the breakfast dishes and get ready to hit the road.

Holly came back a half hour later with several slabs of fileted fish. "Look what he gave me," she said, opening a drawer and sliding the fish into a Ziploc bag. "Looks like we're gonna be eating well tonight." She turned. "So. Do you want to drive today, Camille?" she asked.

"Don't let her. You *really* don't want her to. She's a terrible driver."

Camille laughed. "It's true," she said, nodding.

"Okay. You're out. Barb?"

Barb shook her head, no. "Me neither. When you told us yesterday that we're gonna be driving on skinny, two-lane roads with hardly any shoulder all the way to San Jose del Cabo I nearly lost my lunch. I couldn't even handle driving my own car on these roads. You two are doing a great job behind the wheel. I'd get us all killed."

"That's encouraging," said Holly, frowning. "We were supposed to share the driving."

"Yeah but you disqualified Camille. I want to be disqualified too. How about if I do extra duty doing dishes? Cleaning? Dumping the holding tank? Anything."

Dana and Holly looked at each other. "Well, it's not as though we have to go too far in any one day. I imagine we can handle it," said Dana, scowling.

"Okay. I'll give you guys each a massage once a week for doing all the driving. How's that?" suggested Camille.

"Now there's a deal. I guess we can let them off the hook."

They finished rolling up the awning and hauled the kayaks back onto the roof. "These things feel like they're made out of Tupperware," said Camille. "I'm amazed at how sturdy they are for being so light."

"Yeah. You'd have been munched if they'd been made of fiberglass, your klutziness," teased Dana.

"No kidding. Where are we headed today, Holly?"

"San Quintín. It's only about 120 miles away, so it will be a real easy drive. Once we get south of Maneadero, we head through the Santo Tomás River Valley, up through the foothills and across a huge agricultural valley where they grow strawberries, grapes, tomatoes, barley, potatoes, peppers and all sorts of other produce. Then we'll head out toward the ocean and camp right at Playa Santa María, which is an excellent clamming beach."

"Oh yum," said Camille. "Dana makes the best stuffed clams on the grill."

"*De veras, amiga. Almejas son algunas de mis comidas favoritas. Son sabrosas y tienen muchas, muchas sensualidades*— that's right girlfriend. Clams are some of my favorite foods. They're tasty and they're very, very sensuous."

"Quit showing off. We know you can speak Spanish, smart ass."

They drove back to Mex 1 and headed south. The highway was two lanes now. Every town they came to had *topes*—speed bumps guaranteed to make all travelers slow down. Three hours later they passed through the towns of San Quintín and Lazaro Cardenas, marveling at the number of workers picking tomatoes and fruit in the fields on both sides of the road. Holly pointed out a green truck on the opposite side of the roadway. It had stopped and was helping a four-by-four pickup truck with a flat tire. "That should calm your fears somewhat, Barb," she said over her shoulder. "These guys are called the Green Angels. They're funded by the Mexican government. They patrol the highways twice a day and help out stranded motorists. They have spare parts. Gas. They really are angels."

Several miles south of town, they turned and headed west at the La Pinta Hotel sign, drove down a semi-paved road through a thick canopy of overhanging trees and pulled into the Cielito Lindo Motel and RV Park. Holly went inside to register.

"We can park over there," she pointed. "The space closest to the dunes. We can't get Boris any closer to the beach than that 'cause he'll get stuck."

"Do we have hookups?" asked Barb.

"Yeah we do. So you're not gonna have to dump that holding tank today! But you can be in charge of hooking everything up, okay?"

Barbara grimaced and nodded. "Will you at least watch me so I don't make any mistakes?"

They drove into their space, parked, pulled out, turned around and backed in. "Now we have a better view," Holly said. Dana agreed. Holly, Camille and Barb set up camp like well-trained veterans, pulling out the awning, unrolling the green astroturf carpet. They unfolded the camping table and four chairs, brought the barbecue out from one of the underneath storage compartments and then sat down, popping open four Pacifico beers to go with the guacamole and salsa-filled quesadillas Dana had just finished preparing.

"This was great," said Camille as she finished her lunch and mopped the salsa off her chin. "I really am in the mood to go look for some clams. I can't stop thinking about those sexy little al—what are they?

"Almejas."

"Almejas. Anyone want to come?" Everyone did.

They got their hats, put on their sunscreen, grabbed plastic bags and spoons for digging, locked up the motor home and headed off toward the ocean. Halfway to the shore, they stumbled across a camp-site tucked into a huge crevice in the dunes. There were three four-wheel-drive trucks, two with trailers, five tents, a bunch of gear and an awning spread across four tall poles bearing a banner that read: "Warning: You are now entering Margaritaville. Party Zone ahead."

Dana pointed and laughed. "Uh oh. Vintage Buffett. Looks like we have some serious party animals camped here." Just then two quads roared up and cut across the dunes, skidded sideway and stopped in front of the foursome, spraying sand within inches of their faces. "Hey!" Dana shrieked, jumping backwards and nearly falling down.

The two guys laughed and dismounted. "How ya doin'?" the short, stocky one with his hair in a ponytail asked in Holly's direction. He looked to be in his late twenties.

"Good. We're off to get clams."

The guy pointed toward the west. "Tide's about halfway out.

Should be some decent clammin' out there. Where you girls stayin'?"
Holly's reply was drowned out as the other two quads roared in and
slid to stop much the way the first two had. She finished her descrip-
tion of their Baja tour and the guys gunned their engines and took off.

"Hey! C'mon by later," yelled the ponytailed guy after them.
"Have a cerveza. We'll take y'all for a ride down the beach if you
want. And do some fireworks!"

The women split up, Camille and Dana striding off down the
beach at a brisk pace and Barb and Holly lagging behind as Barb
chased the receding waves, dug gleefully into the bubbles like a child
and unearthed large, succulent Pismo clams. She filled her bag half
full and then began to collect sand dollars, lingering over each spec-
imen she found, oohing and aahing in delight.

Holly snapped a few photos with her new digital camera. Her
irritation mounted. She wondered to herself for about the fiftieth time
why it was that Camille and Dana had become so inseparable. She
was sick and tired of being left with Barb who fussed about her sun
exposure, fussed about what she ate, fussed about the dirt, fussed
about overdoing it physically. Hell, she fussed about everything period. She was becoming a monumental pain in the ass. Why, she asked
herself, when Dana and I have so much in common, am I saddled
with *her?!* It's like Camille has miraculously transformed herself
from a lazy, out-of-shape couch potato into Xena, the Warrior
Princess. She's fearless! She's even tan already! And she'll do *anything!*

But here I am, stuck babysitting this prissy little pale-faced slow-
poke. Doesn't anyone give a shit about *me?!* Have they all forgotten
that it was me who instigated this whole trip and that it wouldn't be
happening without *me and my book contract?!*

Barb seemed to read her mind. "I know I'm holding you back,
Holly. Why don't you go on ahead? I think I have the hang of digging
for clams now. And I enjoy being by myself, so I don't mind at all if
you go. I know I'm a putterer."

Holly arranged her face into what she figured resembled a smile,
spun and took off at a full run toward the north, the opposite direction
that Camille and Dana had gone. Her bare feet sunk into the damp
sand and the warm surf splashed onto her legs as she raced through
the waves. Soon her shorts were wet and her breath was coming hard
and fast. Her lungs began to burn and her chest to ache, but still she
ran.

A few minutes later she felt the endorphins kick in. Almost
instantly she was flooded with a sense of well-being. And power. Her

anger and frustration evaporated. She had reached her runner's high. She turned and ran in place while she searched for the others. The salt haze from the huge breakers exploding offshore obscured her view. She squinted, barely saw them, over a mile down the beach. She turned again and scrutinized the waves. Safe or not? She shook her head, no. A jagged line of white foam ran perpendicular to the shore sure sign of a rip. There was no way she wanted to be sucked out to sea here. No thank you. Not only were there no lifeguards to rescue her, but the waves were over eight feet high. Big mothers. She knew they'd pulverize her. She turned and ran north for another ten minutes, then turned and headed back.

As she ran, her thoughts drifted to her first extended trip to Baja back in '86. In 1981 her dad, Ed Maguire had moved to San Felipe, a town on the northern edge of the Sea of Cortez, a couple of hours south of Mexicali and midway between San Diego and Yuma, Arizona. He came with his girlfriend, Betty, the blowzy bleached blonde. Holly'd never liked Betty. The woman was coarse, unattractive and smoked like a chimney. Trailer trash for sure. She'd lived with Ed for who knew how many years and seemed to exist solely to watch TV, smoke and drink copious amounts of Oso Negro Vodka. Both of them were what she considered to be fairly functional alcoholics—usually doing okay until after dark—when it was best to ignore them or get the hell out of Dodge.

Holly had shown up just after her third marriage disintegrated, a mere four months after it began. She didn't mention it to her dad. It was later annulled on the basis of fraud (the guy was a consummate con man, that was for sure) and they'd lived together in a remote part of Idaho only for a little over a summer so no one knew they'd gotten married. It was better that way. She had no desire to listen to her father's endless ribbing about her parade of marital failures.

In her mind she was there again, at his trailer-house on the edge of an arroyo just north of San Felipe at a place called Pete's Camp. *She pulled her brand new Land Cruiser up to his door. The lights were on and the waning last quarter moon was rising pale over the water, sending a trembling trail of gold all the way to shore. She'd been here before, but only for a few days. This time she had nowhere else to go. Didn't have a clue what to do with herself. With her life. All she knew was that she wouldn't tell him about Kenny—wouldn't. No way.*

He knew she was coming because she'd called. She got out of the car and stretched after the long drive. Looked at her watch. Ten o'clock. She'd come all the way from Idaho in two days. She pulled the keys out of the ignition and walked past a thorny fence made of ocotillo arms, through a half-dead cactus garden and to the front door. The roughly hewn stone and wood structure looked deserted. No lights were on at all. She wondered if they were asleep—passed out already. She knocked. Nothing. She knocked again.

A dog began to bark softly, but without enthusiasm. Still no one came to the door. She touched the door handle and it opened a crack. It was ajar. She pushed it open the rest of the way and stepped into the foyer. A big room opened up before her, furnished with two mis-matched, decades-old, orange, brown and black plaid couches. They were threadbare and the stuffing was popping out here and there. As her eyes adjusted to the dark, she couldn't help but feel disgust rising up like bile in her throat. The whole color scheme was 70's rusts, burnt oranges and browns. A huge wrought iron and wood wagon wheel chandelier hung from the ceiling over a Formica table sur-rounded by six metal chairs with yellow and green flowered plastic cushions. Here and there pieces of bad Mexican art hung on the walls the painted-on-velvet kind that made Holly want to puke. There were dirty dishes on the table, unfolded laundry spilling off of the couch. Her dad lay sleeping with his head on a pile of it, his old, fat, gray-muzzled Labrador Charlie nestled up against him. The house smelled like stale cigarettes. A film of dust covered everything. There were huge spiderwebs hanging from the corners of the ceiling and off the spokes of the wagon wheel.

Shuddering and hugging herself, Holly moved to the front win-dow and opened it, letting the chilly November air clear her head. Over the rooftops of the other houses she could see the shimmering surface of the Sea of Cortez. The tide had already begun to recede, leaving a vast, ever-widening expanse of beach in its place. The moon was nearly straight overhead and there were lots of stars. She breathed in the salt air. She stooped and walked through a narrow, low doorway into the kitchen, which was part of the original trailer. She looked in the sink. Full of more dirty dishes. She turned on the water and mechanically began to wash them.

By midnight she had the kitchen, dinette and living room areas all cleaned up. Still her father slept on. She went prowling into the back bedrooms and heard Betty snoring. She veered away from that doorway and found the room that had been prepared for her. The bed was made, at least, with what looked to be clean sheets. She undressed and fell into it, asleep the moment her head hit the pillow.

As she neared the trio of women, Holly got ready to snap herself back into the present. She fast-forwarded through the rest of that six-month stay with her dad and Betty. It had been okay, actually, once they got used to each other. Her dad had compiled an extensive library on Baja and Holly read every single book he had. Then she went to the library at Pete's Camp and read every book they had too. Her dad's friends began coming by and loaning her their favorite books. By the end of January she was as close to being an armchair expert on Baja as anyone else in all of San Felipe. She'd also learned to ride a four wheeler, a motorcycle, a dune buggy. She'd become a decent jet skier and windsurfer and she could out-fish half of the guys.

Holly amazed everyone there at Pete's Cantina with her stories of her escapades over the years. Having dropped out of college at Oregon State University in Corvallis after less than a year, she'd moved to Aspen, Colorado and taken up skiing. With a vengeance. She worked as a lift operator. An instructor. She was on the ski patrol. For the six summers she was there, she worked for the white water rafting companies that ran tourists down the relatively easy rapids of the Arkansas River. She led backpacking expeditions and hiked up most of the highest peaks in Colorado. She dabbled in rock climbing. Although she always left this part out, she'd met her first husband, Pat Marshall, in Aspen, at the Hotel Jerome one sodden summer night in 1975. Instantly smitten, they went home together and were pretty much inseparable after that. They married three months later, just as the Aspen leaves turned from gold to red. The marriage was over a year and a half later, when his money ran out and he left her to go back home to Cleveland.

Holly moved on then, to Taos, New Mexico. Then up to Durango and Telluride where she worked for a helicopter skiing company. Then on to Flagstaff, Arizona where she was a Colorado River rafting guide in summer and led cross-country skiing tours in winter. She met her second husband there. They got married after she became pregnant and gave birth to a daughter, Hillary, in 1979. However, because of their jobs and their lifestyles, they sent the baby to live with Hal's mother in Prescott. She'd raised Hillary all these last 18 years. Holly saw her occasionally maybe once or twice a year but their relationship was strained. As usual, when she thought of the daughter she'd essentially abandoned, Holly felt a huge knot lodge itself right under her heart.

With a burst of speed, she raced past her traveling companions and pounded on down the beach, willing the pain of it all away. No one in the entire Baja world (except her husband, Rick, of course) knew about her former marriages (and he only knew about two of them). No one except him knew about Hillary either and she really regretted having told him. He got on her case constantly for not spending more time with her daughter and she was sick of it. There were things that were better off kept to oneself, she reminded herself as she turned and slowed her pace, removing her t-shirt and walking now, mopping the sweat from her forehead. "How many clams have you guys gotten?" she asked.

The other three showed her the treasures they'd taken from the sea. They headed back to Cielito Lindo, chatting amiably. They passed the Buffett campsite. No one was there. They returned to the motor home and Dana and Camille pulled up their chairs, popped beers and lost themselves in their books while Holly typed furiously on her laptop computer. Barb went inside to take a nap.

Barb poured lighter fluid on the odd-shaped mesquite coals they'd bought at Calimax in Ensenada. She counted to 50 and lit a match, tossing it onto the coals. They flamed up and then died down soon after. She went inside to help Dana prepare the clams.

"Okay. Here we go," said the chef. "Lift the clam meat out of the shell like this. Remove the membrane and dice it up into tiny pieces." Barb stood over the cutting board that fit perfectly onto the top of the left side of the sink and chopped. Dana sat down at the table and began chopping on another board. Next to her was a large plastic bowl. Into it she dropped diced jalapeños, cubes of cheddar cheese, finely chopped onions, tomatoes and pieces of ham. She sprinkled garlic powder, salt and pepper into the bowl. Then she reached for the tiny Mexican limónes, cut several in half and squeezed the juice into the bowl using a pewter limón press.

Barb passed her the cut-up clam meat and she dumped it into the bowl, stirring everything together. "Now we'll scoop this yummy mixture up and put it back inside the clam shells," she explained. "And wrap each one in foil."

"Do we cook it in the coals or over the grill?"

"Grill. Who's in charge of making the salad and wrapping the potatoes? We need to get them into the coals pretty soon."

"Me."

"Cool. You get on that. I'll finish up here."

"What about the fish that guy gave Holly this morning?"

"She's gonna cook some of it tonight. I have it marinating in olive oil and spices. The rest I'll use tomorrow to make ceviche."

"What's that?"

"You'll see. It's to-die-for."

As the last of the light faded from the sky, they finished up their meal. Holly went inside to get her sweatshirt and brought out a bottle of El Presidente. She popped the top off and poured two fingers of brandy into each of four plastic cups. "Let's have a toast," she said. "To our first incredible meal from the sea." They toasted and drank.

"To the chef!" cried Barbara. They toasted again.

She sat down with the bottle off to the side of her chair, on the ground. After a few minutes she refilled her glass. No one said anything. They were all watching the hugely full, bright orange moon as it began its parade across the mid-October sky.

Suddenly there was a loud crack, like a gun going off and the sky exploded with color. "Fireworks!" squealed Camille. "The Buffett boys are having a party!" A second long skinny skyrocket howled across the sky and exploded into a pink ball.

CHAPTER ELEVEN   San Quintín, Baja California
                          October 17, 1997

Camille awakened at 6:30 the next morning when the alarm she'd stuck under her pillow began to beep in her ear. She was sleeping in the cabover bed with Dana, both of them having decided after the first night that it was easier to share the big queen-sized bed than to dismantle the dinette every night. Being careful not to awaken her friend, she rolled out of her sleeping bag and tiptoed to the bathroom to pee. Then she tapped Barb in the top bunk. Holly was snoring softly. She'd drunk nearly half the bottle of brandy the night before and Camille figured she'd be happy to sleep in.

The two women each downed a quick cup of coffee and set off for the motel office to use the phone. Barb knocked on the door. No answer. She knocked again. Still no answer. Camille looked at her watch. "Shit on a shingle. I'm supposed to call in by 7:00 so we can prep before the 7:15 bit. I'm gonna be late."

"Here," said Barb, "use my cell phone. We're supposed to in case of emergency. This qualifies."

Camille punched in the number of AT&T in Houston. Then, following the computerized directions, she punched in the numbers on her calling card. Within moments she was connected, via the station hotline, to Mark Hendricks. "Wise Guys. Mark here. Who calls on my most private of lines?" he boomed into her ear.

"Cinnamon Breath," she whispered. "Calling from the outer limits of Baja California. *La Frontera*—the frontier, if you please."

"Lemme put you on speaker phone, oh Red Hot Pants. How the

hell's it goin' down there? Anyone out in your neck of the woods out howlin' at the moon the last coupla nights?"

Camille laughed. Barb inched closer to her, trying to get her ear up next to Camille's so she could hear too. "Sure enough. How'd ya know?"

"I *always* know, Cinnamon Girl. Haven't you figured that out yet? How's the PMS comin'?"

She and Barb looked at each other. She mouthed silently, "Holly." Out loud she said, "None of your beeswax. I refuse to let you go there. Hey, Johnny!" she called into the phone.

"Camille," he purred back at her. His voice wasn't nearly as overpowering as Mark's, but far more seductive. "How's my favorite sexy lady? The airways in San Diego are pretty boring without you, babe."

"C'mon Johnny. I've been gone less than a week."

"So report. What's the haps?"

"What do you want to hear first? The straight-forward tourist stuff or the juicy gossip?"

"Hang on. Song's over. Gotta go for a sec." He came back a minute or so later. "Give us a rundown of everything. We have six minutes 'til you're on." She did.

They were live.

"We have a treat for our listeners this morning. Our very own Camille Fleming, the Cinnamon Girl of RockSteady 102.9, is, as we've told you, off on a female bonding jaunt in Baja California. She left on Tuesday and is calling in live via cell phone from San Quintín. Bienvenidos, Camille! We've missed you on our 10:00 a.m. show closes."

"I doubt it," she said, chuckling. "Anyway, I sure don't miss you overgrown frat rats with your obscenely high testosterone levels!"

"Hey!"

"Just kidding."

"Where are you?"

"I'm standing outside the lobby of the Cielito Lindo Motel in San Quintín, about 200 miles south of the border. I tried to get someone to answer the door so I could use their phone, but they're obviously smarter than I am and are still sleeping! We're camped in an RV park adjacent to the motel."

"So. Have you dumped the holding tank yet?"

"No. That's Barb's job. And here we have hookups, so we just flush and that's the end of it! I got excused from ever having to drive this beast yesterday."

"Word got out about the time you backed into the pillar in the parking garage here and took out the rear end of the station van, huh?"

"Yup. Dana told 'em." Laughter.

"For all of our listeners, Dana is none other than Dana Wallace, executive chef at the award-winning restaurant by the sea in Cardiff, Hacienda Gaviota. Tell us about her, Cinnamon."

"Dana's my neighbor and best bud. We're in her motor home. She's the reason I'm here, actually. I trust her with my life. She's been traveling in Baja since she was a kid. Her official purpose on the trip is to investigate the Baja cuisine scene and plagiarize some recipes for all of us to enjoy back home."

"Hot damn! And that Bodacious Baja Babe, outdoorswoman extraordinaire your illustrious tour leader and author of the upcoming book, *Baja Cruising for the Occasional EcoTourist* the indomitable Holly Malone? Is she with you this morning?" Mark asked.

Camille and Barb exchanged another glance. "Not today. Get this, though, will ya? We had some weird goings on in our campground last night."

"Aaaaaooooooooh," howled Mark. "Full moon fever. Tell us...."

"There are these much younger guys you know twenty-somethings camped in the dunes behind us. They were total pirates—like characters out of a Jimmy Buffet song."

"This one?" Johnny interrupted.

"Yup. They nearly ran us over with their ATVs yesterday afternoon when we were clamming. The minute the sun went down they came out with the fireworks. Something fierce. They were shooting skyrockets at each other across the dunes. Quite an air war. Then of course they had the tunes going full blast. Ear-shattering."

Barbara pulled the phone out of her hand on cue. "Hey Wise Guys. This is Barb Benton, your off-duty promotions director."

"Ooooh. Baby Doll Benton. How many showers have you taken so far?"

"Seventeen. In three days. You *know* how compulsive I am. I wash my hands every 20 minutes. I only eat Spam and canned peas."

Camille leaned into the phone. "Don't forget the applesauce!"

When the laughter had died down, she continued. "I'm here in Baja with Camille to get over my fear of dirt. To get in touch with the iron maiden inside me. I'm also here to tell you that one of those Buffett boys, as we called them, put an M-80 in a toilet in our campground last night and blew it up! You would not have believed what a mess it made! We all came running over to see what happened. There was smoke pouring out from out of the top of this outdoor can. In the next stall over was an older guy, well—you know—sitting there doing his best to mind his own business."

The Wise Guys put on the Buffett song, "We Are the People Our Parents Warned Us About."

Camille took the phone back. "So what happened?" asked Mark between bellows and snorts of laughter. "If I'd been there, I woulda fudge my undies for sure!"

"I don't imagine he had his undies on," said Camille. "But I bet it scared the poop outta him one way or the other. Those M-80s make a horrific explosion. Anyway, the lady who owns the motel threatened to call the *policía*—the cops, but the most mature and sober Buffett boy talked her out of it. Promised to pay for everything."

"Sounds like a preview for *South Park,*" said Johnny.

"So Baja hasn't changed much from my youth, huh? Full of drunk gringos raising hell...."

"No! We went skinny-dipping in the bay off La Bufadora night before last. We saw a feeding frenzy and watched some fishermen catch more yellowtail the next morning than you would ever believe! The first day we were serenaded by mariachis in Hussong's and heard the story of the origin of the Margarita. And...."

"Slow down! Start at the beginning...."

"Okay, smart ass. Follow me, friends and I will take you on the first leg of our journey down this 806-mile peninsula which has, by the way over 3,000 miles of coastline. Ready. Set. Go. We entered Mexico at Tijuana, the busiest border in the world. It's also the largest city in Baja, with a population guesstimated at 1.5 million. It became famous as a wild and crazy place to party during Prohibition when production and consumption of alcoholic beverages were outlawed in the U.S. Cantinas, casinos and strip bars sprang up everywhere. When Prohibition was repealed, the government made Tijuana into a duty-free port and it quickly became a destination for world-class shoppers. These days you can buy Cuban cigars on every street corner legally because Aeromexico flies to Havana from Tijuana daily.

"We passed by Rosarito Beach and Popótla, where *Titanic* was filmed. Like the rest of the hundreds of thousands of visitors a year that make this drive down, as my favorite crooner, Lyle Lovett, calls it, 'The Road to Ensenada,' we just grooved on the scenery the whole way." She paused as the music from the song began to play.

"Well I'm impressed, Wise Guys. You're right in there with the tunes. We came through Ensenada, a bustling seaport that's visited every week by three major cruise lines and got a free shot of tequila in the grocery store.

"And now, I've about caught up with myself. The only thing I haven't told you...." She stopped and laughed out loud, "is how I managed to botch my kayak landing and plant my face in the sand, with my boat on top of me!"

"How'd you manage that klutzy maneuver?" asked Johnny.

"Camille?! Come on! She's the absolute *klutz* of the universe!" boomed Mark.

"Never mind. And no, I didn't hurt myself in case anyone gives a rat's patooty. This klutz is signing off. I think the restaurant just opened. I don't know about you big Bozos, but we Bodacious Baja Babes need some chewy instant coffee and a coupla platters of chorizo con huevos with a side of refried beans cooked in lots of lard to jump start our engines!"

"Get outta here, Cinnamon Girl! Great talkin' to ya! Can't wait to hear from you again! Bring us Holly Malone next week!" The line went dead.

Camille turned the phone off and handed it to Barb. She reached into her purse, pulled out a cigarette and lit it. Inhaling, she looked at Barb. "I know. I keep it a secret. But call-ins make me major-league stressed and I am breaking the code of silence on this one."

"I already knew that one. I smelled it last night when you came back from your walk."

Camille laughed. "So I'm out of the closet. Well, that's a relief! Living in tight quarters like we are is rapidly exposing all our warts, isn't it?"

"No kidding. Holly must be stressed out about this book thing. She snaps at me constantly. And she drank a lot last night. By herself. The night before too...."

Camille snorted. "Shit. She lives alone most of the time. So, essentially, do Dana and I. I'm gonna put on that George Thorogood song for you when we get back to the motor home. You know, the one about drinking alone?" Barb nodded. "Single women, especially moms, always drink alone. Who else over the age of consent is ever around?! We've had lots of parties over the phone these past seven years. Dana'd have her wine and I'd have mine. We were trapped in our houses, lonely and bored after everyone went to bed. Even though we lived across the street, neither of us was comfortable leaving our kids so we drank alone." She puffed on her cigarette.

"When Drew moved in with me, everything changed. He's very religious, and so was I when we were together. We drank in carefully measured moderation. One bottle of wine max between the two us on weekends only. The one or two times I saw him drink more, he totally panicked. I half-expected him to pick up the phone and call the pastor to confess. Or check himself into a rehab program."

"You sure weren't married very long," said Barb.

She threw her cigarette butt down on the ground and stomped it. "We're still legally married. But we only lived together as husband and wife for 11 months. I really need to talk about it if you don't mind listening."

"Not at all. Let's go inside and get some breakfast."

They went into the restaurant and ordered. They sipped their coffee in unison.

"There are merits, I believe, to drinking alone. Living with Drew was like living with a cop. It was so bizarre. We had these cast-in-cement rules we had to live by, in order to be good Christians. Therein came the two-drink limit. I actually right before he moved out bought a half gallon of coconut rum and hid it in my closet behind my sweaters!

"Now, don't raise your eyebrow at me, Barbara Goody-Two-Shoes Benton! Let me finish before you slap a negative label on me! I hate being *monitored!* I also hate being treated like a child. It brings out the rebel in me. I would drink when he was working just to prove he couldn't control me! I'd sneak over to Dana's for a toke and a few drinks with her after he went to bed. I did it to get back at him for being so closed-minded. And of course, I did it because it was fun and I missed being able to cut loose when I felt like it!"

"Did he ever catch you?"

"No! I'm a serious pro at hiding things. Holly probably is too. It's just that on this trip we're all crammed like sardines into Boris and we aren't gonna be able to hide *anything!* If I go on a PMS binge and pig out, everyone'll know. Except Mark of course!" They shared a conspiratorial laugh. "If I decide I want to cop a buzz, same thing. We hear each other snore. We hear each other fart. If one of us dares to masturbate, you can bet money that at least one of us'll hear that little moan of release too!"

"Or feel the motor home rocking and rolling as we grind our hips into the mattress!"

They laughed again. "No kidding!"

Their food arrived and they ate in silence for a few minutes.

"When did you become so religious?" Barb asked.

"About a year after my divorce. Drew and I had been friends for a while. I had a major crush on him. For a couple of years I'd gone to

Coffee-by-the-Beach to hear him sing and play his guitar. Then a Christian bookstore and coffee house opened in Encinitas and Drew was hired to run the music department. He started performing there too. I went there a lot to hear him play, or just to visit with him. He started talking to me about God. Jesus. I was feeling pretty empty and confused and I was really hungry for something to sink my spiritual teeth into. He invited me to his church one Sunday."

"Were you dating yet?"

"Oh no. He kept me at arm's length for years. But the church it was an upbeat, creative and funky place. They held their services in an old strip center, in what used to be a grocery store. The pastor spoke my language. The people looked like us you know mostly our age. Not yuppies. More down-to-earth. Lots of long-haired guys like Drew. Women in long skirts like me. I felt at home there. Found myself going every Sunday and then to Bible studies on Wednesday nights. To a Spiritual Gifts Seminar. I was raised a Catholic and I've always prayed, read the Bible and tried to live my life by the Golden Rule. I stopped going to church when I got divorced because of the Pope's stand on divorce. I've always considered myself a Christian. But to make Drew happy, I said this prayer with him, asked forgiveness for my sins and accepted Jesus as my savior. I was officially 'born again.'"

"Mistake?"

She shook her head. "No. I believe in the Bible. I just have a hard time with the endless rules and regulations. However, I didn't see that at first. I joined the drama and singing troupe. I loved it, except that I had to be careful not to cuss. After a while, some of the women began to make these weird comments about my job. You know how raunchy the jocks on RockSteady can get—even me! And we promote artists that are considered very un-Christian. I was *encouraged* to leave my job and go to work for a Christian radio station. Even Drew started getting after me. But I never listened. I couldn't afford the pay cut. That was my excuse. The truth was I'm too stubborn. I *hate* being told what to do. And I *like* my job!"

"You're outrageous, Camille. That's your charm. That and your big mouth! I can't imagine you being able to play by anyone's rules but your own."

"I know. I really wanted to fit in with this crowd, though. Drew and I started playing music together. He played guitar. I played piano. His friend Bart played the drums. It was a dream come true. And we were *hot,* believe me. Not just musically. The music turned us on. Sexually. Big time. That's when we started dating. Or rather, we fast-forwarded from friends to lovers one night when we ended up naked and all over each other on his living room floor!" She looked at Barb and laughed. "Believe me, Drew was equally horrified *and* hooked. We both were consumed with lust, to borrow a phrase from the born-again crowd. It was *great!"* She laughed. "Drew and I were always *unbelievably good* in bed...."

"How in the world did he reconcile that with his religious beliefs?"

Camille shook her head. "He didn't. He was all twisted up about it. We both felt like hypocrites. Ha!" she snorted. "We were. I'd esti-mate that 99 per cent of the singles at our church who were dating were having sex! But we all faked celibacy."

"Your church intruded on your sex lives?!"

Camille nodded. "Oh yes. They did. They really did. Or rather the singles' pastor did. He was incredibly intrusive. He treated us like teenagers only without the zits. We were supposed to maintain our *purity* and that was that. If we didn't, we weren't *committed Christians.* It was ever so black and white."

She finished her food and pushed her plate away. "Do you care if I smoke in here?" she asked. Barb shook her head, no.

"The whole thing made Drew nuts. We tried to abstain from sex, but we failed. Miserably. He hadn't been laid in over five years and he was as horny as a high school boy, let me tell you! Finally, he moved in with us. It was our *big secret.* No one at church knew about it. He wanted me and the boys to come to his house. It was bigger and nicer, but I love my house and I wasn't about to move my boys to a different school. He asked me to marry him, finally. To assuage his guilt, I think. We got married in December of '95 and split less than a year later."

"Why? Didn't he love you?"

Camille shook her head. "I don't know. To be honest, I think the sex blinded him. We were both lonely. I wanted a husband. I hated being single. *Hated* it. He wanted to rescue me, convert me. Fuck me. If we hadn't been trying to *do the right thing,* the whole thing would probably have just run its course. But we were trying to be good Christians, so we got married. Big mistake."

"But I found you in the bathroom at work. Remember? On more than one occasion. You were locked in the handicapped stall bawling your eyes out. I felt so bad for you, having to go on the air when it was obvious you were devastated."

She nodded. "I was. I cried for practically the whole past year. I so desperately did *not* want to fail at this marriage. I wanted to love

Drew—and I did—I do—in lots of ways. Sometimes, still, I cry for him at night. Sometimes, still, I think I'm not gonna be able to live without him. But, when I'm really, really honest with myself—and I hate to admit this—I think it's mostly fear and loneliness talking. Frosted over with a mega-dose of twitchy twat."

"Twitchy twat?!"

Camille laughed. "Acute horniness. I miss his maleness. I miss the sex. We finally stopped playing music together a couple months ago, because we ended up in the sack every single time we played and that caused us both too much pain."

"Do you still miss him?"

"Usually. But not today. Not yesterday. Only once since we crossed the border three days ago! Something's changing inside of me and I'm not sure what it's about yet. Things that were so blurry are starting to come into focus. The pain's gone for the first time since he left. I'm still horny, but it feels different. One thing I see is that I don't miss living with him. In fact, I gotta admit that I *hated* living with him! I have come to see—just in the last day or so that *maybe I don't love him.* Not in the way a wife should love her husband. And maybe Drew never loved me that way either. Or he wouldn't have gone against his faith and left me...."

"If you don't mind my asking, what was his reason for leaving you?"

She took a deep breath. "I don't mind. He had several. He was living in *my* house and when he argued with Matt or Eric, which was often, I would side with the boys against him. Three against one. He expected to be number one— head of my kids in every way. He was over 50 and he'd never been married before. He resented my relationship with my boys. He couldn't comprehend that they'd been around longer than he had and that we were used to functioning as a team. I retaliated by shutting him down in the bedroom.

"I know—me," she said in response to Barb's look of disbelief. "We got progressively more polarized. I took late massage appointments and left him alone with the boys—trying to force them to bond. I made sure he'd be asleep when I got home. Then I'd go over to Dana's when she got off work and we'd hang out. I took extra shifts at work or scheduled piano lessons on his days off. It wasn't a good scene."

Barb made a face. "Doesn't sound like it."

"He got fed up. Talked to the couple who were renting his house—they were from church—and they moved out. He moved back in. I got so pissed off at him for leaving that I filed for divorce."

"You did?!"

"I immediately regretted it, believe me. Especially when he invited Sylvia MacNamara to sing with him instead of me. That about drove me nuts. I tried to stop the divorce, but he wouldn't let me. I've managed to drag it out for nearly a year now, but I've run out of ploys...."

"Is he dating this woman?"

"He says they're just friends. I believe him. He's not a liar."

"Camille," Barb asked, "do you still go to church?"

She ground out her second cigarette. "No. Not lately. I haven't been able to pry myself out of bed on Sunday mornings to go. I was too humiliated. I felt like a colossal failure. Once I ceased being a married woman, the other women at church backed away from me. I didn't feel like I fit in with the singles, because I didn't *want* to be single and I didn't fit in with the marrieds, because my husband had left me. It was too weird. I felt abandoned. Rejected. I'm really struggling with my spiritual belief system right now...."

"I admire your honesty, ya know?"

"Well, it didn't come easy. Trust me." She tilted her head and looked sideways at Barbara. "Watch out. Tomorrow I may take you aside and tell you that everything I said today was hogwash, that I truly am still in love with my husband and ask you to join me in praying for God to bring him back to me."

Barb laughed. "Affairs of the heart. They defy logic, don't they? They absolutely refuse to conform to our little agendas."

Camille laughed with her. "They certainly do." She pushed back her chair. "Where are you coming from spiritually? Do you mind my asking?"

Barb shook her head. "Absolutely not. I was about to impose it on you anyway! I came from a non-religious, liberal family. I'm an only child. My dad is chairman of the International Business Department at Southern Illinois University in Carbondale. My mom is an interior designer. An excellent one. They're both very open, loving people. One hundred per cent real. I'm their only kid and they're my best friends. They took me to Protestant and Catholic churches when I was growing up. We went to the Unity Church too for a short time. One of my best friends growing up was Jewish, and I went to synagogue with her too. My folks wanted me to have a broad-based spiritual foundation so I'd have the tools to make up my own mind.

"I did the Young Life thing in high school and I was seriously gung-ho. Then when I got to college, I took a class on philosophy in religion during my first semester. I got hooked. It was my major for a year and a half, 'til I switched to Communications. I studied Zen and other Eastern religions, Islam and Christianity. Even the ancient Egyptian, Greek and Roman religions. I've checked out the New Age movement since then. I guess I've taken a little bit from each one."

"I had no idea."

"I am not fond of organized religion in any form, to tell you the truth. I think what happened to you and Drew is sadly typical. I'm reminded of the passage in the Bible where Jesus goes into the temple in Jerusalem and berates the Pharisees. Do you know it?"

Camille nodded. "I sure do. I was just reading it yesterday afternoon, as a matter of fact. Matthew 23. Goes something like this: 'Woe to you, teachers of the law and Pharisees, you hypocrites!' He goes on to call them 'blind guides' and 'blind fools' and describes them as clean on the outside and dirty on the inside. It's a pretty powerful speech."

"Definitely. In other parts of the gospel, Jesus told us loud and clear that if we judge others, we should expect to be judged right back in the same way. He knew that every single one of us is imperfect. We all sin and fall short of the mark. Perfection does not exist on this planet. But, religious fanatics of all denominations and sects fall into the same trap the Pharisees did. It's a recurring religious phenomena. The thing I've come to see is that we humans create these vast, intricate codes of behavior for ourselves in the name of God. Then, like those lunatics in the Spanish Inquisition who burnt people at the stake, we persecute—and even murder—anyone who fails to conform to them."

"Is that ever the truth."

"I'm convinced that God is far greater, more loving and more mysterious than we give him credit for being. He's so much more than the sum of every religion that man has ever conceived or ever will conceive."

"What do you think he wants from us?"

Barb half-smiled. "Who knows? I believe we're here on Earth as part of a spiritual journey. We're infinite spirits living in finite bodies. We have limited intellectual capacities and incomprehensible emotions. Yet, deep inside of ourselves we have this sense of knowing that we're all part of a greater whole, that there is so much that we can't even begin to fathom. So many of us try, especially in this culture, to label, define and rationalize everything so we don't feel so insignificant and out of control. But the key to really knowing, to learning the lessons we're here for, is to let go. Surrender's the key to everything, in my opinion."

"I don't understand."

"Think about it. Surrender's the opposite of control. You can't enjoy sex unless you totally let go, right?" Camille nodded.

"God deals in paradoxes—seeming contradictions. That and metaphors. If we want to know why we're here and what our true life's purpose is, then we need to completely surrender our need to control things. We need to open ourselves up and receive, just as we do when we make love. We let go and we wait. We trust. We allow ourselves to become a vessel for God's love. His truth. His purpose. And the answers come. The right ones...."

"Are you sure you're not a Christian?"

"I am. But that's only part of what I am."

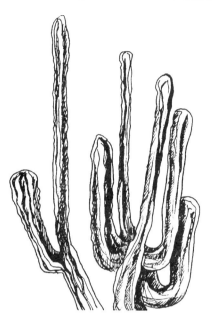

CHAPTER TWELVE   **San Quintín to Cataviña, Baja California**
October 17 and 18, 1997

Camille plugged Pink Floyd's "Atom Heart Mother" into Boris' stereo and cranked it up. Eerie, symphonic music reverberated through the RV as Dana drove south out of San Quintín, through farm lands and east, toward El Rosario. Expansive views of blue ocean and brown hills were visible to the west, while jagged, misty-looking peaks rolled into the eastern sky. They rounded the corner and came into the tiny town of El Rosario.

"Stop at the Pemex station on the left," ordered Holly. Dana put on her blinker and pulled across the lane of oncoming traffic. A smiling Mexican came up and looked at her questioningly. *"Lleno por favor*—Fill it please. *Con magna sin*—With unleaded," she said. He zeroed out the dial and began to feed gas into Boris. A small, dirty boy came up to Dana's window and offered her tiny packets of colored gum.

"No gracias," she said.

"How many gallons does this beast hold?" asked Camille from across the passenger seat.

"Thirty-four. At seven and a half miles to the gallon, that gives us a range of about 250 miles on a tank of gas. When you factor in the 20 extra gallons of gas Ellen made us bring—we have a 400 mile radius, which is a good thing."

"Why's that?"

Holly spoke up. "Cataviña, where we're headed today, sometimes has gas. Sometimes it doesn't. Punta Prieta doesn't anymore. So we need to be careful. That's our most treacherous stretch. If we have to go from here to Bay of L. A. and back, then all the way to Villa Jesus María or even Guerrero Negro before we can find an operable Pemex Station, that's over 300 miles. We need the extra gas. We need the reserves too, just in case...."

"This is in liters," Barb called from outside. "How do we know when it's full?"

"Grab the calculator out of the glove box," Holly told Camille. She handed it out the window. "Multiply by .26 if you want to be right-on. Or divide by four if you want to estimate it the easy way."

"Okay. He's full. It's 108 liters. 28.08 gallons doing it the fancy way or 27 doing it the lazy way. I think I'll do it correctly and keep track of our gas expenses in both liters and gallons in my notebook. Okay, Holly?"

"Cool."

Just then three rigs turned into the Pemex station. Two bore Idaho plates. One had California tags. All were driven by couples who appeared to be in their late 50s or upwards. "Joe! Joe Jennings!" yelled Holly from inside the RV. One of the men from Idaho looked up and smoothed his hair.

Holly yanked open the door, flew down the step and bounded across the asphalt to the faded Winnebago. She threw herself into the man's arms. They hugged. The man's wife came out and hugged her too. They talked for several minutes, and Holly gestured repeatedly toward Boris. Finally she waved for the others to come over.

She introduced them around. "This is Joe Jennings. And his wife Darlene. They live in Mulegé, practically next door to Rick's and my trailer. They're headed back down south for the winter."

The couple shook hands with Holly's three friends. "Sounds like y'all are gonna have a great time. Joe said. "Just keep to the main roads. Don't camp off by yourselves."

"And don't talk to strangers, right Joe?" she teased.

"No. Ya gotta do that. Hell, ain't no such thing as a stranger here, Holly Babe. You *know* that! Just don't talk to strangers out in the middle of nowhere and don't drive at night!"

She poked him. "No duh!"

"Y'all wanna join us for lunch at Mama Espinoza's?" he asked.

"No. We ate less than two hours ago. We'll have to hit her place on the way north."

"Best damned lobster burritos on the penisula," he said in Dana's direction. Her mouth watered at the thought.

"I'll remember that," she said. "Thanks."

"When can we expect you at the Villa María Isabel?" asked Darlene.

"Next Saturday."

The Jennings looked at each other. "Isn't that the day of the Las Glorias Chili Cook-Off?" Joe asked his wife. She nodded.

"I planned our itinerary with that in mind," said Holly. "Rick's coming down for it too." She turned toward Dana. "Want to enter?"

"A chili cook-off? Sure. Why not?"

"Darlene, will you sign her up? Spell your name for her, Dana."

"You have to come up with a name for your chili."

"Oh. Right this second?" The two women nodded. Dana closed her eyes and thought a moment. "I can't think of anything new and innovative on short notice. I'll do my Fifteen Bean Chili," she said. "It's my predecessor Todd's recipe, but it's a good one."

Darlene wrote everything down. Dana slid into the driver's seat and restarted the engine. She wondered how many times her dad and Ellen had run into friends at these remote, infrequent gas stops. There was nearly always an excellent restaurant nearby where travelers could eat, drink and catch up on things. She wondered if Bud knew these people. Thanks, Dad, she said inside her head. Thanks for Boris. I am loving this trip more every day....

She drove along the Arroyo del Rosario for a ways, crossed it and began to climb up into the barren, deeply eroded foot hills. She kept her eyes open for potholes and *vados*—dips that were really arroyos and were frequently washed out or filled with slippery sand. Within minutes, the giant *cardón*—cacti began to appear, their long thick arms reaching skyward. Holly emerged from the back and sat down on the floor between Dana and Camille. She motioned to Barb to sit behind her.

"I'm in tour guide mode now, ladies. We have just officially entered the Central Desert of Baja California. As I've told you before, over 100 species of cacti grow here, 80 of which grow nowhere else on Earth." She pointed to what looked to Dana to be a 25-foot-high cardón. "These big fellas are related to the saguaro we have in Arizona. The difference is that cardóns have multiple trunks. They have strong hardwood skeletons that are used around here as building material on the ranchos. When it rains, they retain water worse than a woman with PMS. They become rotund and succulent. They get as tall as a six-story building and can weigh up to 12 tons. In the dry sea-son—like we're in now—they get dehydrated and shrink up like contration camp victims." She chuckled, obviously pleased with her similes. "See," she pointed. "You can almost see the skeleton peeking through on that giant one over there."

Next she directed their attention to the odd-looking plants popping up with amazing frequency on both sides of the road. "These are called *cirios*—or boojum trees. They live nowhere else on Earth, except here and in Sonora, across the Sea of Cortez. Proof positive that the peninsula was connected to the mainland at one time in the distant geologic past."

Dana looked as best she could. The cirios looked like dancing creatures from another galaxy. They had chunky bases that thinned rapidly to one or more gangly branches long ones that waved about like arms and shorter ones that wiggled on tapered ends, like fingers. "In the winter when it rains, these dudes are covered in green leaves. Right now all you can see is the bare thorns. On top of their heads they grow these luscious yellow flowers that look like pompadours."

Dana remembered. She drove on in silence, soaking up the stark, alien beauty of the scenery. The mountains kept rising up before her, purple and hazy. Ocotillos appeared. Dried-out bushes. Chollas and other cacti.

Suddenly, Camille pointed. "What's that?" she asked. "It looks like a fat cirio without all the wavy branches."

"It's an elephant tree."

"Oh. I love it. It's so cute!" she exclaimed. "Where's my camera? Can we stop?"

"Soon. We'll get all the photo ops we want around Cataviña."

Dana drove up over a rise and down. In front of her, cutting off traffic on both sides of the road, was a canvas-covered, earth-colored Hummer. Soldiers dressed to match were sitting inside and standing on the pavement. They motioned for Dana to stop. She braked. "Let me do the talking," Holly instructed.

"What is it?" asked Barb, her voice edged in panic.

"Nothing," Holly hissed. "Mellow out."

"Hola. ¿Hablas español—Hi. Do you speak Spanish?" a tiny, dark man asked Dana.

"Sí," she said. *"Un poco*—Yes. A little."

"Yo hablo también," said Holly. "I speak too."

"Bueno—Good," he said, smiling. *"¿A dónde van*—Where are you going?"

"Cabo San Lucas. Estamos viajando por una mes. We're traveling for a month."

"¿Tienen drogas o armas—Do you have drugs or arms?" Holly

shook her head, no.

"*¿Quieren mirar*—Want to look?" she asked. He nodded. She motioned to Barb to open up the door and the soldier and his buddy came inside. Holly stood and showed them around.

"*¿Ningunos hombres*—No men? *¿Solamente mujeres*—Only women?" the buddy asked, his face a mask of surprise.

"*Sí. Ahora. Pero tenemos amigos en Mulegé y también en Los Barriles y Todos Santos. Mi esposo va a encontrarnos en Mulegé* —Yes for now. We have friends in Mulegé, Los Barriles and Todo Santos. My husband will be joining us in Mulegé."

"*Ay. ¡Que bueno*—Good!" the two poked around a bit more. As they backed out of the motor home, Holly passed them each a handful of candy. They smiled broadly. "Oh. Gracias."

"*De nada*—You're welcome."

"*Que les vaya bien*—Hope all goes well."

"*Mil gracias*—A thousand thanks."

"What was *that* all about?" Barb asked. "Those guys had big guns. Were they Federales?"

"No," Holly said. "Army. They're just young kids stuck out here in the boonies trying to do their job. They're friendly for the most part. They even like to flirt a little when the big boss isn't around. And they love those *dulces*—sweets!"

"What'd you say to them?"

Dana answered. "He asked her where we were headed. She told him Cabo. Said we have friends along the way. Said her husband was meeting us in Mulegé. They asked if we had guns or drugs and she told them no. They took our candy and wished us well. Pretty simple."

Barb rubbed her arms and shook her head. "Wow," she said. "My adrenaline was pumping something fierce. Will we have more of these roadblocks along the highway?"

"You betcha," said Holly.

"Oh God. Warn me next time, will you?"

Holly, Dana and Camille laughed. "We're about 30 miles north of Cataviña. Make a note of it in your little green book there. That way, when we're driving north, you'll know where they'll be ahead of time."

A few minutes before they reached the Hotel La Pinta, they saw the first of the boulder fields. Monstrous granite rocks rose up out of nowhere and were strewn randomly between and around the cactus forest. It was even more beautiful than Dana remembered from her trip with her dad, back in the late '70s right after the road was paved. Then it had been February and everything had been lush, green. The arroyos had been overflowing with water, making driving through the vados hairy. The cirios had been leafed out and crowned in gold and the cardóns had been plump and sassy. There had been purple, pink, yellow and orange explosions of wild flowers off to the side of the road. She remembered the lupine especially. "Hi lupine, lupine, lupine," she and Bud would say as the periwinkle blossoms rushed by them. Everything was dry and gray now. Even the palm trees at the oasis to her right looked withered.

They stopped at the hotel and topped off the gas tank at the Pemex station out front. Holly went across the street to a truck stop and came back out with a grizzled old Mexican man with no front teeth. She introduced him as José Luís. "He's my amigo," she explained. "He'll take us back a couple of miles to the first cave paintings we'll see on the trip. You want to go now or tomorrow?"

The other three looked at each other. "Tomorrow," said Dana. "I'm pooped." The others agreed. They got back in the RV and continued down highway for half a mile. "Turn left here," Holly instructed. She turned at a sign that read, Rancho Santa Ynéz. She headed three-quarters of a mile up a road and passed a small restaurant. There were four other motor homes and a half dozen tents on the smootheddown lot. She pulled into a likely spot and parked.

They got out. It was hot in the mid-afternoon sun. They rolled out the awning, pulled out their water bottles and sat in their lawn chairs, soaking up the view.

When Dana awoke it was still dark outside. She tapped Camille and they slipped out of their sleeping bags, changed into t-shirts, jeans and hiking boots, grabbed their cameras and tiptoed out the door. They closed it softly behind them. The darkness was barely beginning to fade as they headed up the path that led northeast, away from their campsite. The moon was gone and so were most of the stars.

They worked their way up, down, around and between the huge boulders. They hiked up and down several hills and found themselves in a dried-out river bed, populated by parched-looking palms. They walked upriver a ways, trying to identify the different types of cacti. There were tiny drops of dew on everything that glistened like diamonds in the predawn light.

Dana pointed. "Look," she whispered. At the top of the hill above them, a line of eight tall, straight cardón peered down. Two equally tall, skinny palms seemed to sway sensually between them, both holding themselves at exactly the same 75-degree angle. The towering silhouettes were black against the horizon. Both women snapped pictures.

The sun inched its way out from behind a ravine to their east. Almost instantly they could feel the air warming up. They headed back toward camp, taking another route this time. By the time they saw the restaurant lights flicker on, they'd found themselves in the camp dump. Black ashes, burnt tin and aluminum cans were strewn everywhere. They picked their way around the edge of the garbage heap. Suddenly Camille cried out. "Shit! I'm stabbed!"

Dana came over and took a look. Camille had run right into a jumping cholla and a spine as large as a darning needled protruded from her jeans, just above the knee. "Here, let me," Dana said and gave the thorn a yank. Camille squealed again. "Don't be a wuss," she said. "You're okay!"

"I know. It hurts though. Look," she pointed with one hand while she rubbed at her sore thigh with the other. "We're back!"

They found Barb and Holly sipping coffee together under the awning.

Holly stood and put her hands on her hips. She looked annoyed. "We're supposed to leave in twenty minutes. We made you coffee." She stepped into the motor home and brought out two steaming mugs. "Hurry. Drink up. José Luís will be here soon. We don't want to keep him waiting."

He showed up right on schedule in his ancient, rusted out *troque* —pickup truck. The four women picked up their hats, cameras and water bottles. They put the chairs and table inside Boris and locked him up. Dana grabbed Camille's hand and pulled her into the bed of the pickup with her. Holly and Barb sat up front. José Luís eased the truck into gear, drove out of the campground, turned right onto the highway and headed west. A little while later he turned right again and headed down a dusty, rutted dirt road.

After less than a mile, the truck lurched to a stop. They got out. José Luís led them up a trail that meandered between another boulder field. He stopped at an opening in the granite rocks that was barely three feet high. He motioned them to follow him, chatting all the while to Holly and Dana in Spanish. Soon they were inside a cave. It was big and roomy and there was plenty of room to stand up. It was open on both ends, so that sunlight poured in, lighting it up. Dana looked around. Looming up at her from the sides of the rocks were pictographs of the sun, surrounded by lines that zigged and zagged all over the place. She noticed other geometric shapes too, painted in varying shades of red and edged in black and faded white. The mural was high, about 12 feet, and covered two walls of this semi-outdoor cave.

"There aren't any people or animals in this cave, like most of the others found further south," Holly explained.

They took pictures and sat down in the cool cave to rest. José Luís talked and Holly translated. "The cave paintings of Baja extend from here to just west of Mulegé. These are the first we'll see, but they're by no means the most dramatic. In others we'll see people." Holly explained that one could tell the women from the men because they'd been painted with their breasts sticking out of their arm pits like an extra set of pointed appendages. Their feet poked out at the same angles. "Paintings of animals, such as birds, rabbits, deer and fish are found in lots of the caves. Some have whales and even big horn sheep."

"Will we see those?" asked Dana.

Holly nodded. "When we go to San Ignacio we'll visit *Cueva Pintada*—Painted Cave, the biggest and most famous of all the caves. And *Cueva de las Flechas*—Cave of the Arrows, right across from it." She listened to José Luís a moment and then continued. "There are four main areas in the mountains of central Baja where cave paintings have been found: the Sierra de San Borja just south of Bay of L.A.; the Sierra de San Juan, about two-thirds of the way between there and Santa Rosalía; the Sierra de San Francisco to the north of San Ignacio and the Sierra de Guadalupe, due west of Mulegé. We're north of all of them right now, on the farthest outer edge of the region. Jesuit priests from Spain, who built most of the missions in Baja, were the first white men to discover the cave paintings. They were padres from the mission San Francisco de San Borja, which was built in the mountains southwest of Bay of L.A."

"When was that?"

Holly pulled her backpack off her shoulders. She unzipped it and took out a guide book. She thumbed through it for a few moments. "Here it is. The mission was established in 1762. The cave paintings at San Borjitas were first written about in 1767."

Dana interrupted. "Wait a sec. When did the Spaniards first arrive?"

"The Spaniards tried to colonize Baja in the 1500s. Guys like Cortez, Ulloa, Vizcaíno and Cabrillo. But none of their settlements lasted. It wasn't until October 25, 1697 that Father Juan María Salvatierra, a Jesuit priest, established the first permanent settlement in either Alta or Baja California. It was the mission in Loreto."

"Where's Loreto again?" asked Barb.

She turned to a map and pointed. "Right here. Pretty close to midway between Santa Rosalía and La Paz, on the Sea of Cortez." She took a sip of water and wiped the sweat from her forehead. "There aren't any cave paintings that far south. The most dense concentration of them is around San Ignacio."

"How old are they?" Dana asked, running her hand across the granite rock.

"Most are believed to have been painted between 3,500 and 5,000 years ago, with the newest being about 1,000 years old."

"How many of them are there?"

She conferred with José Luís. "We aren't sure. Way over a hundred."

"I read about them in Erle Stanley Gardner's book, *The Hidden Heart of Baja*," Camille said. "You guys should check it out."

"There's a new book coming out—right about the time we get back home," Holly explained. "A book called *The Cave Paintings of Baja*, by Harry Crosby. He's studied them for decades. I've seen the galleys. And the photos. It's gonna be awesome."

"How many missions are there?" Barb asked.

"Let's see." She flipped through the pages. "Twenty-eight in Baja. Twenty-one in Alta California—from San Diego to San Francisco."

"Wow," said Barb. "Which came first? Ours or theirs?"

"She said that the first one was in Baja. In Loreto—in 1697—right?" asked Dana.

"Yeah. The padres built the missions so they could be reached within a day's travel on foot. They built up southern Baja first, then northern Baja. The Jesuits built 19 missions altogether before they were kicked out—for abuse of authority."

"What'd they do?"

"Basically, they mistreated the Indians. Nearly wiped them out. The ones that weren't killed in skirmishes were killed off by disease. After the Jesuits came the Franciscans, headed up by San Diego's own Father Junipero Serra." She flipped through the book again. "He took over in 1767. It says here that he built only one mission in Baja before heading north to Alta California, where he built 21 missions. He did all that in six years! In 1773, the Franciscans gave control of the mission system over to the Dominican padres, who headed south again and built nine more missions in Baja."

"Wow. That's a lot."

"Twenty-eight. The era of the mission was over by 1846 because war and disease had killed off most of the Indians. There were only a few hundred left. The whole concept was no longer feasible and the missions were nationalized by Spain."

Dana got up and stretched. "You mentioned something the other day about Loreto and a big fiesta marking the Tri-Centennial. Will we make it down there in time?"

"It starts on the twenty-fifth. That's a week from today—the same day as the Las Glorias Chili Cook-Off in Mulegé. We're committed there. I figured by the time we get to Loreto, on the twenty-ninth, we should be able to catch the tail end of the partying without getting too caught up in the insanity of it."

"Wow. Three hundred years. There's no way we can miss that!" said Camille, jumping to her feet. "It's a once in a lifetime thing! And I hate chili anyway! It gives me gas."

"No. We're gonna be in Mulegé. Dana's cooking, remember?" Holly said.

"But it's not fair! You should have told us about the Tri-Centennial *before* you roped Dana into cooking at this Las Glorias thing," Camille said. "Don't you agree, guys?"

Barb gave her a blank look. Dana closed her eyes. "Come on," Camille fake-whined. "You aren't even using your own recipe, for God's sake, Dana. Wouldn't you rather go to Loreto?"

Dana raised her eyebrow at Camille. Camille ignored her. "Let's vote! Who wants to go to Loreto instead of a dumb chili cook-off besides me? Barb?! Dana?"

"I...." Dana started.

Holly interrupted. Her voice was loud and trembled with irritation. "People are expecting us in Mulegé on the twenty-fifth. My husband is one of them. I'm the leader of this expedition and I've made commitments, Dana's made commitments and we will all honor those commitments. Am I understood?"

Camille pressed the point. "Oh Holly, get real!" she said. "You made us commit to this gig prematurely—without giving us the whole scoop. That's not fair! This Tri-Centennial a big deal! It's the 300 year anniversary of colonization in the Californias! Surely your friends in Mulegé will understand and let us off the hook."

Holly's face flushed red. Dana felt the skin on the back of her neck prickle. I better do something, she told herself quickly or we're gonna be in for trouble. "Come on you guys," she said. "I did sign up to cook and we all know Holly's in charge."

"Dana! *It's your motor home!* You have more power here than you're willing to admit. It's the *Tri-Centennial,* dammit!"

"*Camille!*" Dana willed her to get it. C'mon Cinnamon Girl.

Wake up. Shut up and quit pushing, she begged inside her head. She prayed that Camille would read her mind, or her facial expressions. Something.

She didn't. Things had already gone too far.

"Is this about us honoring our commitments, Holly, or is it really about control? You manipulated Dana into cooking at this cook-off so you could spend a few days with your husband. You don't give a shit what the rest of us want to do." She stopped and looked hard at the tour guide, "Ellen told me and Dana that you two'd agreed we'd run this trip by committee. The way I see it from here, you're behaving like a dictator!"

Holly looked like she was ready to deck Camille. She didn't speak for at least ten long seconds. When she did, her words came out slow, clipped and dripping icicles. "You know, Camille—when you and Barb have earned the right to have a say so in things, I'll listen to you. And—just because your husband got sick of your big fat mouth and walked out on you doesn't mean I don't have a right to see mine now—does it? For the last time, we are going to be in Mulegé for the Las Glorias Chili Cook-Off." She turned and ducked through the opening to the cave and took off down the path.

When the rest of them got to the troque, she was long gone. They headed back to the campground. About halfway there, José Luís pulled over to the side of the road. Barb, who was in the front with him, leaned out and asked Holly if she wanted a ride. She shook her head and kept on running.

CHAPTER THIRTEEN Bahía de Los Angeles, Baja California
October 19, 1997

They passed over a rise. Barb gasped from the passenger seat of
the motor home. She felt as though the barren desert had heaved itself
wide open and given birth to the sea. The contrast of severe granite
and sandstone mountains against the dancing surface of the Sea of
Cortez made her breath catch in her throat. Pale purple and white
islands rose up out of the turquoise water and consumed most of the
horizon, looking to Barb like chunks of the moon that had splashed
down to Earth. This was a place where life and death walked hand in
hand.

"It's beautiful," she whispered. "I had no idea...."

"It is, isn't it?" agreed Dana. "It's been about nine years since I
was here last. It never ceases to knock me sideways."

"It's other-worldly...."

"Yes. I know."

Barb turned and looked at Holly. She was pounding at the keys
of her laptop again, and her headphones were on. She'd been cold and
distant since the incident the day before, refusing to make anything
but the smallest of talk. Camille was in the top bunk, sleeping off a
hangover that was threatening to turn into Montezuma's Revenge.

Things were easier without them for now. Camille had been devastated by Holly's remark. She'd cried all the way back to the RV park
and kept on crying until dinner was ready. Holly had stopped off at
the restaurant on her way back and didn't come home until well after
dark. When she did, she acted as though nothing had happened. She
sat down at the fire with the others and chatted for a few minutes,
ignoring Camille completely. Then she yawned, excused herself and
went to bed. All evening Barb had felt like she was walking on egg

shells. She felt useless and out of place. Dana knew Camille much better than she did. She wanted to say something to ease Camille's pain. She wanted to do something to mend the rift between the two women. It was obvious that Holly had ripped the scab right off Camille's healing heart. Her feelings for Drew were still strong, and her wounds raw. Barb could tell that Holly blamed Camille solely for their fight. While that disturbed her, what really bugged was the recurring thought that Holly actually *enjoyed* Camille's suffering. Just the thought of it gave her the creeps.

Barb had some ideas about what had caused the altercation, but she'd kept them to herself so far. She couldn't quite see the entire picture yet, and she was waiting until she could. It was obvious that Holly had expected to have Dana as her buddy on this trip. Barb had seen the resentment burning in her eyes every time Dana and Camille took off together. She knew that Holly considered *her* a wimp and felt like she was forever getting stuck babysitting her. While Barb didn't like Holly's put-downs, she was able to ignore them for the most part. After all, she'd never represented herself as an outdoorswoman. There was more to it than that though, she was sure of it.

She pushed the thoughts aside and soaked up the magnificent landscape in front of her. There was a small town toward the south end of the wide bay. Houses and trailers dotted the shoreline in either direction. She squinted against the late morning sun. There were at least four colorful boats, which she now knew were called pangas, in the water offshore. A lone pickup truck worked its way up a dirt road, a trail of dust chasing it. She heard the whine of an airplane engine and turned her eyes skyward. Suddenly a single engine plane swooped down and circled, flying low over the ocean. Moments later it landed on a dirt strip near the town. Barb opened her mind as wide as she could and willed herself to remember this scene always.

Something inside her shifted and she squirmed in her seat.

Stirrings of desire ignited and burst into flame inside her. Streamers of white lightning shot up and down her spine. She wished it was Bob beside her driving and that no one else was with them, because if that had been the case, she would have had him pull off to the side of the road right then and there. She would have taken him up to the bunk overhead, climbed on top of him and made love to him until they were both spent. Who cared if anyone wondered what they were doing, here on the outskirts of town? She smiled a secret smile. Would he be surprised, or what?! His proper little wife—who never initiated sex—suddenly turning to him with a passion as bare and untamed as this place. It would shock him right out of his socks. Most definitely. She couldn't wait to write him and share her fantasy with him—in detail.

Her body hummed as she played with the words in her head. Moments later another series of images assaulted her. She sat up straight and looked out the window again at the bay. For the first time on this trip—heck, for the first time ever probably—she *wanted* to go in the ocean. She wanted to swim, to walk from one end of that endless stretch of beach to the other. To learn to kayak and snorkel. She wanted to know the people who lived in this fiercely beautiful outback. She wanted to run, to dance and to sing at the top of her lungs.

They were almost there. Holly came forward, pulled off her headphones and crouched down between Barb and Dana. "I want to camp north of town, toward La Gringa." She paused briefly. "It's not so crowded there. Okay with you two?"

They found a spot just off a road that hugged the shoreline. Dana parked Boris between a gold VW Vanagon and a faded Winnebago that looked just like the Jennings'. There were several other rigs parked here and there along the beach and a few tents too. But it wasn't as crowded as the area to the south of them where the houses and trailers were wall to wall. Holly explained that there weren't too many campers because it was still a little early in the season.

Barb got out of the motor home and nearly gagged in the heat. It wrapped itself around her and threatened to suck her breath away. She brushed her bangs back. The temperature had to be well over 100 degrees. She grabbed her hat, walked to the shore, took off her flip-flops and waded into the water. Oh. It was perfect. Warmer even than the pool where she took aqua aerobics at the sporting club where she and Bob worked out.

She heard Camille moan from the cabover bed and turned. Her head appeared against the screen and she called out, "How hot is it here anyway?! I'm dying."

"Turn on the fan," Dana called back at her. "It'll cool you off. Are you too sick to go for a swim?"

Camille groaned. "Yes."

Holly motioned to Dana to help her unroll the awning. They set up camp, hauled the kayaks off the roof and unfastened the mountain bikes. Barb watched from the shore, unable to drag her feet from the water. She turned and looked out toward the islands in front of her. The surface of the sea was as still as a sheet of blue glass. A flock of sea gulls circled overhead, screeching. To the south of her came a flock of brown pelicans, flying in a V formation. They rode the air currents up and down, up and down, like an invisible roller coaster as they searched from on high for their lunch.

Without warning, less than 50 feet in front of her, the surface of the sea broke. A shiny snub-nosed dolphin arched flawlessly out of the water, through the air and back into the sea—without making a splash. Another followed. Then a third. She stood on the shore transfixed, holding her breath. The pelicans began to dive, one by one, sending up huge explosions of white water. The contrast between the two species reminded her of the difference between an Olympic champ executing a flawless dive and a kid doing a cherry bomb or a can opener one moved with a pure fluidity and grace and the other a primitive but intentional awkwardness.

She noticed, from the corner of her eye, a skittering near her toes. She looked down and saw a trio of stingrays darting across the sand like odd-shaped flying saucers with barbed tails. She squealed and threw herself backwards. She fell onto the wet sand, landing hard in a sitting position. A wave came and washed over her legs. She scurried backwards like a crab. Holly's laughter echoed in her ears.

"Yeehaw!" she yelled. "Classic move, Barb! Let me guess! Those cute little stingrays spooked you!" Barb turned her head, her cheeks stinging in humiliation. Holly was leaning against one of the bikes, dressed in shorts and a sports bra. She wore a visor and sunglasses and a carried a small pack on her back. A water bottle was strapped onto the bike's frame. She swung her leg up over the bike, mounted, waved and pedaled off down the dusty road, still laughing.

Dana came over and pulled Barb to her feet. "She said she needed some space," she explained. "She went to look for some friends of hers. She says they're gonna take her out diving and not to expect her back 'til late."

Barb heaved a sigh of relief. "Thank God," she said. "What are we gonna do, Dana? What's with her, anyway? She can be so nasty...."

Dana shrugged. "I dunno. I've never seen this side of her before. We've always had a superficial, easy relationship. She's intelligent and competent, but—shit—Barb this mean streak of hers is real and it's making me uncomfortable as hell."

Barb nodded. "I hate to gossip, but the way I see it, she's a control freak. She punishes anyone who gets in her way. Maybe I'm wrong. I hope so. Maybe she'll come back tonight and be ready to talk things through...."

"I'm not counting on it. I'm thinking that the three of us are gonna have to sit her down and somehow make her see what she's doing."

"That'll be a trick. She seems to have the art of nailing someone with a zinger—and then bailing—down pat."

"I know. And the last thing I want us to do is make her feel like we're ganging up on her. Or mutinying...."

Just then strains of "It's a Small World" came at them from down the road. In a slow-moving cloud of dust, came a miniature white van. The name *Helados Super Ratón*—Mighty Mouse Ice Cream, was etched in black between enticing and colorful pictures of ice cream cones, fresh fruit popcicles and other chilling delights. Dana waved him over and they each bought a banana split for six pesos, or 75 cents. They sat their beach chairs down right at the waterline and ate, their legs and feet in the surf.

"All you have to do is shuffle your feet," Dana said.

"Huh?" Barb asked, her mouth full of whipped cream and nuts.

"The stingrays. They're way more scared of you than you are of them. Just shuffle your feet when you're in the water. There's tons of them in this bay—more than anywhere else I've been in Baja. They'll take off if they see you coming."

"Don't they hurt when they sting?"

Dana nodded. In between bites she said, "I got stung once when I came here with my family as a kid. I remember it vividly. My dad cleaned my foot with saltwater and cut out the barb with his fishing knife. It hurt! Then he make me soak my foot in hot water for over an hour. By that time the pain was pretty much gone and he was able to disinfectant it and bandage it. But I had to keep it clean for the rest of the trip."

"Do you think it's strange that she bailed on us this way?"

"I'm not sure. I think it's good she's gone for the day. It's better than putting up with her annoyance. I've been here before. I can always go ask the neighbors for help if we need it. We'll be okay."

"What do you do with someone who won't talk?"

Dana shrugged. "I asked her if she wanted to talk when you were standing in the waves. She said no, that everything was fine. She just wants to be the undisputed leader, I think. I don't think the team concept works for her at all."

Barb was quiet for a moment. She wondered how to say what she wanted to say next. Taking a deep breath, she began to speak. "Dana. Forgive me if I'm blunt, but in Holly's defense, you and Camille haven't been exactly fair to her. You've been inseparable, like Xena and that sidekick of hers...."

"Gabrielle."

"Yeah. You've been having such a good time together, it's like you've forgotten that we're here too. Holly and I are nowhere near compatible in this adventure. I'm a complete and utter neophyte. She's an expert. You're close to that and Camille's somewhere between you and me. To leave her and me together all the time is to court disaster."

"I know. I hear how she talks to you. It bugs me. But I'm not gonna be bullied into hanging out with her and leaving you two behind all the time when you don't know your way around—just because Holly wants a playmate. She knew how tight Camille and I were before we left. This is the first time the two of us have ever gone on vacation together—or done anything major together without our kids—in seven years! I'm not about to let Holly's moods define my trip."

"You're aggravating her."

"Shit," said Dana. She finished her ice cream, got up and walked into the water. She bent over, washed her hands, came back and sat down. "I hadn't thought of that. I guess I'm partly to blame for this. I've been pretty selfish."

Barb nodded. "Yes ma'am. But I'm not blaming you entirely. Holly's a bitch when she doesn't get her way. Granted, Camille went a little overboard, but you have to admit, she was right. Holly should not have committed to the Chili Cook-off without telling us that we'd miss the Tri-Centennial because of it. And what she said to Camille was cruel. She knew that remark about Drew dumping her would hurt her—badly. She had her gun out and she was shooting to wound. She did the same thing to me today when she made fun of me when I got scared by the stingray and fell on my behind."

"She doesn't mock me."

"No," said Barb. "She doesn't want you out of the way. Just us."

"She sabotages things. I guess she doesn't realize that when she trashes you guys, it pushes me away. So how do we tell her all this without alienating her further?" Barb shrugged.

Dana stood and brushed the sand off her backside. "Let's drop it for now. You want me to teach you to kayak and snorkel today, kiddo? We can take the boats out to that rock outcropping over there...." She pointed toward the south at the end of the La Gringa point, "then we can beach them and go explore the undersea world. What do you say?"

Tentacles of fear gripped themselves around Barb's heart for the briefest of moments, then relaxed and let go. "Sure. I'd love to," she said. They went inside to check on Camille and get changed. Fifteen minutes later, Dana had pushed her off from shore. She showed her how to dip, first the right end of the paddle into the clear sea and then swoop it up and dip the left end in.

At first, Barb shifted her weight from one side to the other, making the boat rock precariously. It nearly tipped over and visions of herself landing on the sand, only to be stabbed by a giant stingray, flashed through her mind. Next she saw images from the movie *Jaws* and came within half a breath of begging Dana to take her back to shore.

"Don't move your torso so much. Just your arms and shoulders. You're making it harder than it needs to be," she explained. "And you have a life jacket on, so you'll be okay even if you do fall out. Follow me...."

They stroked off, with Dana in the lead. Barb glued her eyes to Dana's arms and mimicked her every movement. Within ten minutes she had relaxed. Wow, she said to herself. I'm really doing this! And it's fun! She wished Bob could see her now.

The ironwood fire burned slow and hot. Crickets chirped loudly. The moon was just beginning to rise over the peaks of *Isla Angel de la Guarda*—Guardian Angel Island. Barb twirled her marshmallow ever so slowly over the flames, being careful not to let it catch fire.

"So what else did you see?" asked Camille. She'd just awakened and eaten some canned chicken soup. She was bundled up, in spite of the warmth of the evening, still fighting the effects of a fever.

"Sea turtles! A whole bunch of 'em! And two seals...."

"Sea lions."

"Oh. Okay. Sea lions. We saw something jump. Dana wasn't sure if it was a marlin or a sailfish but it was *big!*"

"Tell her about the best thing of all."

Barb groaned. "Oh my God. You wouldn't have believed it, Camille. We saw a sperm whale!"

"You're kidding."

"Nope. Dana recognized it cause it has a square head, long nose and no dorsal fin. It came within about 50 yards of us and blew sky high. Then it rolled and rolled in the water, showing us its backside. It was so huge it seemed like it went on *forever!* We could see its barnacles even! Then it whooshed its tail at us and it was gone. Just like that."

"I tapped on the side of my kayak for the longest time, trying to get it to come back. It didn't, but you should've seen Barb, backpaddling like a maniac. It was hilarious. She was just sure it was gonna come up from under her and smash her and her boat to smithereens!"

Barb nodded. "I was."

"I explained to her that they're playful creatures. Intelligent and gentle and capable of navigating via sonar systems far more complex than any invented by man. This guy wouldn't hurt her. *But she didn't believe me!*"

Barb laughed. "Nope. I did not. That whale was huge! Let me tell you!" The three women laughed together as Barb pulled her coat hanger from the fire and nibbled at her marshmallow.

Just then Holly and her mountain bike materialized in the fire light. "Hello all," she said.

Barb's eyes sought out Dana's. Holly sat down. "May I?" she asked. She took Barb's coat hanger and mounted a marshmallow on its end. She stuck it in the flames and it caught fire immediately. She waited a moment and then pulled it out, blew on it and ate it right off the stick. She jumped up then, ran over to the cooler and pulled out a beer, popped the top off with the opener dangling from its handle and sucked down the cold liquid. No one said anything.

She sat down again, beer in hand. "So what'd you do today?" she asked.

Barb repeated the story of their kayaking trip. Holly's eyes widened in envy as she described the variety of wildlife they'd encountered.

"Did you take them to the *museo*—museum, Dana?"

"No."

"Well maybe tomorrow. It's worth a visit. It has a great collection of mining remnants from the Las Flores mine, plus Indian artifacts, seashells and other natural phenomena. And then there's the sea turtle preserve...."

"Will you take us?" Dana asked.

Holly reloaded her coat hanger and stuck another marshmallow in the fire. "Sure."

Dana got up. "Hol, would you come for a walk on the beach with me?"

Holly looked at her, confusion clouding her features. "Yeah. Let me eat this and get another beer."

"So what do you think?" Barb asked Camille as they listened to Jimmy Buffett's "One Particular Harbor."

"Dana talked to me while she was cooking dinner and you were taking that saltwater bath of yours. How was it, by the way?"

"It was wonderful. She gave me that coconut soap we bought back in Ensenada to use. It lathered up really well. I used regular shampoo and conditioner and that didn't work quite as well. But I have to admit, I actually feel clean."

"Good. I'm gonna try it first thing in the morning. I'm extremely sick of my own stench, believe me."

"Then we have to go into town, get ice and dump the holding tank at Guillermo's."

"I know. I even offered to drive." Camille was quiet for a few long seconds. Then she spoke. "She asked me to tell you that she's following most of your suggestions. You were right. She is the logical one to talk to Holly. If all of us converged on her at once, it would be a another bad scene. Dana said she's not even gonna bring up the Chili Cook-Off incident. It's just not worth it. Hopefully we'll be able to catch the tail end of the Tri-Centennial. She does intend to apologize to her for spending too much time with me, and to suggest that we switch off."

Barb cringed in spite of herself. "Isn't that kind of co-dependent?" she asked.

"I suppose it is. But we have to choose our battles. We committed, as Holly keeps reminding us. We need to learn from this. We all know she's a control freak now. We all know she gets real mean when she's crossed. We need to make sure we have all the facts before we let her talk us into things."

"Good call."

"She doesn't like either one of us, you know," Camille said with a slight grin.

"I know. She thinks I'm a total wimp. But I think I shocked her when I told her about our whale encounter."

Camille giggled. "You pretty near shocked the shit out of her, is what you did!"

"We'll let her spend some quality time with Dana. You and I can find ways to entertain ourselves."

"True. I'd like to go for a long walk down the beach tomorrow and take some pictures. Talk to some of the folks that live here. You up for that?"

Camille nodded. "Yes. Most definitely. I feel a lot better tonight. Give me one of them saltwater baths in the a.m. and I'll be good as new. Just keep me away from the tequila bottle for a while."

"You certainly drowned your sorrows."

"Well, hells bells, woman. She hit a nerve. A couple of 'em. What can I say?"

"How do you feel about it now?"

"As confused as always. I would give *anything* to be over Drew

—once and for all. But I'm just not there yet."

"Baby steps."

"Ah yes. And the old adage, one day at a time. Patience has never been my strong suit. Neither is failure. I swore I'd never ever ever get divorced again...."

"Well, perhaps that's one of your lessons this time around."

Camille leaned forward. The firelight illuminated her face, showing her freckles in what looked to be three-D. "Lessons?!"

Barb nodded. "I believe everything that happens to us happens for a reason. To teach us something. If we reach deep down inside ourselves and ask for the lesson in every adversity or challenge that confronts us—I believe we'll be shown it. And we'll not only be stronger and wiser, but we'll see life more clearly too."

"Huh?"

"That way we don't hang on so tight to the outcome we want. Because all too often we don't get our way. It's like the Stones song, you know? About not always getting what we *want,* but always getting what we *need."*

"You mean I may not want this divorce, but I might *need* it...."

"You *need* the lesson. Otherwise, in the circular motion of life, it will come back to you again and again in a different form, and in a louder, more dramatic voice until you surrender to it and learn it."

"You and your surrender stuff. I swear...."

"Just think about it Camille. Especially when you're walking on the beach tomorrow. Go into that quiet place inside you where your inner voice speaks. You know that place?"

Camille nodded. "Sure I do. We Christians call it the voice of the Holy Spirit."

"Of course it is. Doesn't matter what anyone calls it. It's there for us nonetheless. Instead of begging him to bring Drew back, ask God for the lesson. Drew may not be the right life mate for you. You may need to be alone, as Dana's been. This is a time in history when the roles of men and women are changing. Not just economically, but spiritually too. I read somewhere recently that we, as a species, are exiting a period of 52,000 years of male-dominated energy and moving into a period of 52,000 years of female-dominated energy. You know, more intuitive, down to earth, in tune with the ebbs and flows of nature. The men have come close to annihilating this planet. Maybe it really is up to us women to turn things around. Maybe it's time for us to embrace our own brilliance instead of embracing the brilliance of men. Maybe we can start functioning more like planets than moons orbiting the sun ourselves, instead of orbiting our men, who in turn orbit the sun."

"Whoa. Most people I know would disagree with you—but I think you're on a roll, girlfriend! So you mean it might be a *good thing* for me to raise my kids alone?"

Barb nodded. "Maybe so."

They were both silent, lost in the spiraling circles of their own thoughts. Suddenly Camille stood up, arms raised and eyes closed. She began to hum, then to sway. In a sweet, ever-so-soft voice she began to sing:

You are the diamond in my mind
you are the love I long to find
you are the light that shines so bright
though I try with all my might
I can't forget you, I can't forget you.

You are, you are, you are,
the diamond in my mind
You are, you are, you are
the light that shines so bright.
I can't forget you, I can't forget you.

You are with me where I go
and if there's one thing that I know
all these years you've been away
my thoughts never seem to stray
away from you.
Always with you, always with you.

You are, you are, you are
the diamond in my mind
You are, you are, you are
the light that shines so bright
I can't forget you, I can't forget you.[1]

She stopped singing, opened her eyes and looked straight at Barb. "It's called 'Diamond in My Mind.'" I thought I wrote it for Drew," she said. "I think I meant it for God."

CHAPTER FOURTEEN

Guerrero Negro to
San Ignacio, BCS
October 21, 1998

Dana read aloud from Holly's notes. "Guerrero Negro, a community of approximately 11,000, is located in the midst of the immense Vizcaíno Desert. It is the world's leading producer of salt. Just south of town are thousands of evaporating ponds, each about 100 yards square. They are flooded with three to four feet of sea water. The desert sun causes the water to evaporate rapidly, leaving a residue of pure salt, which is scooped up by dredges and taken to a nearby wharf. The salt is then loaded onto barges and transported 52 miles to Cedros Island, where it is transferred to oceangoing freighters. Salt from Guerrero Negro is used in Mexico, the United States, Canada and Japan."

"So do we want to stay here or not?" Holly asked from the driver's seat.

"Where do we go otherwise?" Dana asked back.

"We can go on ahead to San Ignacio and spend an extra day there. That'd be my choice. But I want to offer you all the option of spending the night here."

Dana spoke from the passenger seat. "I flew in here once with Francisco Muñoz on the way to Puerto Vallarta with my dad and Ellen back in '67. It was desolate beyond belief."

Holly shook her head. "It hasn't changed much. Damn. I'm so sorry Mr. Muñoz wasn't in Bay of L.A. I wanted to interview him for the book."

"I was supposed to interview him too," said Camille. "So who comes here anyway?"

"Surfers. Diehard fishermen come to fish in Vizcaíno Bay. The Audubon Society does some birding out by the old pier 'cause there are some really nice marshlands there. During whaling season Guerrero Negro caters to ecotourists. Then you can catch a panga out to Scammon's Lagoon—called Laguna Ojo de Liebre by the locals—and play with the gray whales. I only work out of San Ignacio Lagoon myself. I like everything about it better. Of course, if the Japanese are allowed to build their salt refinery there, they could ruin it too. And endanger the gray whales."

"Really? asked Dana. "The Mexican government is gonna let them do that?"

Holly nodded. "It appears so. It's all about dinero, you know." She sighed. "Guerrero Negro's a friendly town. But I can't tolerate the smell of diesel fuel. I've been to Malarrimo Beach a few times, and I was thinking of taking you there, but everyone tells me it's been picked over and it's not really worth the trip. So...."

"Pass," called Barbara from the behind her head. "This desert depresses me. I've never seen anything so desolate in all my life."

Dana looked back at her. "It's actually pretty in the spring," she said, "if it gets rain. But right now it's bleaker than bleak." Holly looked out the window at the vast emptiness, uninhabited except for the rare yucca válida and some salt brush. She didn't like it much either.

"What's Guerrero Negro mean anyway?" asked Camille.

"Black Warrior," said Dana. "After a gringo whaling ship that was wrecked at the entrance to the lagoon nearly a hundred years ago."

"So what we do?"

"I vote with Barb to blow on through," said Dana.

"Me too," agreed Camille.

"Write this in your notebook, Barb! We all actually agreed on something! However, we need to stop for gas and we may as well eat lunch too. Our mileage today, if we go all the way to San Ignacio, will top 200 miles. We're in the red zone."

They drew closer to the twenty-eighth parallel, which divides the states of Baja California and Baja California Sur. In the distance, rising 140 feet up out of the desert haze, was a monument of an eagle—the national bird of Mexico. It cried out to the heavens with its angular steel beak and hovered precariously on an off-center concrete body with small, chunky wings. It hung in the blazing midday sky like a ghostly sentry.

Holly instructed them to all set their watches an hour ahead and she pulled up next to the monument, at the military check point. Several men in uniforms descended upon the motor home. One asked for their tourist cards and carefully inspected each. A second asked Holly what kinds of fruit and vegetables they had. Others just milled around and stared at the four women. She bantered back and forth with the agricultural inspector for a few minutes before he waved them through. "I'm taking you to the Malarrimo Motel and RV Park, ladies," she said. "After we hit the Pemex station."

Holly and Barb ordered chicken tacos. Dana and Camille ordered fish tacos. Holly noted their disappointment when their lunches showed up twenty minutes later. The chicken tacos were good and Holly was hungry. The corn tortillas were lightly fried and the chicken was topped with lettuce and tomato and served with a creamy combination of guacamole and salsa verde, or Mexican green sauce. She spooned extra guacamole on her tacos and began to munch them down.

It didn't go quite as well for Dana and Camille. Both picked at their fish tacos and ordered extra Cokes. Unlike their northern Baja cousins, these didn't come breaded and garnished with cabbage, radishes, tomatoes, cheese and cilantro and smothered in mysterious Mexican white sauce. No. These were simply pieces of dried, salty shredded fish wrapped in equally dry flour tortillas.

"Seen enough?" asked Barb as they piled back into the motor home.

"Sí," said Dana. Her words were echoed by the other two. "Let's blow this pop stand. How far to San Ignacio?"

"Look on the map."

"Eighty-eight miles."

"We'll be there by four at the latest."

The first sight of San Ignacio always dazzled Holly. After so many monotonous miles of bleached-out desert, the sight of the extensive date palm groves and lush oases, the palapa-roofed huts and colorful storefronts was like taking a tropical vacation in the dead of winter. It snapped one's senses into instant wakefulness—eyes, ears and noses numbed and sluggish after a season of desolation were suddenly alert and astonished. She loved the town's mission and the cool, tree-lined plaza that fronted it. She loved the people of San Ignacio. It was one of her favorite places on the peninsula and the departure point for the whale-petting and cave painting tours she led in winter and spring.

She drove past the Pemex station, pulled off Mex 1 and veered to the right. She headed through thick palm groves, passed the La Pinta Hotel and a bird-filled lake that was really an upwelling of an underground river and approached the town. She made a right turn into the Trailer Park El Padrino. The park wasn't very full. There were only six other rigs and half as many tent camping groups. She pulled into one of the 20 sites with hookups. "We're in luck, ladies. Here we have full hookups. This place offers one flushing toilet, four excellent, hot showers, a modest restaurant with okay coffee and not too many bugs."

"Scorpions?" asked Barb.

"No. Just mosquitos and no-see-ums. We'll be all right if we put on our repellant around sunset."

The owner, Don Abel, and several of his dogs came over while they were setting up camp and collected the $8 fee. Barb fawned all over the dogs while the rest of them worked. They changed into sundresses. They were, after all, in a Mexican town now and life was more formal than in the other out-of-the way places they'd visited. Holly pulled her camera out of the case and took shots of the others setting up camp. They walked back toward the lake and took pictures of each other in front of it. All sorts of ducks paddled about on its surface, poking their heads underwater from time to time to chomp down some critter or another. Holly snapped photos of them too, and then pressed the viewer and checked out her work. Good enough, she thought as she mentally patted herself on the back. It felt good to be here.

They walked back toward the center of town, marveling at the green everywhere. The roadway was shaded by towering palms. As they neared the mission, Holly heard the others gasp, almost in unison. There it was, the most majestic mission of all, in her opinion, rising up out of the palm oasis like a mediaeval castle. She explained that the San Ignacio Mission had been founded by the Jesuits in 1728, but the present church was built by the Dominicans and completed in 1786. "It has lava block walls that are four feet thick," she explained. "That's why it's so well-preserved. They still hold church services here."

"Can we go inside?" Camille asked.

Holly nodded. "You bet." They walked up rough, hand-hewn stone steps and stepped up toward the tall wooden door. Camille caressed the darkly stained wood. She was the first one inside the church, walking as if in a dream. She drifted toward the urn that held holy water, dipped her fingers in it and crossed herself. She curtsied toward the altar with its larger-than-life replica of the crucified Christ. She took a seat at one of the long wooden benches and knelt down, her hands on the back of the seat in front of her. She dropped her head onto her hands, closed her eyes and prayed. Dana followed a few moments later, omitting the holy water and curtsying ritual. She was obviously not Catholic, Holly noted. Barb stood next to Holly, her eyes sweeping the vast room, taking in all the art on the walls, memorizing the intricate designs on the carved ceiling, the altar, slipping off her sandal and the rubbing her bare foot against the worn stone floor.

Holly motioned to Barb and the two of them stepped outside. "Let's go sit in the plaza and wait for them," Holly suggested. Barb nodded, quiet. They sat on a bench and listened to the breeze rustling through the leaves in the tall trees that shaded them from the hot sun. A dark-skinned man came by pushing an ice cream cart and they stood, walked over to it and bought frozen fruit bars. Holly chose coconut, with fresh strands of fruit sticking out of it. Barb chose mango.

"This is the best thing I've ever tasted in my whole life," Barb said after two bites.

"It is."

Camille and Dana came out of the mission just then and bought their own fruit bars. Camille's watermelon popsicle had a few black seeds in it. Dana got coconut. They strolled through the park. It was getting close to sunset and people began appearing from inside their homes. They walked across the plaza and into the office of Kuyima and the *Instituto Nacional de Antropología e Historia*—the National Institute of Anthropology and History. The receptionist greeted Holly and she set about obtaining their permits to visit the caves while the other three went next door to check out the Cave Painting Museum. She found them there a few minutes later.

"We're all set," she said. "Our guide will be by first thing in the morning."

Dana gestured toward the map on the wall. "Where are we going?" she asked.

Holly pointed. "We're south of the region knows as La Sierra de San Francisco right now. Right here. " She showed them the route they'd be taking the next day and gave them a little background on the caves they'd be visiting. "We're going to Cueva de la Flechas and Cueva Pintada, which is, as I said before, the biggest and most famous cave of all. They're located on opposite sides of the Arroyo de San Pablo. "

They walked up the street to Renee's Restaurant, sat down outside at a table and ordered. As they sat sipping Pacifico beers, a trio of highly made-up, heavy-set women in very tight pants and halter tops appeared out of a doorway across the street and disappeared into another doorway next door to Renee's. Holly and Dana raised their eyebrows at each other.

Holly got up a few minutes later to go to the restroom. She came back and peeked in the door, looking for the women. It took her eyes a while to adjust to the dim light inside the night club. Mexican rap music was playing at mid-volume on a fairly decent sound system. When she was able to see clearly, she bit her cheek to choke back laughter. The three of them were helping each other into costumes of royal blue, yellow, orange and hot pink. The clothing looked to have been made for women at least two sizes smaller than they were. Excess flesh oozed out at their bare midriffs. Stomachs bulged over too-tight miniskirts. Chubby legs found their way to chubby feet jammed into high, high heels. But the feathers that they draped over themselves next—well—the feathers somehow transformed them from too-old, too-fat women in absurd apparel into magically exotic creatures. She motioned for the others to come look.

They all sat back down at their table and ordered another round of beers, this time with some quesadillas and guacamole to go with them. "Since we won't be able to have a whale encounter on this trip," Holly said, "I want to tell you what it's like."

She began. "The gray whales make a 6,000 mile trip every year from their home in the Arctic to the protected lagoons of Baja to mate and calve." She looked up. "That's a 12,000 mile round trip. They're some of the most playful of all the whales and are really well known for their spyhopping and breaching behavior."

"What's that?" Barb asked.

"Spyhopping is when they lift their big old heads out of the water to spy—or to check things out on the surface. Then they slap them down again with a major splash. Breaching is when they throw themselves out of the water like dolphins. They're truly amazing to watch."

"How big are they?"

"The females are larger than the males. They can grow to about 50 feet and weigh 35 to 40tons. The males only get to be about 46 feet long and weigh around 30 tons. They have these filters in their mouths that are called baleens that they use to sieve food from the water. They blow about three to five times in a row, then they flip their flukes, which are their tail fins, and dive for three to five minutes."

"How long can they stay down?"

"Up to 15 minutes. And they can dive to about 400 feet, although they prefer shallower water."

"How big are the babies?"

"About six feet long when they're born and they weigh about 2000 pounds. They nurse for eight months off their mothers, whose milk contains—by the way—53 per cent fat. Ours contains only two per cent fat."

"Wow," said Dana. "How long is a gray whale pregnant?"

"Thirteen to fourteen months. They become sexually mature somewhere between five and 11 years old."

"Is it true that it takes three of them to mate?" Dana asked.

Holly chuckled. "Oh yeah. It sure enough is. The adolescent male comes alongside the female and holds her steady while the mature male—well—for lack of a more delicate way to put it—while he puts it to her!"

Laughter erupted around the table.

"A ménage à trois!" exclaimed Camille. "How kinky!"

"Yeah, but have you ever tried to get it on in the ocean?" Holly shot back. "It's a real trick for humans when we're floating around with no way to anchor ourselves, and we have two arms and two legs each to hold on with. These are massive cetaceans who have no appendages to use to balance themselves. They need the help of a third party. They've obviously perfected this way of playing the mating game over more years than we could ever conceive of."

"Think of all the up close and personal practice those young boy whales get. Why, I'll bet that by the time they get their turn up at bat, they don't have any doubt whatsoever about what they're supposed to do!" said Camille, still laughing.

"No kidding. And I bet they're hot to trot too!" added Dana.

"Aren't they on the Endangered Species List?" asked Barb.

Holly shook her head. "No. They were put on in 1946 because there were less than 500 of them left, but they were taken off in 1994. Now the Mexican government estimates that there are at least 24,000 of them."

"Good Lord but they're prolific!" exclaimed Barb.

"I know."

"How did the whale petting start?" asked Camille.

"I was just getting to that. My good friend Francisco Mayoral is a local fisherman who lives on Laguna San Ignacio. He must be in his mid-50s now. He was supposedly the first one to have an actual whale encounter, back in '72. You see, the gray whales had a bad reputation among the Mexican fishermen. They were called Devil Fish by the whalers who hunted them here from the mid-1800s 'til the mid-1900s. The females were fiercely protective of their young and were known to charge whaling boats, often injuring and killing their crews. It was horrible the way the whales were slaughtered, actually. San Ignacio Lagoon, just to the southwest of us, is only three miles long and one mile wide. The whalers would block off its entrance and turn the entire place into a killing ground. People say the water in Laguna San Ignacio and Scammon's Lagoon used to turn red with the blood of the dying whales."

Camille and Dana looked at her and shuddered in disgust. "How horrible," Dana said. "How did the whales ever come to trust humans again?"

"I have no idea," said Holly. "According to Francisco, the first 25 or so years the whales were 'protected,' no one dared to go near them. The locals were terrified that the whales would smash their pangas with those powerful flukes of theirs. They didn't know of anyone who'd ever gotten near a gray whale and lived. Until Francisco, that is. He was out in his boat with some other fishermen one day, rowing to catch the outgoing tide. A whale swam up to their boat. He rowed like crazy for shore, just like Barb did the other day when she saw the sperm whale. Only this gray followed him. He and the other guys in the boat fell to their knees, made the sign of the cross over themselves and started praying like dead men. Francisco told me that he opened his eyes, only to see the whale's nine-foot head with its huge unblinking eye staring right straight at him. Then it slipped back into the water and started rubbing itself up against the boat. It did this, apparently, for nearly an hour. Then it swam away.

"The local fishermen discussed this phenomenal event among themselves, but the lagoon was so isolated that word didn't leak out to the scientific community for a few more years. It was a crew member from a whale-watching boat out of San Diego, the *Salado,* who was the first person to actually touch a gray whale, in 1976.

"Over the next five or so years, scientists descended on the area with greater and greater frequency. The playful whales—the ones who loved to be stroked and who put on shows for the humans—they started being known as the 'Friendlies.' Lots of them are recognizable. We've named them and they remember us too. We look forward to seeing each other every year."

"Do the mothers let your near their babies?"

"Oh yes! It's amazing! They teach the babies to come to us. The babies love to be petted. And so many of the older ones love to have their baleen stroked. I've had my boat picked up and carried on a mama whale's back before. And then spun like a toy."

"Wasn't that scary?"

She laughed. "Oh no. It was a rush and a half!"

"What did they kill whales for?" asked Barb.

"Blubber, which was boiled to use as oil. Whalebone and baleen were used for corsets, brushes and the spokes of umbrellas. After whale oil was replaced by petroleum, whale meat was used as cat food."

"Eeew," groaned Barbara.

"No kidding."

"So when do they show up in the Baja lagoons?"

"About December or January. And the last stragglers take off by late April."

"I want to come back with you on one of your tours. People do have to come on a tour, don't they?" asked Dana.

"Oh yes. Absolutely. The Mexican government is incredibly strict about that. The local fishermen like Francisco are the only authorized guides. They have to accompany us gringos out on the water. Then there's always a group of government observers who watch all the tourists from shore with their high-powered telescopes to make sure no one hurts the whales or ventures into the off-limits areas of the lagoon."

"How much does it cost?"

"Last year it was $48 for a whale-petting tour. That included lunch." Holly stood up, stretched and yawned. "It's getting dark. Why don't you three head back and put some bug repellant on? You can stop in at the La Pinta and use the phone if you want to call home. I'm gonna go up the hill say hi to some folks. I always make the rounds when I'm in town. We have to hit the sack early. The trip we're taking tomorrow is a '90s, condensed-version cave painting tour. Used to be we'd be out in the wilderness for up to a week. But, in honor of our 'occasional ecotourists'—folks who're not only short on time, but who'd never last two days on the back of mule, we're doing it the fast and easy way."

Barb groaned on cue. "What?! I have to ride a mule?!"

Holly nodded. "Yes. You do. It's much easier than hiking, I assure you."

"Will I be bucked off?"

"Hardly." She turned and looked at the others. "We better get a move on. We need to be on the road before daylight."

"I miss my boys," Camille said. "But what I'd really like to do before I call 'em is go with you and interview this Francisco guy for the radio. Can I, Holly?"

Holly nodded slowly. "Yeah, I guess that'd be okay."

"I'm going to La Pinta. I need to call home, " said Dana.

"Me too. Wait 'til I tell Bob I'm going for a mule ride tomorrow. He'll keel over backwards, I'm sure."

CHAPTER FIFTEEN   San Ignacio, Baja California Sur
                            October 22, 1997

The day was already promising to be a scorcher by 5:30 a.m. when their guide and his young son showed up in a battered, rusted out old troque that looked like it could easily be a first cousin to the one they rode in at Cataviña. All four women were dressed in jeans, t-shirts, hiking boots and hats. Each carried a backpack with sunscreen, a camera, water and a fairly gourmet lunch that Dana had prepared for them. Holly introduced them to their guide, Chuy, and his grandson Chuyito. She explained that both names were short for Jesus, which in Spanish was ,pronounced Hay-SOOS. Chuy shook hands with everyone. He spoke perfect, lightly accented English. His grandson was shy and spoke little. He hid behind his grandfather's legs when Dana addressed him in Spanish. His mumbled reply was barely intel-ligible.

Barb got into the front with the Mexicans. The other three climbed into the back. Chuy drove out of the campground and head-ed northwest on Mex 1. Dana looked at the map. They were gonna head 26 or so miles back toward Guerrero Negro before turning due east toward the caves. A little over a half an hour later, Chuy slowed the truck and turned right onto a graded, washboard dirt road. They bounced along for another hour or so, arriving at the village of Rancho San Francisco de la Sierra just as the sun was inching its way up over the mountains.

The truck ground to a stop and Chuy and his grandson got out.

Immediately a dozen dust-colored dogs rushed the truck, barking like crazy. The boy stooped down to pet the closest ones. A scrawny, leather-faced woman appeared in the doorway of one of the huts, followed by several children. Three men in cowboy hats sauntered over. Within two minutes a crowd had gathered. Everyone talked and gestured with great animation. Finally, Chuy and a trio of men unloaded sacks of flour and sugar from the bed of the pickup, along with five cases of Tecate beer and three cases of Coca Cola. The villagers waved goodbye as the truck lurched off toward Rancho Santa Teresa, further up the arroyo.

A while later the road ended and Chuy parked the pickup. Two teenage boys leading six fully saddled mules appeared as if by magic from behind a cluster of boulders. Chatting non-stop with Chuy, they adjusted the stirrups to match the length of each women's leg. Then they tied down their packs and hoisted them up onto the crusty leather saddles. The group organized itself into a line with Chuy in the lead and Chuyito taking up the rear. Holly and her mule followed Chuy and Dana preceded his grandson, with Camille and Barb in between. They headed down the arroyo along a wide trail. Holly explained that the two caves they were going to visit, along with *Cueva Ratón*—Rat Cave had been selected by the Getty Conservation Institute in L.A. for archaeological preservation. That's why the trail was wide and well-manicured. The rest of the caves were as undisturbed as they'd always been. They headed west and then climbed up, along the wall of the *barranca*—canyon. A while later the mules stopped at the steps marking the entrance of Cueva de las Flechas.

Dana dismounted after Chuy tied her mule to the post in front of her. The sight before her took her breath away. She stared, open-mouthed at a mural that reached to at least five times her height. Three ancient, human-like figures stared down at her. The head and left side of the largest figure, on the left, were reddish in color. His right side was black. The middle figure was all red with a black face or hat and the smallest was pure red. All had their arms raised to the sky. Behind the large figure was an enormous deer. Below him was a figure that looked something like a frog—half red and half black again. There was a smaller deer on the far right.

Chuy began to explain in slow, measured sentences. "If you will look very carefully, you will see that two of these 'monos,' as the human figures are called, have other inverted figures on their shoulders." He pointed to the one of the left. "This one has a human figure on its left shoulder and a sea turtle on its right. The center mono has a human on its left shoulder and a deer on its right." He gestured. "Notice how this mono is shot through with arrows. That is how this cave was named. It is called, in English, The Cave of the Arrows. It is not common in the caves of La Sierra de San Francisco to see humans shot with arrows. Usually here it is only the animals that are shown being killed. We do not know why this is."

Dana looked at Chuy. *"¿Qué es esto*—What's that?" she asked, pointing.

Dark eyes smiled at her from under his wide-brimmed hat. "It is a frog, perhaps. We are not sure of so many things about these *indios*—Indians. They are a mysterious people. Most of them were killed by disease or by the priests who ran the missions during times of rebellion. Their culture was very primitive and the Catholic padres were not interested in *mágica*—magic or legends. They wanted nothing to do with the pagan gods of these Indians. They wanted only to make them Catholics. And," he said, smiling, *"de veras*—of course, to make them to work in their fields. The ones who are left have lost their identity as a people. They have become one with us here in these mountains. We are all one people now."

As he was speaking, Dana raised up on her tip toes on the wooden floor. She ran her fingers over the smaller figures below the monos. She traced the faded replications of deer and what looked to be dogs or rabbits and other animals. Her thoughts drifted as she tried to imagine what these people had been like and what had compelled them to paint like this. Someone tapped her on the shoulder and she turned, startled.

"Please do not touch the murals," Chuy said to her.

"Oh. *Lo siento*—I'm sorry," Dana replied. She backed off.

"Dana, look...." It was Barb.

Dana turned. She walked the opening of the cave and peered out. She squinted in the bright light. For the second time in less than an hour, her breath caught in her throat. Majestic cardón cacti stood sentry over the steep canyon walls. Below them stretched colorful layers of striated rock, dotted here and there with tough desert shrubs. At the bottom of the deep arroyo a grove of native palms stood tall, proud and green against the faded dryness, the fronds rustling in the breeze. They continued around a corner and disappeared from sight, just below the point where an opening in the rocks occurred. She had never seen anything so incredible in all her life.

"That's Cueva Pintada," Holly said. "It doesn't look all that big from here, but it is. It measures 50 feet across at its opening." She pointed. "Can you see the ramps? The Getty people built them. They run the full width of the cave. There are wooden floors inside too." Dana nodded. They soaked up the view for a while and turned back to study more of the art in Cueva de las Flechas. They went to the center of the cave and sat down. It measured, they were told, 50 feet wide and 30 feet deep, but it was less than four feet high in most places. Chuy pointed out a magnificent bighorned sheep with curled horns on its head. It was done in black and red with dual sets of front legs. There were several pairs of rabbits, a large black deer and lots of small creatures.

When they'd seen enough, their guides hoisted them back onto their mules and led them out of the cave. They followed the trail down the canyon wall and through the mostly dry riverbed, which was, surprisingly, filled with several small, deep pools of water, nestled between outcroppings of boulders. The mules expertly skirted the ponds and began to climb the opposite wall of the arroyo. At the entrance to Cueva Pintada, they stopped again. Dana turned to check out the view from this side. It was even better, she thought, from this slightly lower vantage point. She could see everything in greater detail. She pulled her camera out of her pack and snapped several pictures, including a couple showing the entrance to Cueva de las Flechas. She wanted the twins to see as much as possible. She knew she'd be back here again for a longer visit, and she promised herself that they'd be with her. No doubt about it.

Cueva Pintada was 50 feet long inside, but, as Chuy pointed out, it wasn't very deep—only 40 feet or so. Half the cave had a low ceiling. The other half was much higher. Dana's eyes swept the chamber as he lectured. Because of the density of the rock and the degree of protection offered by the cave itself, most of the murals were still vibrantly colored and easy to discern. He led them to the northern part of the cave. It had a low ceiling and was covered in pictographs. Dana sat as she had before and craned her head back to look. The colors were barely faded at all, but the Indians had painted the ceiling in so many layers it was hard to tell one figure from another in places. She saw birds, rabbits and small deer.

"This cave does not contain all of the images found in Baja cave paintings," said Chuy. "Other caves are larger inside but do not contain the large number of well-preserved paintings of this one. It is the most famous and most visited of all the caves."

"My butt aches," moaned Barb, stretching and prancing as she caught up with them. "But this is totally worth it. How many are there?"

"In this region, there are 20 major caves and many more smaller ones. In all of Baja we number well over 100 caves discovered. More are discovered all the time."

Dana followed Chuy across the multi-leveled wooden floor and leaned against the railing in front of a mural at the south end of the cave. It went on for about 100 feet horizontally and stretched even higher toward the ceiling than the paintings at the entrance of Cueva de las Flechas. She wondered again at the array of people, some red, some black and some half and half. All had their arms raised to the heavens. She could indeed tell the women from the men by the pointed breasts that protruded from their armpits. They danced in front of her, over or underlaid with a variety of wildlife—mostly deer with antlers and big-horned sheep. A figure, looking like some kind of monstrous sea mammal, leered down at her. It was obvious to Dana by the delicacy of the painting and the attention to detail that these Indians had felt great love and respect for the noble animals that shared the mountains and coastal waters with them.

"Where do you think they got the scaffolding so they could paint so high up?" she asked.

"Scientists believe that they made ladders from the palms down in the barranca."

"Ah," she said. *"Claro*—Clearly."

"Was this cave discovered by the missionaries?" asked Barb.

Chuy shook his head. "No. Their roads were much higher up, on the mesa. They did not visit these deep canyons."

"So who discovered this place?"

"We are not sure. We believe that by the year 1890 that several of the rancheros in the area knew of it. The American, Señor Gardner, the writer of Perry Mason TV shows was the first person to photograph these caves. He came here by helicopter in 1962 and my people in the ranchos were very much afraid at first. But he was a good man and very generous too."

They explored for a while longer and picnicked at the edge of the canyon, playing and taking pictures of one another after they ate. Chuy and his grandson hoisted them back onto their mules and led them back to the pickup truck. There they turned the mules back to the mysteriously reappearing teenage boys, piled into the truck and began the bumpy ride home.

Dana pulled flour tortillas out of the cupboard. She heated up the *borrego*—lamb meat and homemade tortillas that Holly had been given as a gift by a rancher's wife. She spooned red and green salsa into bowls and crumbled some white queso fresco onto a plastic platter. She sliced two avocados and an onion, then walked to the water container on the front of the motor home and rinsed a tomato and a bunch of cilantro. Back inside, she chopped everything up and arranged it on the platter. After checking on the meat, she opened a can of *frijoles refritos*—refried beans and scooped them into a small saucepan. She lit the fire under the burner, went back outside to the cooler and pulled out two ice-cold, dripping bottles of Chardonnay. Carrying them inside, she popped out the corks with a professional twist of her wrist.

She called to Barb to set the outdoor table. Minutes later, the buffet had been prepared and the foursome sat down to eat.

The campfire was burning low and the tunes were cranked up high. The third quarter moon rose in the sky, bathing the campground in pale moonlight. They'd worked their way through both bottles of wine and had been sipping brandy ever since. "The Eagles Greatest Hits" tape was playing. "Tequila Sunrise" came on and Camille stood, moved her chair and began to sing and sway in time to the music. Dana stood up, and without consciously even willing it, found that she'd materialized next to Camille and was dancing and singing along with her. The two visibly loosened in each other's presence and began to spin in ever-expanding circles around the campfire, arms and bodies moving in unison as they reached together for the stars. Before the song ended, Barb and Holly joined them.

Next played "Take it to the Limit" and the movement intensified. Dresses and hair swirled. Every face was bathed in a blissful glow. A man from the campsite over grabbed Barb's hand and began to twirl her around in a swing dance. Two surfer boys from down the way inserted themselves in between Holly and Camille. A foursome of snowbirds from Alberta joined in and so did the young kids from over by the showers. The song ended and the music switched. Suddenly the first strains of "Pretty Girls Don't Cry" from Chris Isaak's "Baja Sessions" CD came on. By the time he got to "South of the Border— Down Mexico Way" Holly let out a huge whoop which was followed by a chorus of "Brrrrrrreeeeeeeehaaaaahs!"

A half hour later the coals to the fire had died down and so had the revelry. All the other campers had gone back to their sites and most of their lights were already out. None of the four women were tired. The high of the day hadn't worn off yet, so they went back to sipping brandy and talking quietly.

"Anyone want to play cards?" Holly asked.

"Nah," said Barb. She sat up straight. "But I have an idea!"

"What?"

"Remember as kids how we all used to sit around the campfire and tell ghost stories?" Everyone nodded. "Well, how about if we take a slightly different approach to it. A more mature and womanly approach, if you will...."

"What do you have in mind?" asked Dana.

Barb giggled. "Well, I was thinking that maybe we could each take turns telling about the most bizarre place we ever had sex."

Dana jumped to her feet. "Oh me! I wanna go first! I have a great story!"

Holly shook her head. "Go for it."

"Okay." She flashed back in time 22 years to her first construction job. She'd been hired as a project clerk on a museum renovation in San Diego's prestigious and elegant Balboa Park. She worked in a trailer, the only female among a group of 50 plus guys—most of them near her age. She'd just broken up with her boyfriend of four years and was feeling ripe for a fling. He was the only person she'd ever slept with and she doubted that he'd been a very good lover. Either that or there was something wrong with her.

She laughed to herself as she remembered the first trick the crew had played on her. It was her first day on the job and she had to use a port-a-potty to go to the bathroom—the same one all the guys used. Not one to act chagrined, she stepped inside and locked the door. It had just been pumped out, so the pit inside was clean, empty. They knew that. They didn't miss much.

As she was sitting there minding her own business, the outhouse began to tip and sway, almost keeling over. She screamed, yanked up her jeans, buttoning and zipping them faster than she'd ever dreamed possible. Laughter echoed all around her. She tried to open the door, but it was locked from the outside. She screamed, cussed and beat on the door. Finally, her boss, Jack Kennerly, came up and chased the culprits away. He opened the door and let her out, a wily grin spread across his face.

No matter how hard she begged, he never told her who did that to her. Not even after they became lovers. She made him guard the door for the next week whenever she had to use the bathroom, but it never happened again. She'd been initiated and accepted into the group.

Dana's mind flashed to their Friday afternoon beer parties. They all worked from 7:00 to 3:30. About 3:15 one of the guys would collect money for beer and Doritos. By 3:40 at least 50 grungy, sweaty men would be squatting together sipping beers and smoking cigarettes on the small patch of remaining asphalt behind the skeleton of the museum. By 4:00 the contests would start. Their favorite was the hammer slamming. Out of their tool belts they'd pull massive hammers and huge nails, slamming the nails into pieces of scrap lumber in one blow. They cheered each other on, their camaraderie a delight to watch.

It was after the Bobcat incident that she and Jack had first acknowledged their burgeoning attraction for one another. It wasn't even supposed to have been there, but her dad's rental company had not gotten around to picking it up that afternoon. One of the guys stole the key out of the job site trailer and scrunched himself into the tiny forklift. The cage was barely large enough to accommodate his oversized frame, but he could've cared less. Fired on by the cheers around him, he started it up and hooted and hollered like a maniac as he made that Bobcat dance. He did wheelies, 360s and chased Dana around what was left of the parking lot as the other guys rooted him on. After a few minutes, Jack showed up and stopped everything. He confiscated the key and told the guys to knock it off. Then he grabbed Dana by the hand and told her he was buying her a drink.

"Hello?! Are you gonna tell us or what?" Camille demanded.

"Oh sorry. I was just remembering." She reiterated the background information to them and then got to the juicy part. "He was married and that was a tragedy. I never got involved with a married man after that. But I don't know if it was the forbidden fruit part of it or what, but I've never had sex like that—before or since. We would sneak out of the office and go inside the walls. They were framed and dry walled, but they weren't sealed up yet. We had all these little hiding places where we grabbed ourselves some quickies. We were insatiable—hot, hot, hot! And in love too. I don't think anyone's ever loved me like he did. But I ended up getting another job and breaking it off with him after his wife found out. He had two little boys and I just couldn't bear to be a home-wrecker. Having been cheated on repeatedly by my own former husband, I now understand how she felt. I'm at least grateful that I did the right thing at the end. Because he would have left her and married me if I'd insisted."

"So get to the point," Camille said.

"Okay! Okay! My favorite, most unbelievably wild sexual encounter was when we were adding the new top story onto the building. The roof was just in the process of being completed, and it was a flat roof too—by the way. We went up there one afternoon about this time of year after work and drank a bottle of Champagne together. Smoked a joint."

"You did?!" Barb interjected.

"Yeah. I did. I still do sometimes. It's hard not to, having a pothead for a neighbor."

"Hey. Don't blame me for your transgressions, bozette."

"Get on with the story," said Holly.

"Okay. Okay. So, anyway, we were out there right under the flight path of the jets landing at Lindbergh Field."

"Oh my God! You didn't...."

Dana laughed. "You're darn straight we did. We got it on right there, stark naked on the roof, with the planes flying low overhead. There's no way the pilots could've missed seeing us. We were sure they were passing the gossip about what we were doing back and forth between the cockpits of the approaching jets and the control tower."

"And you had intercourse?" Barb asked, her eyes wide in amazement.

"Yes ma'am. We did. And more! In all sorts of positions and from every angle—if you know what I mean. It was the absolute, ultimate turn-on of a lifetime!"

"Well, shit howdy, girlfriend. And all this time I thought it was me who was the sex fiend. What happened to you, Dana?"

"What else? I dated around for a few years. Then I married Brad and the wild woman inside me curled up in a little ball and died."

CHAPTER SIXTEEN   San Ignacio, Baja California Sur
October 23 and 24, 1997

In her dream she was lying on her back in bed, naked. There was a pillow jammed over her face, cutting off her air. She reached to pull it away, but her hands were tied behind her back. Her left arm was asleep. She kicked her legs, but they'd been forced apart and were tied to something—each of them. She lay there, helpless and spread-eagled. She couldn't breathe. A black horror enveloped her and she twisted her body from side to side, trying to break free of the bonds, to break through the darkness. She couldn't do it. She was trapped.

There was something crawling up her leg. Something big and hairy. She jammed her feet into the mattress and threw her entire body up into the air. The pillow came off her face and she bumped her head against something hard. On her stomach was a tarantula. He was at least six inches in diameter, and so close to her face that she could count the hairs on his immense, double-jointed legs. His fractured eyeballs stared into her, his beak pointed toward her breasts. His spider mouth opened in an evil, ravenous leer.

She felt a burning, stinging sensation between her thighs as the spider positioned himself above her. She kept thrashing against her bonds, trying to jolt the tarantula off of her. His face melted. His grin twisted and embedded itself in a stocking face. The eyes of the man who'd raped her back in college stared at her. A mute scream erupted from her mouth.

The masked man taunted her, laughed at her and thrust himself into her unwilling body. He was punishing her, he said. She was a worthless slut and he was gonna make her pay for it. He slapped her face hard and she screamed. He slapped her again. And again. "Noooooooooo...."

The terror in her voice rung in her ears. She awoke to find Barb standing over her. "Holly? Are you okay? You were having a nightmare."

The overhead light in the cabover bed flashed on. "What's going on back there?" called Camille, her voice froggy with sleep.

Holly leaned over the side of the bed and threw up onto the sheet-vinyl floor. Barb sidestepped the puddle of vomit and rushed for a dish towel. She mopped it up. Dana materialized with a bowl in her hand and a placed a cold, damp cloth on her forehead.

There was an excruciating streak of pain running from Holly's left ear down the side of her neck. She was stranded somewhere between the dream and reality, lost in a maze of fear. Of bone-crushing desperation. She squinted. The ache in her head was unbearable. She fell off the bed and onto her knees as her eyes spun out, making things tilt and reel crazily in front of her. She dry-heaved into the bowl on the floor. Struggling to orient herself, she looked at the watch on her wrist. The numbers were swimming in circles and she could not read them. She closed one eye and the numbers slowed down and moved into focus: 6:05 a.m.

"Show me where it hurts," Barb commanded as she sat beside Holly on the floor and cradled her head in her lap. Holly touched her jaw. It was tender to the touch. She pointed to her left her ear. Barb began massaging Holly's jaw and neck muscles, working to undo the knots there.

"Every muscle in your body is rigid. Totally tensed up. I have some Valium in my duffel bag. You want some?" Holly nodded and Barb whispered to Dana who returned with them and handed them over with a glass of water. Barb fed them to Holly. Camille filled the teakettle with water and lit the burner.

"Tell me about the dream."

Holly started to cry. The door banged shut as Camille and Dana went outside.

"We're going over to the restaurant to get some breakfast," Camille called as they left. "Coffee water's on."

Barb held Holly while she sobbed. "I'm cold," she choked out.

Barb pulled the blanket off her bed and wrapped her in it. They sat together on the floor. Eventually Holly's crying slowed down. She looked up, her face a blotchy, red color, slick with tears. She wiped her running nose on the edge of the blanket and pulled it tightly against herself. She stared at Barb. Neither of them said anything for several long minutes.

Holly broke the silence and began to speak in a dry, rusty monotone. She felt like her mouth was disconnected from her body. She recited the ugly scenes as they replayed themselves in the cinema of her mind.

"I knew him," she explained. "We'd been out a few times. He gave me the creeps and I wouldn't even take his calls after he pushed me down on the bed in his frat house one night and threw himself on top of me. He was horrible, Barb. Drunk. An animal. I'm sure he would've raped me then and there if his roommate hadn't come back." She went on to tell Barb how this 20-year-old man, whose name she refused to say out loud, had broken into her dorm room that night in early January of her freshman year when she was the only one present on her floor. "I was a virgin, you know," she said. "And he was the devil. A twisted, sick monster that got his rocks off by torturing me and hurting me. After he left, I threw up for what seemed like hours. And I screamed for help, but no one came. I finally managed to get my hands untied. Then my feet."

"What happened next?"

"I got dressed and went to the school infirmary. They called the police. He was arrested and eventually sentenced to five years in prison."

"That's all?!"

Holly nodded. "I'm still afraid he'll find me and come back. I never did well in school after that. I dropped out before finals. I can't tell you how many times I've had that nightmare." She shook her head. "That and the one about my mom...."

"What's that?"

Holly shuddered.

"It's okay. Just get it out. All of it." Her voice enveloped Holly in a cocoon of softness.

"I can't tell you. I haven't told anyone in years! Not even my husband knows about any of this! Please don't force me to tell! Please!" And the crying started again in earnest. "I hate you, God!" she screamed to the heavens. "If you really exist, why did you make this happen to me?! Why, God?! Why?!"

The teakettle Camille had put on whistled. Barb disentangled herself from Holly and stood. She made coffee and brought them each a steaming cup. She grabbed a napkin from the holder and hand-ed it to Holly, who mopped at her tears.

"Jeez Louise. I haven't cried like this in over 20 years," she whispered.

"Will you tell me about your mom?"

"Only if you swear to never tell a soul. I'll never forgive you if you do...."

Barb crossed her heart. "I promise."

Holly shuddered again. "It's not a pretty story. It's definitely not gonna make your day."

Barb patted her hand. "So what?" she said. "I'm a big girl."

Holly sighed long and hard. "Okay." Out of her mouth poured the story of her mother's suicide over Christmas vacation, her freshman year in college, ten days before the rape. "I didn't find her. I was at the Christmas tree lot helping my dad. He owned it, you see. We lived in Bend, Oregon back then and that's what he did. He ran a Christmas tree farm. My brother Jeremy was three years younger than me. Sixteen. He found her. He was working at McDonald's and had an early shift. I don't think she meant for him to find her. He never recovered from it...."

"How did she do it?"

"Pills. Jeremy said she'd gotten really sick before she died. There was puke everywhere. And shit too. She shit herself, Barb." Holly's crying started up anew. Sniffling, she continued to speak as the tears coursed down her cheeks and dribbled onto her blanket. "Her face was all purple too, he told me. My dad flipped out afterwards. He took Jeremy and moved to our aunt and uncle's in Oklahoma City. Then Dad started drinking a whole lot. He still does. Jeremy, he hated it there. He lost his mom. I was gone and Dad was hiding out in a bot-tle. He did the usual thing kids did in those days. Still do, I guess," she mumbled. "He turned to drugs. Pot. Mescaline. Peyote. You know, hallucinogens. Acid was his escape route of choice. He did one of those swan dives out the eighth story window of our uncle's office when he was 17. He never even made it through high school."

Silence descended on the motor home as the reality of what she'd just told Barb struck Holly like a lightning bolt. She took a deep breath. Exhaled slowly. She looked at Barb. Barb's level gaze came right back at her, full of compassion. Holly felt an easing in her heart for a split second as a chink broke away from the fortress she'd so carefully constructed around it. Barb hugged her and she stiffened, the barrier shifting back into place.

She struggled to stand. "Please. You can't say anything to anyone about this. I'd die if Rick found out."

"I promised you. I keep my promises. But I think you should really tell your husband sometime."

"I can't...."

"But Holly. He's your husband. He deserves to know. If you can trust me, you should be able to trust him—don't you think?"

"No. I don't want him to know. I don't want Dana or Camille to know either. Tell them—tell them what I told Rick. That I have this recurring nightmare about being buried in an avalanche. I was once, but it wasn't that a big a deal. I dug myself out. Will you do that?" She yawned as she felt the Valium kick in.

Barbara nodded. She helped Holly climb back into her bunk. As she drifted off to sleep, Holly remembered exactly how it had felt when she was little and her mom comforted her after she'd had a nightmare. It felt just like this....

Holly slept the entire morning. She told the others she planned to spend the afternoon working on research for her book and sent them out for supplies. She gave them directions to the local *carnicería*—meat market, *frutería*—fruit store, *panadería*—bakery and *mini mercado*—mini-market. Their first stop was the meat market. It was located on a dusty, winding back street at the top of a hill. There were two mangy-looking yellow dogs crouched out front with a dirty little girl selling gum. Camille exchanged looks of mutual alarm with Barbara as Dana waltzed right into the carnicería and began chatting with the proprietor.

Camille stood in the doorway and gawked in horror. There were flies everywhere. Plucked chickens hung upside down from hooks on the ceiling with gaping wounds where their heads had once been. Behind them, entire sides of beef were lined up, their cow shapes still recognizable. There were pigs too—whole ones with their heads still on—hanging in between the chickens and cows, and dismembered ones inside a glass display case up front. Camille cringed at the sight of pig parts, including feet, being offered for sale. She noticed tripe for *menudo*—a soup guaranted to cure hangovers—liver, brains and all sorts of other disgusting delicacies on display. At the far end of the case she saw long strands of intestines stuffed with *chorizo*—spicy sausage, and lamb, along with bacon, ham, pork chops, ground beef, precut roasts and steaks.

It was enough to make a vegetarian out of anyone, she thought to herself and backed out of the shop. It was obvious to her that the third world standards of sanitation didn't phase Dana. She functioned like the pro she was, bargaining and joking with the butcher and his wife. You'd think she lived here or something.

When she was finished, the three of them walked around a corner to the frutería, where they planned to stock up on fresh fruit and veggies. The woman who ran the store was out front, sweeping up pieces of trash from the hard-packed dirt. She swept the aluminum cans and scraps of paper into a pile, scooped them into her dust pan, then stood and looked up at the women, breaking into a mostly gold-rimmed smile.

"Buenas tardes," she said—wishing them a good afternoon.

"Buenas tardes," Dana answered back as she walked inside and grabbed a shopping basket.

"This is much easier to handle," Camille said as she looked, impressed and instantly hungry, at the wooden crates that had been stacked six high on top of each other so that their open sides all faced front. The produce was exquisite and the selection excellent. One wall of the minuscule store front was lined with crates full of oranges, papaya, mangos, bananas, coconuts, pears, peaches. Then there were tomatoes, jícama, limónes, avocados, cabbage, lettuce, radishes, cilantro, potatoes, onions, dried pinto beans, celery, carrots, beans and at least six types of chiles on the other walls.

They filled three baskets with fresh produce, paid and moved on to the bakery.

"The panadería is always my favorite stop," Dana explained to Barb and Camille. She picked up a round silver tray and a pair of tongs and began plucking golden, oblong-shaped hard rolls from a bin. "The bolillos in these little towns are always way better than the ones in the big cities like Ensenada. The coarser the flour, the better-tasting the bread. With a little butter, these rolls will melt in your mouth, I promise! This is about as far from Bimbo Bread as you can get!"

She added odd-looking cookies and breads from off the metal shelves located around the edges in the tiny, hot shop onto the tray. She chose round cookies with multi-colored sprinkles on top. "Here. You guys pick some too."

"How do we know what they taste like?" Camille asked.

Dana laughed. "Just wing it. Pick out whatever tickles your fancy!"

They did that, paid and then it was on to the mini-market, where they bought toilet paper, canned goods and all sorts of other staples. Dana rented the services of two young boys for a total of six pesos and two candy bars. The boys helped them carry all their goodies back to the motor home.

Dana made a scrumptious dinner of what she called her Pacific Rim Flautas—chicken marinated in coconut milk and curry and rolled in flour tortillas, deep fried and served with a fresh mango salsa that was to-die-for. Everyone ate ravenously as they told Holly about their afternoon's adventures.

As they ate, Camille couldn't help but notice that Holly and Barb seemed to have reached some kind of an understanding, because everything seemed different between them. Barb was solicitous of Holly and in response, Holly was subdued and polite. It was like she'd been abducted by aliens and been replaced by an android. Her hard edges had softened. Gone was her sarcastic bossiness, and in its place was a tentative and compliant fragility. What a change! Camille liked her better this way and wished that at least some of the new Holly would stay with them, but in her heart of hearts she knew it was just the Valium—that and the high of her newfound closeness with Barb. She figured Holly had revealed a hidden part of herself to Barb, and in doing so, they'd bonded. But from what she'd seen of Holly— any intimacy would be short-lived. As soon as she regained her strength, she'd take up her rightful place at the helm and her attitude of superiority, not to mention her barbed remarks to the rest of them, would resume. She was sure of it.

The next morning Camille, Dana and Barb were up and out early. It was Friday. Time for call-in number two. The trio grabbed a quick cup of coffee at the El Padrino restaurant and walked down to the La Pinta Hotel where they knew they'd be able to use the phone. Dana spoke in Spanish to the gerente—manager, and he dialed the number to RockSteady. He handed the phone to Dana who handed it off to Camille.

The call-in started off about the same as the last one. Camille regaled the Wise Guys with stories of their escapades. She told them about the sunrise hike in Cataviña, the cave paintings and the sights they'd seen from the road. Barb got on the phone next and described the view coming into Bay of L.A. Camille had missed it the first time around and could see it now in her mind's eye as the scenery was repainted in words for the listeners back in San Diego. She went on to tell of her kayaking experience with Dana and seeing the giant sperm whale.

"Where were you during all this, Cinnamon Girl?" boomed Mark. Barb held the phone between them. That way Mark's voice wouldn't blow out her ear drums.

"Camille had a slight case of the tourista," said Barb. "Holly Malone, our tour guide seems to have it now. We'll be hearing from her next week instead of today."

"Ah! The Revenge of Montezuma hits the Bodacious Baja Babes. How long'd it keep you out of action, sweet pea?"

Camille took the phone. "One day is all. I am woman. Wanna hear me roar?" She roared into the phone. They left out the part about the dancing in front of the campfire, not wanting to open that one up for Mark or Johnny's interpretations and then it was Dana's turn.

"We now introduce you to Baja Chef Extraordinaire from our very own Hacienda Gaviota. Dana Wallace. How are you?"

"I'm doing great, Mark. This is absolutely the most fun I've ever had in my life. You know that my dad passed away a couple months back. He left me his old motor home. Ostensibly to get me off my butt and out into the big wide world again. It's the single mom syndrome, you know!"

"Dana and Camille are both single moms," explained Johnny.

"Yes—we are and we're in the process of proving that we can have adventures and go places like Baja right now—while we're both unattached—without waiting around for Mr. Right to show up and escort us!"

"Hear that you single forty-something men out there?! Take it from me, I *know* these women. They are available and they are *babes!"*

"Middle aged babes with wrinkles, rolls and cellulite. Ugh. Hey, Johnny, throw a pail of water on him and cool him off, will you?"

They heard a hideous squealing in the background as Mark pretended to melt like the Wicked Witch of the East in the Wizard of Oz.

"He's dead. I killed him. I have the broomstick. Now can I go back to Kansas?"

"Ignore him," mouthed Camille to Dana. "Ignore him."

He ignored himself and changed the subject. "How's the highway? Lots of potholes? Any mechanical difficulties? Flat tires? Close calls? Tell us...."

Camille pointed to Dana. "Go for it," she mouthed.

"Fine. Some. No, no, and no. We've been very fortunate. We

did, however, stop between Guerrero Negro and San Ignacio—on a very desolate stretch of road—for an old Pontiac Trans Am whose radiator had boiled over. A young Mexican couple with a brand new baby were stranded out there in the middle of the desert in temperatures well over 100 degrees. We gave them water to drink and filled their radiator for them. You wouldn't have believed how grateful they were!"

"You should have some good road karma coming your way now," Johnny said.

"It's the rule of the road in these parts!" Dana said. "Help and be...."

Before she could finish, Mark interrupted her. "What? Cool! Russell back there on the phones has just told me that we have a call from a listener who has a line on the chef who's solely responsible for turning Dana here into the culinary genius she is today. Says he's hanging out down in Baja too."

"What?!"

"Put her on the line."

"Hello? Who's this?"

"This is Margo."

"Howdy Margo. So who is this mysterious chef and what's he doing down south?" asked Johnny. Camille leaned in closer to listen. She looked at Dana out of the corner of her eye. Her tanned face had faded to a bleached white.

"His name's Todd Hayward. He's my brother. He was the executive chef at Hacienda Gaviota from the time it opened until a little over three years ago. You remember him, Dana?"

"Of course," she said. "Last I heard, he was working on a Love Boat cruise."

"Right," Margo confirmed. "He jumped ship in Cabo. He lives in Todos Santos now, about an hour north of there. He owns the Cafe Todos Artes, which is a restaurant, art gallery and recording studio."

"Wow. Thanks." said Dana. "I'll look him up."

"You better. And give him a hug for me," his sister said.

"Oh. I will. Don't worry. I will."

They finished the call-in, told Mark about the interview with Francisco Mayoral and signed off.

The trio walked over to the lake and sat on its bank beneath the date palms. While Camille smoked her cigarette, they watched the ducks in silence as they bobbed and dipped their heads underwater to gobble up their breakfast. A snowy egret had flown in on its way to or from somewhere, and stood alone—tall, elegant and aloof in the shallow water.

"I remember him," Camille said. "A little younger than us. Dark hair. Tall. Really nice. Funny. Cute. Very, very sexy."

Dana smiled dreamily. "Give me a hit," she said and took a puff of Camille's cigarette. "You think every man is sexy, you horndog," she said. She got up. "I'm going for a walk. I'll meet you back at camp."

A mosquito buzzed Camille's ear and she waved it away with her cigarette. "I'm ready to hit the road," she confided to Barb. "I've loved staying put a couple of days. And there's no doubt about it. San Ignacio is one very trippy place."

"It sure is. Must be the spirits of all those Indian artists wandering around in the vicinity. You know Indians. They're rooted firmly to dear old Mother Earth, but they're total mystics too. They can spin through the cosmos on the back of a coyote and stay grounded at the same time."

Camille shook her head. "You act like you've been smoking loco weed. I was just thinking how that the Indians preyed on the animals and the Spaniards preyed on them. That doesn't sound cosmic to me at all."

Barb shook her head. "No, no, no, no, no. You missed the point entirely. The Indians hunted the animals for food. They would've never wiped out the gray whales the way the white man nearly did. They've always understood the balance of nature and lived in harmony with it. Like the wild animals, they believe that some creatures must die to feed the ones who live. The weaker ones in every species are consumed by disease. Others are consumed for food. The thinning-out process forces each species to keep improving genetically. Humans are the only ones who kill each other off for purely egocentric reasons. And we're the only ones who've allowed our population to explode beyond reasonable parameters. In many ways, the less civilized people of this Earth have always been closer to understanding the basic truths of life than we are."

"Thank you, Professor Doolittle. That's 'cause they're closer to nature."

"Yeah. We first world folks have created so many wonderful and complicated toys—we think we're equal to or greater than God."

Camille finished the thought. "Ah yes. Herein arrives the concept of original sin. We so deeply hunger for answers that we can't resist eating the forbidden fruit the serpent offers us. We all play God and we get mad as hell when we can't make things go according to our elaborately concocted little schemes."

Barb clapped her hands together. "Bravo amiga! You are moving beyond your paternalistic mindset and expanding your global consciousness. We'll get you orbiting the planet on the back of a coyote yet!"

Camille pretended to hit her on the knee. "I beg to disagree, ma'am. I wouldn't count on it!"

"Cosmic. She's cosmic," Barb explained to the female mallard duck in front of her. "She's gone totally cosmic on me. And she doesn't even know it yet."

Camille put out her cigarette. She stood and pulled Barb to her feet. "Come on, my little space cadet. It's time to blow this galaxy." She started to walk toward the RV park, then stopped and looked back at Barb. "You know what?"

"What?"

"I'm getting some very funny feelings about Dana and Todd. They got along awfully well together."

"Did they date?"

"No. He had a girlfriend for most of the time they worked together. She was involved with RockSteady's own Peter Mays. What a mismatch that was. Orchestrated by me, none the less. I think they broke up right before Todd took off."

"So you think...."

"Who cares what I think? Dana hasn't let a man near her in years. Her divorce really messed her up. And then there was that hideous custody battle. Brad cheated on her—big time. Then he trashed her—big time. Peter was a louse too. He couldn't resist his fans and he cheated on her too—every chance he could get. I saw him drag a scantily clad young girl outside at a party once and I know for a fact he had sex in the bushes with her—and Dana was there the whole time."

"Did she find out?"

"In the end."

"Ouch."

"Yeah. Ouch is right." She shook her head. "I don't know if she'll ever be able to trust a man again. Still—I have the funniest feeling about Todd resurfacing after all these years. He was a stone cold fox and a talented chef with a heart of gold. I always thought he and Dana would've made a great couple. But, hey. What can I say...."

"Say nothing for a change, Camille! Puh-lease! This is obviously a very sore subject with Dana. Let's give her some space and let things sort themselves out! In the meantime, it's time to go to Santa Rosalía."

CHAPTER SEVENTEEN   **Santa Rosalía, Baja California Sur**
                          October 24, 1997

"Listen up! As soon as we pass by these three mountains, which are known as *Las Tres Virgenes*—The Three Virgins, by the way, we're gonna head down a steep grade and then we'll be in Santa Rosalía. This is what I wrote yesterday for my book. I want you to hear it." Holly squatted down between Dana, who was driving and Barb. Camille sat cross-legged on the floor behind her.

"Here goes: Santa Rosalía, a town of over 11,000 and located almost two-thirds of the way down the east coast of Baja, is the only place on the peninsula that can boast a French heritage. It was settled by the French in the late 1870s, who received permission from the Mexican government to mine and process the copper ore found in its nearby mountains. The town's buildings were constructed of wood imported from San Francisco, California and roofed with galvanized iron from France. The French-owned and managed El Boleo Company not only built the town, mines and refinery, they also put in a pipeline to import water and built a seaport to export the processed ore.

"For nearly 80 years Santa Rosalía flourished as a copper-mining town. Although the mines closed down in 1954, it is still a bustling community. Its church, La Iglesia de Santa Bárbara is world-famous. It was designed by Alexandre-Gustave Effeil for the Paris World's Fair and was actually constructed out of galvanized iron by one of his fellow students. After the fair's completion, the church was dismantled and shipped in pieces to Santa Rosalía around Cape Horn in 1897." She looked up. "By the way, did you guys know that Eiffel not only designed the Eiffel Tower in Paris, but he also designed the locks for the Panama Canal and the framework of our Statue of Liberty?"

They all shook their heads. "Interesting bit of trivia. Okay. Here I go again: These days the town still has the best bakery in all of Mexico, named El Boleo, after the French company that settled it. Visitors can stay in the historic, elegant Hotel Francés, situated on top of the hill overlooking the ocean. Santa Rosalía has a new marina that has begun to attract a few of the yachties who travel the Sea of Cortez in their sail boats and power boats during the pleasant fall, winter and late spring months. Ferries travel regularly back and forth between Santa Rosalía and Guaymas, on the mainland. Other than that, Santa Rosalía is pretty much off the beaten tourist path, as no major airlines fly in. Caravans of motor homing travelers stop in to rest and stock up on supplies."

She finished reading and looked up. "What do you think?"

Dana looked over at her. "I'm intrigued. Isn't this the place you told us was the street food capital of Baja?"

"Yes. It is. I'm not gonna write about that part though until we've all lived it." She pointed, "Look. As soon as we come around this bend we should be able to see the Sea of Cortez again."

There it was. Beautiful, bold, blue and as beckoning as always. Dana counted backwards. Had it only been three days since they'd left Bay of L.A.? It seemed like a lot longer than that. For her, time was frozen—or rather, it was spinning backwards. She couldn't wait to get off by herself.

They took a vote and decided to go find a place to camp before they checked out the town. That way they could spend the day at the beach and come back for dinner. It had only been a 45-mile drive from San Ignacio to Santa Rosalía, so they had the whole day ahead of them. Holly drove them to the Las Palmas RV Park on the south end of town. They pulled in to take a look. "It's either here," she said, consulting her camping book, "or we go south another seven or so miles to the San Lucas Cove RV Park. That would be my choice. It doesn't have hookups, but we can pull right up to the beach and, if we're lucky, snag ourselves a palapa next to the water."

"Yes!" shouted Dana.

"Ditto!" shouted Barb.

"I'm there!" echoed Camille.

Dana pulled out, turned back onto Mex 1 and headed south. At Kilometer 182 she turned left off the highway and eased Boris down the steep slope of a dirt road. A half a mile later they were there. Holly was right. The park was set in a protected cove bordered with palms and mesquite trees. There were a dozen other rigs camped there. The usual camp dogs came barking up to greet them, followed by a Mexican man in a cowboy hat and two dusty-faced, barefoot children. They collected the nightly fee of $6 and watched as Holly got out and guided Dana as she backed into a perfect site with its own palapa and fire ring on the sand.

They got out. It was already hot and they unrolled the awning, pulled down the kayaks and boogie boards and changed into their bathing suits. There were no stingrays in sight, which Dana quickly pointed out. At the count of three, they raced to the water and dove in.

While the others frolicked in the warm, shallow water, Dana swam off toward the south by herself. She wanted to think about Todd, the chef who'd mentored her—the one who was in Todos Santos—the one she was certain to see in another ten days or so, but all she could see was Peter Mays. Why him? she wondered to herself. I haven't thought of him in eons. But, as her arms propelled her rhythmically across the ocean's surface, they became twin movie reels, replaying the film from the day she met Peter in the cinema of her mind.

It was Cinco de Mayo—the fifth of May—the holiday celebrating Mexico's defeat of the French at the Battle of Puebla in 1862. They were at the Princess Hotel in San Diego where the festivities were being held. They walked down to the Barefoot Bar and Dana was overwhelmed by the beauty of the place. Built on the edge of Mission Bay, it was a tropical paradise of lush palms, hibiscus, daisies, ranunculus and a proliferation of other flowers dramatized by the day's unseasonably warm weather. A bridge spanned a saltwater lagoon that emptied into the sea via a waterfall. Baby stingrays and parrotfish cruised through it. The bay beyond it was a summer shade of periwinkle blue. The sky was cloudless.

She inhaled deeply as the delicate, delicious Hawaiian scent of plumeria blossoms drifted her way. The heat penetrated her like a long-lost lover, warming her through and through. Her gaze wandered to the fleet of the pleasure boats nestled up to the docks surrounding the bar. Others cruised by, their passengers basking in the sun. It was crowded. RockSteady was throwing the party. Barb Benton, the pro-motions director, had hired a reggae band for the occasion instead of providing the traditional Mexican mariachi sounds. Somehow, the Caribbean tunes were just right for the day. Some people were danc-ing. Others were bellied up to the bar, drinking beer, rainbow-colored Margaritas or doing tequila slammers.

Camille introduced her around. She met the Wise Guys, Barb, the station manager. She met a very extroverted woman named Holly Malone who led whale tours in Baja and asked Dana a hundred non-stop questions about her travels south of the border. She met everyone she was supposed to meet and then, suddenly, they all disappeared. She was alone. Her eyes circled the bar area. No one. Recollections of her only other singles outing assaulted her. Here she was, stranded at another social function. She took a quick gulp of her drink and, determined to look relaxed, pasted a smile on her face and focused her attention on the band. She swayed to the rhythm of the conga drums as the lead singer, a great dancer with long dread locks, belt-ed out a Bob Marley song. She sang along under her breath.

Two songs later a hand touched her shoulder and she turned. It was Camille. With a guy. One about her height with hair somewhere between the color of ripe wheat and desert sand. It was wavy and hung below his collar in back. He was dressed in white shorts and a faded Hawaiian style flowered shirt. He was nice-looking, no doubt about it. But what got her most were his eyes. He had melt-in-your-mouth brown eyes that locked into Dana's. They reminded her of a koala bear and a deer at the same time: vulnerable and tender, alert and intelligent—but overly wary and guaranteed to bolt at the drop of a hat.

"Peter Mays. Dana Wallace." So this was him....

Suddenly, out of nowhere, she was struck with an overwhelming urge to kiss him. She took a sip of her drink and swallowed hard. They stared at each other, neither saying anything for several long seconds. Dana shifted her weight, held in her stomach, felt the smile stretching tighter and tighter across her face. She wondered what to say next.

He moved closer and touched her hand. The aroma of his Old Spice aftershave nailed her. A lightning bolt of pure passion passed between them. Her knees shook as her body vibrated with desire, the intensity of which she'd never known before. She blushed from the tips of her toes to the top of her head. She stepped back and looked him over carefully. He was rangy and well-muscled. Tan. Magnetic some-how. What was the deal here? Her eyes stopped at his mouth. For the second time in two minutes, she wanted to feel that mouth on hers.

A lazy smile caressed his lips.

She shifted her weight. She hated this. Couldn't be this stupid. Not again. She had no use for infatuation, that vile serpent who'd cursed her past. If she wanted anything from men these days, it was friendship. Lovers she would do without. It was too soon, too soon. She wasn't even legally divorced yet.

He watched her wrestle with herself, watched her look him over. He was looking her over too. His amusement at her discomfort seemed to merge into discomfort of his own. They were both tongue-tied. The silence stretched between them like a rubber band. It encircled them, drawing them together and forcing them apart in an invisible mating dance. Advance.... Retreat.... Advance.... Retreat....

Still he was silent. What was she supposed to say? Dana scanned the patio, frantically searching for Camille. She couldn't find her.

He spoke. "I can see you're not used to this. How about if I ask you some questions?"

"What kind of questions?"

"Simple. Harmless. Non-intrusive. Deal?"

She drained her Margarita. "Go for it."

"Do you like to fish?"

"Excuse me?" She'd expected something a little more personal.

"Camille told me you love Mexico. I figured you must fish. Do you?"

"Fish? Yes. Of course I do."

"Ah. Do you ski?"

"Yes."

"Very well?"

"I hope so. I went to college in Colorado."

"Hunt?"

"What?! Hardly."

"Didn't think so. How about football?"

"Playing or spectating?"

"You answer. It's your turn."

"Spectating. Former Charger fan here. Back in the Dan Fouts days when they kicked butt. My ex-husband had season tickets. But I quit going after I had kids."

"Kids? Ages? Sexes? Names?"

She told him.

"Okay." He eyed her empty glass. "Quiz over. You have two choices, Ms. Dana Wallace. Dance with me or buy me a drink."

"Dance."

They danced. One dance. Then he checked his watch. "I have to be on the air at ten tonight. So, it is nap time for me." He yawned to emphasize the point. "I'll see ya."

"Aren't you going to ask me for my phone number?" she blurted out and instantly wished she hadn't.

"Do you want me to have it?"

She nodded as her cheeks flamed red like a 13-year-old's.

"Tell you what. Call me. When I'm on the air. Any night after 12, if you're up that late. After 'Back Seat Memories' are over. Use the hotline. Camille will give you the number. Okay?"

She nodded, mute.

And he was gone.

It never got any easier than that, she reminded herself as she breaststroked toward the beach. A cluster of ugly black turkey vultures with blood red heads circled overhead and dropped down, one at a time, to feed on the carcass of a sea lion that had apparently just washed ashore. She decided not to come in yet and turned, swimming back to the north toward her friends. Peter was brilliant. Sensitive. Talented. He was a painter and his work reminded her a little of Picasso's or Miró's. The tortured parts of his soul twisted and turned and wormed their way onto his canvases. His work chilled her to the bone, yet also fascinated her in an almost perverse sort of way. She shivered as she thought of him. He'd hurt her. Bad.

She got out of the water and walked—not toward the others but in the opposite direction—toward the vultures and their feast. She wasn't finished with him yet, she could feel it. Images kept popping into her head. Of her. Peter. She'd called him all right, a few weeks after they'd met. They started talking on the phone late at night. Dana had just been laid off her job as a project manager at Sundance Homes, a major San Diego homebuilder that was downsizing like crazy in the recession of the early '90s. She was unemployed, divorced and broke. Not exactly the time to fall in love. Especially with someone who was going through his second divorce. But she fell in love with him anyway.

Oh yeah, they were a pair to draw to—she and Peter. They'd ended up hanging out together off and on for over nearly three years. Too scared to ever get close. Too lonely to ever give up. Every time they broke up, it felt to both of them like they were going through drug withdrawal. So they'd slide back together—only to find they could never trust each other. Both had been cheated on by their exes. They could never relax in each other's presence unless they drank way too much. Which was not how Dana wanted to live her life.

Their sex life had been a catastrophe from the get-go. Dana never lost that quicksilver, struck-by-lightning attraction she had for him, but the minute he'd touch her naked body, her desire would vanish—replaced by panic. She pretended and faked her orgasms. He wasn't fooled and eventually called her on it. They finally gave up trying to connect physically after the second year, but still, amazingly enough, her attraction to him persisted. Still, until the end, she fantasized about him constantly, hoping that somehow—someday they would both magically lose their inhibitions and the smoldering sexuality they felt sensed in each other would burst forth into flame. Not! Todd and Camille were finally the ones who spilled the beans to her that Peter had been "doing" other women the entire time they'd been together.

As she trailed her toes in the sand and felt the sun prickle against her shoulders, she remembered that last Valentine's Day. No, I don't want to go there, she told herself. I don't. I won't. I can't. It didn't work. But Ellen's words to her the night before she left for Baja spiraled back at her from across time and space. *The lesson.* "What did I learn from him?" she asked the lone pelican who was skimming inches above the surface of the water to her left. "We didn't part friends. He lied to me. He cheated on me. And Todd—poor Todd. He was there for the whole ride...."

She sat down in the sand. Suddenly she was back in the kitchen at Hacienda Gaviota, on Valentine's Day of 1994.

"Pound that chicken, woman! Harder! Come on. Flatten it. Pretend it's your ex-husband. Or your ex-boss. Anyone or anything you want to beat the living daylights out of. That's it! You've got it! Hooray! We'll make an executive chef out of you yet."

She swung the mallet at him. "Cool your jets, buster, or I'll pound your head."

Todd laughed. "That's the spirit, old girl."

"I'm not that old."

"Five years older than me."

She swung again. "You're asking for it, you know. Watch out! Here I come! You're dead meat!" She chased him around the huge stainless steel and tile kitchen.

"Truce! Truce!"

Hector García, the restaurant's owner walked in. "Jesus Christ! Would you two take it easy?! We can hear you all the way out in the bar."

Dana stood still, wooden hammer in hand and waited for Todd to speak. After all, he was her boss.

"I started it. I was instructing her on how to pound chicken."

"*Well, could you put a lid on it? It's Valentine's Day you know. We have customers out there. Lots of them. They'll think you're in here actually butchering the chickens. Especially if you don't hurry up and get those dinners out. Save the child's play for before and after business hours, okay?*"

"*Sir Hector, forgive me. I was wrong.*"

"*I'm sorry too,*" Dana said.

The double doors swung shut and they looked at each other. Both covered their mouths as they burst into gales of silent laughter.

"*Okay. Back to work, Ms. Assistant Chef. Roll those flattened chicken boobies in chili powder.*"

"*New Mexico or American?*"

"*American. Then fry 'em up and sauce 'em down good with the lime and orange glaze. Is it ready?*" He turned to look at the pot behind him on one of the ten burners. "*Stir it, Dana darlin'. But turn the fire down, will you? Okay,*" he said when she'd complied, "*now where's that orange zest?*"

"*Over there.*" She showed him and turned her head to read the computer screen in front of her. "*We have seven orders for Chili Chicken with Citrus Glaze. Two for Wild West Pepper Steak, three for Blue Corn Tacos, one Medallions of Pork Ixtapa....*"

Another round of orders flashed onto the screen.

"*What's on there now?*" he asked.

"*Taos Enchiladas. Three orders. One Swordfish in Cilantro Butter, two Garlic Shrimp on Skewers and four Chipotle Chile Snappers. Holy Toledo! We're swamped. How in God's name are we gonna get all these out?*"

He touched her shoulder. "*Never fear, my lovely dear. Trust in your chef and he will never fail you. Take a deep breath and remember, we prepped for this tonight. We're ready. We can do this. You can do this. You could do it without me. What's our favorite saying now?*"

She laughed in spite of herself. "*Mise en plac—everything's in place.*"

Later, as they were finishing up the last orders of the evening, Todd ducked out of the kitchen to ask Hector a question. When he came back, he looked upset.

"*What's wrong?*" Dana asked him.

He took her by the shoulders. "*In 10 minutes we'll be done in here. If you want, I'll drive you home. What I'd rather do, if you'll let*"

*me, is take you to the Starlight Grill in Del Mar and buy you a drink.
We'll sit at my favorite table by the window and discuss the fact that
I've been your number one secret admirer for as long as I've known
you. Okay?"*

"What's going on?" she asked, alarmed. "Is Peter out there?"

*"Yes." Todd nodded. "He is. He's drunk and loud and wedged
between two young ladies in very short, very tight spandex mini-
dresses. It's not a pretty picture. Will you forget him and sneak out the
side door to have that Valentine's drink with me?"*

"What about Melinda?"

*"Melinda and I aren't getting along much better than you and
Peter are—although I do have to admit I'm better behaved than he is
and far more respectful of women." He gripped her shoulders even
harder. His brown-flecked green eyes peered into hers. "Look at me,
Dana. Really look at me. I care about you. A lot. I want to be with you
tonight. I won't hit on you. I just want to be there for you. Is that such
a bad thing?"*

*Dana's head reeled. She broke away from him. "Take me home,"
she said. "Out the side door. I don't want to see him. Not tonight. Not
ever again."*

She hugged her knees as she shook her head to clear it. "He was
in love with me," she told the pelican, who'd landed and was strolling
in the surf nearby. "I never even saw it 'til now. How could I have been
so blind? After Camille told me about the rest of Peter's escapades, I
was so angry at him and so disgusted with myself for hooking up with
another womanizer that I missed the truth entirely. Todd," she told the
pelican again, "was in love with me. He told me so that night and I
forgot it entirely until now. Couldn't handle it. Even when he broke up
with Melinda and kept bugging me to go have that drink with him at
the Starlight—I just made a big joke out of it. Our joke, I called it. Ha
ha ha. Oh God. I hurt him. How I must've hurt him."

She got up and began to walk. Her pelican waggled his wings at
her and took flight. She kept walking. She rounded a bend and walked
until she was out of sight of the others. There were dunes. She walked
out into the water, ducked under a miniature wave to cool off, came
back and parked herself between two dunes, under the semi-shade of
a lone palm. There wasn't a soul in sight. She lay on her back in the
sand and flapped her arms and legs, making an angel like she used to
do in the snow.

Her thoughts kaleidescoped back to Peter. He may have had a
weakness for women, but he wasn't all bad. In fact, he was the one
who encouraged me to explore my *artistic* side, she reminded herself.

Peter helped me pick myself up after life dumped me on my ass. I was newly divorced, unemployed, lonely, scared and wallowing in self-pity and he saw me as a successful chef. Just because I loved to cook for him and he loved to eat my food. Just because I'd waitressed, taken some culinary classes and done a little cooking in college. It was Peter who convinced me to have my mom call Hector—Hector who'd bought two of her dead husband's restaurants from her. Hector—who hired me and apprenticed me to Todd! Peter saw my success years before it happened!

"Thank you Peter Mays!" she screamed to the sky. "And I forgive you! I do!"

She got up, dusted herself off, ran into the ocean and did a hand-stand in the shallow waves. Then another one. And another. She ran into the deeper water and threw herself into, up and out of the water, arching her body like a dolphin. Over, over and over again. Then she ran back onto the beach and spun herself sideways through the air, turning her first cartwheel since high school. She stumbled and near-ly blew out her ankle on the landing, but recovered and did it again. By the fifth one she was breathless, but she knew her legs had been straight and she knew her toes had been pointed and she knew she'd gotten it right.

From a ways up the beach she heard the Baja yelp. It was a cho-rus actually. "Brrrrrrrreeeeeeeeehaaaaaaaaaah! Ay! Ay! Ay! Ay!" She did one last cartwheel and botched it totally, landing on her ass in the water, laughing 'til tears ran down her face.

It was a little after sunset. Dana, Camille, Barb and Holly had parked Boris on the outskirts of Santa Rosalía and were walking down its narrow, crowded streets. There were a lot more people around than there had been earlier in the day. They walked to the church first and admired it.

"This was really built by the same guy who did the Eiffel Tower in Paris?" asked Camille.

"Remember? It was designed by Eiffel, built in Paris, disassem-bled and shipped in pieces to Baja. Let's go inside." They did. It was fairly deserted. Camille repeated the ritual she'd gone through in San Ignacio and Dana followed her. This time she too crossed herself with holy water and curtsied toward the image of the crucified Jesus Christ. She found herself kneeling in a French church made from tin, in Southern Baja, thanking God for the revelations of the day.

"Okay, Lord," she said, as she neared the end of her prayers. "I'm not done yet. Please say hi to my dad for me up there in heaven. Tell him I love him and miss him. Tell him thanks a bazillion for knowing how much I needed that motor home. Please help all of us, especially Camille and Holly, to get along and go gently on each other for the rest of this trip. Please keep us safe. Please keep my children safe. Thank you for helping me remember what really happened that night I broke it off with Peter. Oh and please send me a guardian angel or two to stand by me and help me out when I come face to face with Todd. You know how hopeless I am around men—and I want to see him again. I do. Bad...."

She paused and opened her eyes for a second. Saw a lone tear escape from Camille's closed eye. She shut her own again. "Oh. Just a couple more last things, God. Please help Camille to find the strength to be whole and happy without Drew. Help me to forgive my mother for all that she's done to hurt me over the years. Please help me to forgive Brad. Oh," she added, as an afterthought, "and myself too, for all the mean and stupid things I've done. Thanks for listening. Amen."

She stood and walked to the back of the church. Went outside. There, in front of a white hot dog cart that read *"Perritos Calientes—* Hot Dogs," or to use the literal translation "Warm Puppies," she saw Barb and Holly stuffing their faces. She walked over to them. "These carts only come out at night, for some reason," Holly told her between bites. "Six pesos'll get you the treat of a lifetime." Dana ordered one for herself and one for Camille.

She was handed a steaming, fresh bun which the proprietor assured her was from the El Boleo Bakery. Inside was a delightfully spiced Mexican hot dog, wrapped in bacon and grilled to perfection. It was covered in jalapeños, tomatoes, grilled onions, cheese and that mysterious Mexican white sauce. She bit into it and sighed. It was wonderful. Camille was still in the church, so Dana ate hers too.

After this first course, they wandered over to the world-famous bakery and stood in line. Holly got a free flour tortilla from one of the women working behind the counter. Dana popped a piece into her mouth. Loved it. Ordered a couple dozen, along with some baguettes and sweet rolls.

Then it was back to the streets. Holly bought a clear plastic cup stuffed full of sliced cucumber, jícama, coconut, papaya, cantaloupe and sprinkled with chile powder and fresh lime juice from a fruit vendor. Camille bought herself a mango on a stick that had been peeled back and cut expertly into the shape of a flower. They walked along, sharing bites and enjoying the friendly, all-Mexican crowd.

Suddenly Dana's nose went up as she caught a distinctive aroma—one that told her that someone nearby was barbecuing steak. Her olfactories were instantly electrified, her mouth began to water and her head turned to locate the source of the wondrous smell. Less than a block away was an outdoor counter jammed with people standing, hunched over plates of food. Dana moved in for a closer look. Yup, they were scarfing plates full of tacos. The guy behind the counter tossed a few slabs of marinated carne asada onto a grill behind the counter, cooked them, removed the meat to a wooden board and quickly chopped it into tiny pieces with a meat cleaver. Meanwhile, he heated up corn tortillas and heaped grilled meat on top of each tortilla. He handed a plateful of tacos to a couple of young men in front of him and motioned for them to add cilantro, roasted chiles, cheese, onions, tomatoes, any of several types of salsa, cabbage, huge radishes and sour cream sauce to their tacos. They finished loading goodies onto their tacos and moved aside, motioning for Dana and her friends to move in to the empty space. They did.

CHAPTER EIGHTEEN   **Mulegé to Bahía Concepción,**
Baja California Sur
October 25 and 26, 1997

Holly slid out of bed and tiptoed to the cab of the motor home. She turned on the stereo, put a tape in the player and cranked it up, smiling to herself. The Rolling Stones, "You Can't Always Get What You Want" blasted back at her.

"Hey!" Dana mumbled. "What's going on?"

Holly turned down the volume. "Today's the Las Glorias Chili Cook-Off," she said. "It's 6:00 a.m. We need to be in Mulegé as early as possible in order to get our business taken care of before the festivities start at noon." She heard groans all around and chuckled. "I'll turn it back up if you don't hoist your heinies outta bed."

"How far to Mulegé?" asked Camille.

"Less than 35 miles. But I want to get a good spot at the Villa María Isabel for Boris. We need to set up camp, pick up our e-mail, do laundry and grab a shower. Then there's the prep work to be done on the chili."

Dana squinted at her through sleep-filled eyes. "I soaked the beans. I have the rest of the ingredients set aside in baggies. Barb and I did it last night when you guys were hanging out at the campfire with the guys next door."

"So, great." Holly turned and filled the tea kettle with water. "I'm making coffee. I want to be out of here by seven. Who wants to help me break camp?"

Two hours later the Sea of Cortez, which had been out of sight for a few minutes, reappeared, sparkling and majestic, on the horizon.

The road descended into a wide valley. A jungle of brilliant green palms extended all the way to the dark-hued mountains to the west. A broad river split the valley. In the early morning light, it seemed as though the rest of the world was asleep. A deep peacefulness, etched over with exhilaration, crept into Holly's heart. She sighed. They were in Mulegé, home of the lushest palm oasis and the only navigable river on the peninsula. Her and Rick's special place. She fidgeted in her seat as she drove. She couldn't wait to get there. To see him. It had been nearly six weeks this time.

Holly drove through the twisted, narrow streets of town and along the north edge of the river, pointing out the sights. They stopped at a mini mercado for beer, ice and some chiles, and then at the little *oficina de correos*—post office in the heart of downtown Mulegé where they picked up e-mail from their accounts. Everyone had e-mail. Holly and Barb both sent off the mail they'd been saving on their laptops. Camille and Dana answered the mail from their kids on the spot.

Her anticipation building, Holly drove them to the Villa María Isabel RV Park. She waved at Joe and Darlene Jennings on her way in and to several other friends too. "Rick here yet?" she asked Darlene.

"He sure is. He drove in late, night before last. Went out fishing all day yesterday. I'll go knock on your trailer door and tell him you're here."

"Good. He can help us make camp."

Joe had reserved them a campsite in the transient section of the park. It wasn't along the riverfront because all the permanent trailers with their room and porch additions had taken over the choicest spots, but he'd snagged the last site with hookups. It was crowded here. Everyone was looking forward to the big fiesta today. About a third of the residents of the park were cooking. The rest were planning to watch, eat and play.

As Holly had known they would, the other three women loved being in Mulegé. They loved this river, in the middle of the most photographed palm oasis in all of Baja. Their campground felt like a five-star resort with its pool, restrooms, shower, dump station, bakery and laundromat. Camille put herself in charge of laundry. The water was—amazingly enough—potable, so Barb filled all their tanks to the brim. Dana finished prepping for the Chili Cook-Off and after they'd set up camp, Holly and Rick penned a sign for Dana's Fifteen Bean Chili and went off to their own trailer.

As the screen door banged behind her, Holly felt suddenly ill at ease with her husband. She looked hard at him. At 37, he was nearly ten years younger than she was, and while that fact excited her on some levels, it intimidated her on others. He was rangy and tall, and because of his Indian blood and the fact that he lived most of his life at sea, he was as dark as any Mexican fisherman. There were more lines around his dark eyes than she remembered and his face looked gaunt to her, like he'd lost weight. She inhaled and waited to feel that familiar stirring inside.

He caught her staring and reached for her. "Come here, wife," he said. "I'm sorely in need of a conjugal visit." He took her hand and led her through their screened-in porch and into the living room. All the blinds were drawn. "I want you. Now," he said and pulled her down onto the couch.

"Can't we talk first? I want to hear all about your trip to Caracas. I want to tell you how the book's coming along...."

He kissed her. And kept kissing her. Within moments their clothes were off and they were making love—exactly the same way they always did—a few minutes of kissing, a few more minutes of foreplay and then intercourse—with him on top. Of course. Holly's feelings careened between arousal, disappointment, anger and frustration. She wasn't gonna get there, she could tell. She felt as though she were floating somewhere about a foot or so above her body. She could see Rick, she could smell him, she could even feel him, physically. But her soul had somehow disconnected itself from what was happening between them. She opened her eyes and sought his with a hunger born of desperation and loneliness, but they were closed. She felt his urgency as he moved faster and faster inside her and willed herself to move along with him. Within moments he collapsed on top of her, sweating and spent.

He rolled off her, leaned up on his elbow and kissed the tip of her nose. He was smiling. "Boy, I needed that. Was it good for you, babe?"

The answer that came out of her mouth shocked her more than it did him. "If you had to ask, then you know the answer's no. It wasn't good. It was a wham-bam-thank-you-ma'am."

His eyes widened. Then it was his turn to surprise her. He laughed. He actually laughed. "It was, wasn't it? I'm sorry, Hol. I was selfish. Here, " he said as his hands and mouth began to dance across her body, "Let me make it up to you...."

An hour later they were loading up Rick's van with beach chairs, cameras, portable table, camp stove and cooking gear. Holly climbed into the front seat with him, and Dana, Camille and Barb settled into the back. They drove to the site of the Las Glorias Third Annual Chili Cook-Off. There was a huge burnt orange, rust and white Tecate tent stretched across a level spot by the river that looked to have been mowed in anticipation of today's festivities. Loud, Mexican oohm-pah-pah accordion music blared from speakers on either side of the canopy. There was already a large crowd gathered, and it was only a few minutes before noon.

Joe and Darlene waved to Rick and he parked his van behind their dune buggy. They unloaded. Holly looked around. This was the first time she'd made it down here for the cook-off. There was a bocce ball game going on at the far east end of the knoll. Four gringos, two of whom she knew, were playing. One pair gave a loud hoot as an opponent's ball was knocked right out of the court. A trio of mariachis were tuning their instruments nearby. There were cooking stands set up everywhere along the makeshift park's perimeter and white plastic tables and chairs emblazoned with the Tecate logo in the middle. At one end, adjacent to the registration table, was another table over-flowing with things to be raffled off—homemade cakes, pies cookies, toys and all kinds of trinkets. There were piñatas hanging from some pepper trees.

It was gonna be one grande fiesta, she thought. No doubt about it. As Rick helped Dana set up her stand, a voice over the loud speak-er announced that it was noon. Time to start cooking. The chefs would be allowed two hours to cook, and then the judging would begin. Anyone who was interested in judging should sign up at the registra-tion table. Holly considered signing up, but decided not to. She looked over at her husband, hoping that he'd break away from Dana and come hang out with her, but he seemed to be thoroughly enjoy-ing himself as he tossed onions, garlic and roasted peppers into her chili pot. Holly sighed, pulled out her camera and began to take pic-tures. When she finished, she jotted down some notes on a yellow pad before moving on.

At the edge of the grass lot, out of the contest area, she spotted a table where some local Mexican women were selling food. She stopped and watched as one woman chopped tomatoes, onions, chiles and cilantro to make salsa. Another was making guacamole, while a third was cooking quesadillas, along with carne asada and fish tacos, over a large, greasy, flat grill. Holly ordered one of every-thing and wolfed it all down.

Her next stop was the beer stand. The nearly toothless, grinning old man behind the counter was someone she'd known for years. "Hola Jaime," she called to him. *"Quiero una cerveza Tecate por favor."* She bought an ice-cold Tecate for him for 10 pesos, and then, as an afterthought, bought two more—one for Rick and another for Dana. Holly delivered the beers.

"How's it coming?" she asked as she snapped photos of the two of them.

"Fine," Dana answered between poses. "Thanks for the beer. I was really thirsty. Here. Taste this and tell me what you think." She dipped a plastic spoon into the chili and handed it to Holly. Holly took a bite and swallowed.

"Wow. That's tasty," she said. "But the beans are still a little crunchy." She glanced at her watch. "You have another hour though. It should be perfect by then. I have faith in you, Dana. Wanna come walk around with me?" Holly asked her husband.

He shook his head. "Nah. I'm the sous chef today. I promised Dana that I'd be her loyal assistant. Go have fun, babe. You know everyone here. You'll be fine. You don't need me."

Holly's cheeks burned as though they'd been slapped—hard. She spun on her heel and willed herself to walk, rather than stomp away. Where the hell are Camille and Barb? she asked herself. I need to find them. Now. One of them has to take over for Rick. I will not have him standing there, fawning all over Dana while I'm stuck roaming around by myself. No way José. He's my husband. Why the hell is he with her and not me?!

She searched for Camille and Barb and found them drinking beer and playing bocce ball with a group of guys from Colorado. Waving at them briefly, she mumbled to herself, "Screw them all. I need a drink. A strong one." She wove her way through the crowd until she was in line for Margaritas. *"Una Margarita de Hornitos— doble, por favor*—A Hornitos Margarita—double, please," she said. It was delivered to her in a 16-ounce red plastic cup. She walked over to Darlene and Joe's stand and drank it while she talked with them.

By the time the judges were ready to announce the winners at 2:30, she was pretty damn drunk, and she knew it. She worked her way carefully back to Dana and Rick and offered her husband a sip of her drink. He declined. "Would you get me another beer, Hol?" he asked. "And one for the chef here too?"

Her eyes narrowed and she felt the bile rise up in throat. "I'm not your slave," she spat at him. "Get your own goddamned beer!" She grabbed his car keys, walked over to where the van was parked, got in and drove off by herself.

It was morning. It had to be. Camille opened her eyes and blinked. A congregation of crowing roosters seemed to have circled the motor home and begun their Sunday services. There had to be at least a dozen of them going off, one on top of the other like a choir of zealots. She closed her eyes and tuned in to the cacophony. There was a lot more going on than just crowing. There were other birds chirping—pleasant-sounding ones. A foul-mouthed crow. Some sort of meowing too. There was snoring too, coming from the body next to her. Dana.

Camille turned over on her back and stared at the wood veneer paneling on the ceiling. She'd heard from Drew and it disturbed her. Big time. She got out of bed and retrieved the printout from her backpack. She checked the clock above the sink. It wasn't even 6:00 a.m. yet. Oops. Make that 7:00 by yesterday's time. Today the clock "fell back" an hour as Daylight Savings Time officially ended. She slipped outside and looked around. No one was up yet. She walked over to the restroom, used it and returned. She sat down and reread Drew's letter:

My Dearest Camille,

One life, one God. One way or the other we pass from darkness to light. From glimpsing perfect hope and love to living it through a life of humility and obedience. At the urging of my Promise Keepers group, I have begun counseling with our pastor, Bruce Bellows. You and I were guilty of sexual immorality, both before and after our marriage. I have asked God for forgiveness. I beg you to do the same.

I ask you also to consider attending counseling sessions with me after you return from Mexico, while maintaining—of course—our sexual purity. We owe it to our Lord to honor and abide by the covenant of marriage. While it was wise for us to separate, I believe you were wrong to file for divorce. In my confusion, I supported you in that choice. I was wrong. Please forgive me.

It is my abiding prayer that our life together as faithful Christians may resume and that our marriage will be restored, so that we may be a beacon of light for others in troubled remarriage situations.

In His love,
Your husband, Drew

"Man oh man oh man," she said out loud as she ran her fingers through her tangled hair. "What the fuck, over?! What's up with all this sexual purity crap anyway? We're still married!"

The screen door banged and Barb stumbled out of the motor home. Her hair was down for a change, and it was wild. "Whatcha doin'?" she asked, rubbing the sleep out of her eyes.

"Read this. I showed it to Dana yesterday at the party. She just shook her head. Told me I was being *manipulated* in the name of God. She went with me to church a bunch of times but said she couldn't handle all the hand-waving and the holier-than-thou stuff. She has zero tolerance for the born-again set."

"What do you *feel* in your own heart, girlfriend?"

Camille shrugged. "I'm not sure."

"Well, let me make some coffee and let's talk about it." She went inside for a few minutes and came back with two steaming mugs of coffee. She inhaled deeply. "Now that's more like it. Sure is noisy here, huh?"

"Yeah. I can't figure out where that God-awful meowing's coming from."

"Peacocks. Holly told me."

"Well, I can't stand it. I want to leave. I think we should go to Conception Bay today and let Holly stay here at her own place for the next two nights. I really think she and Rick need some time alone together to mend their fences—without us."

Barb looked at her thoughtfully. She nodded. "Yeah. She really lost it yesterday. The green monster bit her something fierce. I still feel bad for Rick. I don't believe he meant to make her jealous. He was just trying to help Dana. Anyway," she said with a sigh, "I'd rather be on the beach. It's only 10 or so miles away. I want to explore a little bit more around here, but after that I'm definitely game for moving on."

Camille laughed. "You're elected to talk to Holly. You're the one she likes best right now." She changed the subject and waved the letter. "What do you think about this?"

"Do you still love him?"

Camille made a face. "I don't know! This e-mail gives me the creeps. It makes me feel like he wants me back because it's the proper Christian thing to do. It feels like he's blaming me for filing for divorce. It feels like he's blaming me for all this *sexual immorality* crap. Ya know what?" she asked, sitting up very straight in her chair.

"What?"

"I'm not buying this shit one bit. I'm being made out to be a slut is what it feels like. It feels like he's doing the *right thing* for all the *wrong reasons!*"

Barb nodded. "That's possible. Do you trust him?"

"No." She shook her head emphatically. "I don't. I see this as being all about him wanting to look really fucking holy in front of the church. It isn't about loving me or my boys at all. It isn't about love, period!"

"Yeah, but if you really do love him—and I think you still do—can't you take this as an open door and just explore it a little? What do you have to lose?"

Camille shrugged. "I don't know. I'm so confused!" She made a face. "The only things I know are that I don't want to be hurt, I don't want to be chained up or put in a cage and I don't want to be blamed unfairly."

"Do you trust this Bruce fellow?"

"Oh, hell no. He and I've had several run-ins. He thinks I'm stubborn and overbearing. Not the ideal submissive wife by a long shot."

"So what will these men do to you? Put out your fire and make you over into a white-bread version of yourself?!"

She nodded. "Yup. Can't you just see it now? My face on the Bimbo Bread truck instead of that snugly little white bear in the chef's hat!"

"You want to know what I *really* think, Camille?"

Camille took a sip of her coffee and nodded. "Yes. Definitely."

Barb pointed to Drew's letter. "This is just the sort of thing that drives me nuts about organized religion. I agree with you. This reconciliation ploy isn't about loving you. It's about Drew being afraid of looking bad in other people's eyes. He wants to tame you, like you said—in order to make himself look good. Love isn't about judging and blaming and controlling. Love's the opposite of all that. It accepts. It affirms. It releases. It surrenders. It trusts. It has faith that in the final analysis, once the negative of life's big picture is developed, we'll all see that everything works together for good!"

"So? What do I do?"

"Look for love at the source, instead of looking for it through a man. Reach way down deep inside yourself. When you face your own neediness and your fear of being alone straight on—then it will leave you, because you'll see clearly how outdated and counterproductive it is. You'll free yourself up to connect with the essence of love inside you—which is God. I know you love God, Camille. But I'd bet money that you aren't sure you're worthy of his love. Am I right?"

Camille nodded, her mind reeling.

"I know this one from my own experience. *God's ability to love you is limited only by your ability to receive his love.* Right now. If you can't receive his love, you won't be able to receive any man's love either. It has to start at the source and flow outward. Does this make any sense?"

"Why can't I feel God's love?"

"Guilt and fear. They build walls that shut out love. Pure and simple."

"What about Drew? Does he shut out love too?"

Barb nodded. "Absolutely. From what I've seen of him, I'd say he's incapable of loving you the way you deserve to be loved. He mouths all that religious rhetoric, but I see him as being much more committed to being *appropriate* than being *real.*"

"So you think he's being appropriate by wanting to reconcile with me—but—in his heart of hearts that isn't what he really wants?"

"Obviously I can't speak for him. But yes, that's my take on it."

Camille was silent. The early morning noises came back at her and she tuned into the chaos for a long minute. She gave Barb a long, hard look. "He's doing the right thing for the wrong reasons," she said.

Barb nodded. "Yes. Exactly. If he comes back to you, let him come with his fears faced and his heart overflowing with love. That's the only way it works. Otherwise you're just trying to outsmart the truth. You'll find yourselves back where you started from with the same unlearned lessons staring you in the face!"

"Puke," said Camille. "I don't wanna go around this block again."

"Are you gonna answer the e-mail?"

"No. I can't."

The screen door banged open again and Dana stumbled outside, holding a coffee cup. "Hey you two. Cock-a-doodle-doo and meow. Did those obnoxious roosters and peacocks wake you up too?"

"No duh."

She sat down. "Wow, that was some party yesterday. My guts are on fire."

"Well, no wonder. That Chuck guy who won the cook-off with his *Pedos de Fuego*—Farts of Fire Chili with the habañeros in it was out to get all of us."

"You got it. It's gonna be one of those white-knuckle mornings."

They reminisced about the party for a few minutes.

"I heard last night from a guy who's on his way north that the fiesta in Loreto has been going on since the twelfth of this month," said Camille. "Today's the last day. Holly fed us a line of shit and it backfired in her face. She made us miss the Tri-Centennial so she could come here and rendezvous her husband and what does she do? Gets drunk, throws a fit and ends up hurling in her trailer all afternoon and half the night." She shook her head. "Poor Holly. I can kinda relate somehow."

"I'm not feeling real sorry for Holly at the moment," said Barb. "She goes off the deep end whenever she doesn't get her own way. I think a few days away from her would do us all good. She's starting to make me crazy—and obviously we're making her crazy too. I want to be on the beach again. From what the guys from Colorado were telling me, Bahía Concepción is the most beautiful place on the entire peninsula. I like Mulegé but I'm in the mood for wide open spaces, white sandy beaches and that pale aquamarine water Dana goes on and on about."

They walked toward the bakery to buy some goodies for breakfast and saw Holly approaching from the other direction. She was bright-eyed and ebullient—as though yesterday had never happened. "Hey!" she called out. "I have the best idea! How about if you go on ahead to Conception Bay today."

They caught up with her. "You're not coming?" asked Dana.

Holly grinned and shook her head. "No. You don't need me. Just go south on Mex 1 for 13 miles 'til you reach K-114. That's Playa Santispac—my favorite place. If you don't find a good spot there, go two kilometers and pull into Posada Concepción. There's a decent RV park there. Check out EcoMundo. It's the biggest kayaking and dive business in the area. There are campgrounds all down the edge of the bay for about the next 10 miles."

Camille and the other two locked eyes. "Yesssss!" she cried and all three raised their hands in unison. High fives smacked all around. "Barb wants to do a little shopping this morning. We talked about checking out the mission and the museum that's in the old prison. We'll head out after that."

"Can you recommend somewhere for lunch?" asked Dana.

Holly kept on grinning. "Oh sure. Go to The Serenidad or Las Casitas. It's an adorable hotel right in the middle of town, just off the river. On your way back, stop at Jungle Jim's for a beer."

Dana drove 25 miles south of Mulegé. Camille rode shotgun and Barb was in Holly's favorite spot, crouched between the two front seats. They oohed and aahed as the miles rolled by. Never had any of them seen a bay so beautiful, so peaceful, so pristine and so empty. Except for the 10 or so campgrounds and gringo settlements scattered along its western edge, and with the exception of a few fishing boats, kayaks and sailboards on the water, Bahía Concepción was unsettled. It was all sea, sky and deserted islands—a true camper's paradise.

At Kilometer 91, Dana pulled into Playa Armenta and turned around. "This is a bit rustic for us," she said. "Where do you guys want to go?"

"I vote for the second place we saw. Or the third."

"Me too."

Dana drove north again. At K-112 she pulled off to the right and drove into Posada Concepción. They parked, got out and walked around. The beachfront property was completely taken up with permanent structures. A middle-aged Mexican man came up to them as they strolled along the beach, admiring the houses and wishing they could stay in one.

"Buenas tardes, señoras. ¿Cómo están—Good afternoon, ladies. How are you?"

"Bien gracias—Well, thanks," said Dana. She introduced herself and the others to the caretaker, whose name was Armando. They chatted a few minutes in Spanish. *"¿Es posible acampar acerca de la playa*—Is it possible to camp close to the beach?" she asked him, finally.

"Oh. Sí." He pointed. *"Las personas que viven en estas dos casas son de la misma familia. Ellos no van a estar aquí hasta Diciembre, para la Navidad*—The people who live here in these two houses are from the same family. They won't be here until December, for Christmas. *Si quieren, pueden estacionar su vehículo en este espacio entre las dos casas*—If you want, you can park your vehicle in this space between the houses."

"What'd he say?" asked Camille.

Dana turned and told her.

"Señora," Armando interrupted. *"Hace muchísimo calor aquí*—It's really hot here." He pointed to the southernmost house which had a huge tile patio in front of it. The patio was walled off from the beach by a rock wall and covered over with a thatched palm palapa. It had a built-in barbecue and fire ring. *"Si quieren usar el patio y la palapa de esta casa, no hay problema*—If you want to use the patio and the palapa at this house, it's no problem."

"Oh. Muchísimas gracias—Oh, thanks so much. *¿Cuanto cuesta por una noche aquí*—How much does it cost per night here?"

"*Oh. Por ustedes mujeres tan bonitas, solamente 50 pesos*—For women as pretty as you, only 50 pesos."

"Gracias," said Dana. "Give me a hundred peso bill, will you, Barb?" she asked. "We're staying here two nights, right? Barb nodded and handed her the money.

"*¿Tiene niños—Do you have children?*" she asked Armando.

"*Sí. Tengo cinco niños y dos niñas*—Yes. I have five boys and two girls."

"*Bueno*—Good. Camille, would you dig out that candy bag? He's doing us a huge favor. I want to give him some goodies for his kids."

Forty-five minutes later they were seated on the tile patio in their beach chairs in the shade, sipping ice cold Pacificos. "This is beyond awesome," said Barb. "When I walked over to check out the restaurant and bathing facilities I stopped by the EcoMundo Center. You can actually get fully provisioned for a kayaking expedition to those islands out there. Or sign up for one of their day tours. They rent kayaks and dive gear too."

"Cool. We need one more kayak and we can have ourselves a kick-ass day on the water," said Camille. "I really need it. My head is clogged up with Drew's mumbo-jumbo and Holly's latest bullshit."

Dana went on. "Well, if it's any consolation. My head's all clogged up too. It's overflowing with images of the men I've loved and lost over the years. I can't seem to stop reliving my sordid relationship with Peter Mays. Or Brad. Jack the married guy. Even my dad's been invading my inner space more than I'd like him to. Every man who's ever inhabited my heart seems to have come back to visit lately. I keep replaying those relationships ad nauseam. Especially the painful parts. It's like a scratched-up old record that keeps on getting stuck."

Just then an ice cream wagon began circulating through the little beachfront community. Strains of "It's a Small World" filled the air. All three women looked at each other and burst out laughing.

"Never fails, huh?" said Dana. "I think every ice cream truck in Baja plays that song! I hate it! Every time I ever took my girls to Disneyland it would be stuck in my brain for weeks!"

"Another old scratched-up record. We do need to go kayaking tomorrow. I'm kinda bugged myself," Barb added. "But I don't know what's bugging me. I priced the kayaks. It costs $20 for one boat for a half day and $25 for a full day."

"Let's do the $25. We can pack a lunch and head out early in the morning."

"The lady at EcoMundo told me there's great clamming out at the islands."

Camille looked at Dana. "I want more of those stuffed clams like you made in San Quintín."

Dana smiled. *"Mañana.* Armando's bringing clam ceviche over tonight around sunset. He swears it's way better than ceviche made with scallops."

"Oh yum," said Barb. "Cool. Let's change into our suits and go for a walk on the beach. We need to clear some serious cobwebs out of our heads and hearts."

"No," said Dana. "To clear out our heads, we need to be underwater. Grab the snorkeling gear. We're going to leave this *loco mundo*—crazy world with its annoying music and visit the undersea one."

CHAPTER NINETEEN   Loreto, Baja California Sur
                                 October 28 and 29, 1997

After coming down from the foothills to the flatlands north of
Loreto, the view once again made everyone sit up straight in their
seats and take notice. To the west the jagged peaks of La Sierra de la
Giganta rose without apology from the desert floor. To the east, past
the town, shimmered the Sea of Cortez. Rising from its depths was
Isla del Carmen, home of a salt producing operation dating back to
the days of the Spaniards.

The roar of a jet engine made it impossible to hear Holly talking.
An Aero California jet swooped from the sky, lined itself up with the
runway and came in for a landing. The left wheel touched down in a
cloud of smoke. The wings wobbled ever-so-slightly and then the
right wheel touched down. The engines reversed and the plane slowed
to a stop. "Ladies and gentlemen," Holly announced, "We have just
arrived at Loreto International Airport. Please check under the seat
back in front you and in the overhead compartment to make sure you
have all your belongings. Do not leave your seats until the 'Fasten
Seat Belt' sign has been turned off."

"Civilization," said Dana. "I knew there was an airport here.
Wow. I'd say Fonatur [the Mexican government tourist agency that
developed the resorts of Los Cabos, Cancún and Ixtapa] has arrived.
How many new gringo hotels are there?"

Holly pointed to one of her many guidebooks. "Okay. Here it is," Dana went on. "Hotel La Pinta. Formerly El Presidente. Beachfront. Four blocks from town plaza. Twenty-nine haciendas, 20 villas. Hotel Oasis. Beachfront. Forty rooms. Hotel La Misión. Waterfront. Thirty-five rooms. Two blocks from plaza. The biggie: Diamond Eden. All-inclusive, five-star resort for adults only with 248 rooms and 62 suites."

"Holy shit, Batman! That place is huge!" exclaimed Camille from behind Dana's head. "Let me see that." She grabbed the book and read on. "My God, are we in Baja? This place has an 18-hole golf course, eight tennis courts, a gym, two pools, a 'clothing optional' beach and more activities than you could ever do in a week! There are more hotels too—Plaza Loreto, Villas de Loreto and Loreto Shores. Phew!"

"Now I know I've been in the boonies for two weeks. This is *weird.*" said Dana. "I'd heard Loreto'd been built up, but I wasn't prepared for this...."

Holly turned left onto the main drag and headed east, toward the Sea of Cortez. "Believe it or not, the downtown part and the *malecón* haven't changed too much. Look," she pointed. "There's McLuLu's fish taco stand. She's been here for about 12 years. We can get five huge fish tacos for 25 pesos. Anybody game?"

All hands went up, so they stopped for lunch. It had only been a 70 mile drive from Posada Concepción, so they had most of the day ahead of them. Dana ran across the street and bought four Pacificos, poured them into plastic cups and they settled down for a scrumptious lunch.

Afterwards, Holly gave them a quick tour of the hotel strip and Nopaló Beach five miles south of town. She told them about *another* new marina being developed in Puerto Escondido, ten miles south of there. They retraced their route back north through Loreto and passed the mission in the center of town, turned right onto Francisco Madero, drove across a big arroyo and stopped at the Loreto Shores Villas and RV Park sign. Holly pulled in, hopped out and chatted with the manager, paid him $20 for four people for one night and followed his directions to a site with full hookups toward the back of the park.

Barb got out and looked around. This wasn't a fancy Fonatur resort, that was for sure. It was back from the ocean, but there were trees, restrooms, showers and a laundromat. That was pretty deluxe, compared to where they'd just been—but nowhere near as pretty. However, she planned to do some serious shopping and sight-seeing here *after* she took a shower and washed some clothes!

When the afternoon siesta was over two hours later, the four went out on foot to explore Loreto. They walked north along the wide oceanfront promenade. It was built of brick pavers and extended out to the rock barricade that formed a seawall or malecón. Every few feet were concrete benches, some facing east and some facing west. There were people sitting on most of them, despite the fact that it was so windy the tops had blown right off the white caps and it was impossible not to taste the spume in the air.

The cool breeze whipped the skirt of Barb's sundress about her legs. The circulating air felt great after two sizzling, perfectly still days on the shore of Bahía Concepción. She was walking faster than everyone else in her excitement to get to the church and the plaza and turned left onto Loreto's main street. It awed her that she was, after all, in the oldest permanent settlement in both Alta and Baja California. She reviewed her history. Loreto had been the capital of both Californias until it was destroyed by a chubasco in 1829—at which time the capital had been moved to La Paz.

Suddenly she was face to face with the mission. *"Nuestra Señora de Loreto. Cabeza y Madre de las Misiones de Baja y Alta California*—Our Lady of Loreto. Head and Mother of the Missions of Lower and Upper California" read the inscription above its main entrance. She walked up the stairs and stood in front of the massive wooden door. She looked up. The clock on the steeple was stuck at 3:41. There was no trace of the Tri-Centennial festivities other than a few tattered posters flapping in the wind. Some were already in pieces on the ground, mingling with leftover potato chip bags and candy wrappers. Gone were the artists, craftsmen, musicians, dancers, vendors and all the others who'd participated in the revelry. Barb heaved an internal sigh and followed Dana and Camille into the church. There was a heaviness on her heart. Today she too felt the urge to enter this historical sanctuary and pray.

Adjacent to the mission church, they found the Museo de las Misiones, a historical and anthropological museum. An impressionistic statue of Christ on the cross, carved from driftwood, marked the centerpiece of the courtyard. All three stopped to look at it. There were wine presses and an ox cart next to Jesus, reminding Barb how challenging life must have been on this peninsula 300 years ago.

Holly materialized and led them into the museum. It was constructed, she said, with materials indigenous to the region: stone, brick, shell lime, mesquite, palm and ironwood. There were several priceless old oil paintings that looked like they belonged in Florence's Uffizi Museum instead of this remote Baja village over 700 miles south of the United States border. There was a portrait of Ignacio de

Loyola, founder of the Jesuit Order, a painting of the Apostle Santiago and another of Archangel Michael. Camille grabbed Barb's hand and led her to a nearly life-size sculpture of the reclining Christ. For a split second he looked so real, Barb was ready to kneel at his feet. Chills rushed up and down her spine.

The museum's ethnographic collection offered up samples of the region's arts and crafts. There was a boat hand-hewn from a single log, saddles, horse-hair halters and clothing typical of that worn by people in the missionary period. Holly led them finally to a huge bell. She explained that in 1875 the bell was lost overboard a ship en route to another mission. It was rescued 100 years later when it appeared in the net of some fishermen.

"Okay gang," she said. "Tour over. I got way behind on my writing while Rick was here, so I'm heading back to camp to work. You don't need me to show you the tourist shops anyway." She made a wide sweep with her arm. "They're all up and down this street."

A bust of Padre Salvatierra, founder of Loreto, faced them from a plaza across the street. What had once been the main street of town was now a pedestrian walkway. Small shops lined both sides of it. Barb squealed in spite of herself. "All right!" she said. "I have waited two weeks to go shopping! Let's go!" And she took off, with Camille and Dana trailing behind.

The noise level in this campground was even more intense than in Mulegé. Loud Mexican and American rock music played until well after midnight. It was far enough away that they couldn't sing along with it. It was close enough that they could hear the constant echo of the pounding bass and drums. Shortly after 4:00 a.m., a dozen roosters began to exercise their vocal cords in anticipation of the approaching sunrise. There weren't any peacocks.

The first glimmer of daylight found Barb and Dana dressed and on the malecón. Townspeople were lined up all along the jetty, loading up hooks with live bait and casting lines into the churning water. Feathery black fins rose from up out of the sea and danced across its surface as the bigger fish fed on the smaller ones. As the sky ever so slowly began to lighten, the horizon became edged with orange, gold, lavender and hot pink. Three fishermen hooked up simultaneously.

"¡Pescado! ¡Pescado!" they cried to anyone who would listen. Their poles bent nearly in half as the panicked fish fled to the south. They cranked for all they were worth. Minutes later there were three roosterfish thrashing in the throes of death on the malecón.

Barb walked up to the closest one and stooped down to take a look. It was nearly three feet long and elegantly striped in maroon and black on top. Its belly was opalescent—like mother of pearl. It had a huge comb on its head that would've made any bird jealous. "They're real fighters," Dana explained. "My dad used to love to catch 'em. They were his favorites, actually—second only to the mighty dorado—or mahi mahi to give you the more familiar Hawaiian name."

"Can you eat them?"

Dana shook her head. "I wouldn't. The meat is dark and strong-tasting. I'm sure these guys will, though. They're not into wasting." She laughed all of a sudden. "I wonder if they crow," she said.

Barb joined in. "I bet they do. I bet they rise up out of the water in the early mornings, just before breakfast time, open their mouths up really wide and crow at the top of their lungs to their brothers, those landlocked roosters who have no manners whatsoever."

They found a bench facing the ocean and sat down to watch the rest of the sunrise. The colors were peaking now. The lavender had intensified and deepened to a wild shade of purple. The hot pink had transformed itself to an intense, vibrant fuchsia. The gold had melted into a luminous shade of orange. Like a sunset in reverse, the sun slid up over the edge of the water and rose all at once—a huge red ball of fire in the sky.

A lone pelican sailed by on a smoothly curving current of air about 12 feet above sea level. Dana pointed to it. "Do you know what? In my next life, I want to come back as a pelican."

"Why? They're so funny-looking."

"I like that about them. They're a curious, unlikely mixture of clumsiness and grace. Like me. Watch," she said as another pelican took off from the rocks in front of them. "He takes off into the wind by kind of pushing with his feet. See? Then he pushes at the air few more times 'til he's up as high as he wants to be. He catches the current and rides it to his heart's content.

"I love watching pelicans," she continued as another eight of them flew by in V formation. They have the most amazing ability to locate those invisible airways. I've always wondered if they can actually *see* the air. They just hop on and cruise up and down, around corners. It's all so effortless, but can you just imagine how much fun it would be?! When they're hungry, they skim low over the waves, looking for food. When they see something that appeals to them, they zoom up. They zoom down. They dive bomb—kaboom! Look!" she exclaimed as two pelicans aimed themselves at the water and landed with splashes that exploded at least six feet into the air. "When they come up, if you look really carefully, you'll be able to tell if they got their fish."

"How?"

"There. Now. The one on the left. Watch his entire body shiver as he tosses his head back and flips that fish from his pouch into his mouth and sends it sliding on down his throat."

They watched in silence for a few minutes. "It seems like whenever I'm at the beach, the first pelican I spot is always a loner. I see it as my totem. The lone pelican. Like me, the lone woman. I keep hoping that one day I'll see a pair first and that'll be an omen that my nights of sleeping alone are soon to be over."

"Really?" asked Barbara. "You? Lonely? I've always seen it in Camille. That man hunger practically oozes out of her pores. But not you. Jeez, Dana you act like you have your life all together—two gorgeous daughters, a great job, plenty of friends...." She looked over at Dana and made a face. "I'm babbling, aren't I?"

Dana nodded, smiling. "It's okay. I envy your life too. The devoted architect husband of 15 years, the 9-to-5 career, the custom home he personally designed for you on the bluffs, plenty of free time and the discretionary income to enjoy it. Yeah. I hate you. I do. I'm forever going in 27 directions at once. Single moms are plate spinners. We're always living on the brink of insanity. We have to make time for everything and everybody but ourselves. This is the first time I've had a vacation without my kids since Brad left me."

"You've closed yourself off from men, haven't you?"

Dana looked at her and nodded. "Well, yeah. Like I said that night we danced like wild women—living with him destroyed something inside of me. He treated me badly, but for some bizarre reason, I was devastated when he left. I built a fortress around my heart 10 feet high. Being with Peter wounded me further. I have an outgoing personality and this mask of competence I put on. But I'm no less lonely—or man-hungry than Camille. She's just a lot more honest about it."

She stopped talking to watch another flock of pelicans fly by and launch an aerial attack on the bait fish churning around on the ocean's surface. Another roosterfish came flying out of the water on the end of a line and landed with a loud splat on the walkway only inches from her foot.

"Oh!" Dana exclaimed as the fisherman scooped up his catch, apologizing profusely. "Barb, I keep sensing some kind of sadness in you. Why didn't you have kids?"

Barb jerked as though she'd been struck hard across the face. Without warning, she was slapped backwards in time. Back to that night when she was a sophomore in college—the night she lost her virginity. The memories sped through her mind in a blinding flash. His name was Kevin and he was her first real boyfriend at the University of Southern Illinois. She'd been the last of her girlfriends to become initiated into sex, to make that mysterious and supposedly magical transition into womanhood. She'd known him about seven months.

They were in a house he shared with three other guys. A Rod Stewart album had just finished playing and someone replaced it with Big Brother and the Holding Company. Janis Joplin's raspy voice belted "Take Another Piece of My Heart" out of the monstrous speakers on either side of the fireplace. They sat on the floor with their backs pressed against the couch, kissing through two entire albums.

"Come on, Barbie." He kissed her again, his mouth stale and sour with the taste of too many joints, beers and cigarettes. "You're so beautiful. I want to see you naked. Let's go into my bedroom. Please...."

She swallowed her fear and drained her can of Miller. They floated down the hallway toward his room. He turned on a black light and pulled off her formerly white, now fluorescent, iridescent, pale blue sweater. Strains of The Who's "Tommy" drifted in through the locked door. Then they were rolling together across his single bed. "Mmmmm," he murmured as he locked his mouth onto hers, kissing and stroking her all over.

"Mmmmm," she murmured back. This was starting to feel nice. Movie frames of their future skipped across her mind. He loved her. She could tell. They'd get an apartment together, be married in three years—have a family. She sighed. Barbara Caldwell. How perfect it sounded! Five weeks later she found out she was pregnant.

Seated on a concrete bench on the malecón in Loreto, she related what she'd just seen in her mind to Dana. "I had an abortion. To this day I get this 'I want to die' feeling in my soul in early November, about the time my baby would have been born. Every year I try not to remember how old he or she would have been."

"It's almost November," Dana said.

Barb nodded. "I know. I'd forgotten. A few weeks after the abortion my doctor fitted me with an IUD. It seemed to be the ideal solution to avoiding another unwanted pregnancy. Except that it perforated my uterus and I had to have it removed in the ER less than a year later. Stupid me. I couldn't take the pill and I hated the diaphragm, so I waited six months and got another IUD. This one lasted two years before it did the same thing."

At that moment a tiny Indian woman carrying a wonderful-smelling tin pail came up to Dana and tapped her on the shoulder. "¿Tamales?" she asked.

Dana looked at Barb. "You hungry?" Barb nodded. *"Sí, señora—* Yes ma'am. *Muchas gracias—*Thanks very much. *¿Cuanto cuestan por cuatro—*How much does it cost for four?" The woman told her and she paid her 10 pesos for the four tamales. "Boy, I could do with a cup of coffee. I don't mean to interrupt your story, but what do you say we go hunt one up, along with some fresh fruit or something to go with these delicacies?"

They walked up the street, passed the mission and found an out-door cafe. They ordered coffee, fresh orange juice and a bowl of salsa for their tamales. Once everything arrived, Dana urged Barbara to continue.

"Right after I had the second one yanked out was when I went to Europe and met Bob."

"You met him in Europe? How romantic!"

Barb smiled. She did love her husband, more today than ever— even though he was over 700 miles away. "It was. Believe me. I finished my MBA in 1981 and my folks sent me to Europe for a year. I met Bob on the boat between Málaga in Spain and Tangiers in Morocco. It was friends at first sight, actually. The lovers part came a little later. We both had someone back home we were trying to be faithful to." She laughed. "We traveled together for three months before we realized we were hopelessly in love. We got married the following September and I moved to San Diego with him.

"Right after that I started trying to get pregnant. Being an only child, I wanted lots of kids. We both did." She stopped and took a bite of her tamale. It was a dense, moist cornmeal pastry filled with spiced beef, tomatoes, onions and olives. It was delicious.

"What happened?"

"I had pelvic inflammatory disease. PID. I got it from the IUDs. Ever heard of it?"

Dana nodded.

"Basically it caused scar tissue to build up in and around my uterus and fallopian tubes. I ended up having two surgeries to try to clear my tubes, but neither worked. I ended up with a textbook case of endometriosis and finally, when I was 31, I had to have a hysterecto-my."

Dana reached for her hand. "Oh God. I'm so sorry."

Barb's eyes were wet. She could feel the tears threatening to come and she willed them to stay away. For now. "We tried to adopt after that. We contacted an attorney who specialized in private adoptions.

After a long wait, he found us just the right pregnant girl. We went through an extensive interview process with her and she decided we were the ones she wanted to have raise her baby. She was 17 and so pretty. I got really close to her during the pregnancy. We paid all her medical expenses. Bob and I were with her during the delivery. Her family wouldn't come. But, as she was going through the final stages of pushing, the baby's dad showed up."

Barb stopped for a sip of coffee. She looked at Dana. This time a tear escaped from her eye. It wound its way down her cheek and dropped onto the remnants of her tamale. "It was a boy. When we were leaving the house to go bring the baby home from the hospital we got a call from the lawyer. She'd changed her mind and decided to keep her baby."

"She could do that?!" asked Dana.

"Oh yes she could. And she did. We were gonna name him Daniel. We had his room ready. His clothes. His car seat—everything." She dabbed at her eyes with her napkin.

"It's weird. I hardly ever think of it anymore. Bob and I—well—we nearly lost it that year. It took a lot of therapy and a whole lot of love, understanding and forgiveness on both of our parts to get through that. We made our peace with it though. We did. Our marriage is stronger and I know we're both better people for it too. We each donate a day or two a month to Voices for Children. We're advocates who lobby in Juvenile Court on behalf of kids who've fallen through the cracks or who are lost in the maze of foster care. We have our three doggies. I'm on the board of the San Diego Humane Society too."

"Good God in heaven. You are an angel. Do you know that?"

Barb laughed so hard at that one that she choked on her orange juice and spit it across the table. Dana raised her napkin in a lightning flash and caught the majority of the spray in it. She wiped the rest of it off her face. "¡Olé! ¡Toro! ¡Toro!" she called out, laughing uncontrollably too as she played bullfighter with her soggy napkin. They laughed until they were snorting. Tears rolled down their cheeks.

Barb got up, went to the counter and returned with a stack of napkins. She plopped them down in the middle of the table. "Here. Blow your nose," she said to Dana. Dana leaned forward in her chair and reached for a napkin just as an enormous gust of wind blew through the cafe. It lifted the napkins off the table and scattered them throughout the restaurant and out onto the sidewalk. Dana and Barb jumped up out of their chairs and chased them as they flew down the side street, onto the main street of town and off towards the mission.

"Hey! Slow down! Come back here!" Dana yelled as she ran,

grabbing up napkins as fast as she could.

"What's with this wind all of a sudden?" Barb asked as she ran alongside.

"I don't know. It comes up like this sometimes."

A dust devil whirled by them, lifting pieces of trash right out of the trash can at the side of the plaza and sending them swirling through the air. Barb's mouth and eyes filled with sand. She wiped at her eyes and spit into a napkin. "Damn! This is awful! Will it stop?"

Dana squinted, shrugged and turned towards the east as she scooped up the last of the napkins and wiped at her own eyes. "I'm not sure. Let's go back down to the malecón and check things out. We can ask one or two of the fisherman what they think. That should give us some kind of idea of what's going on here." They began to walk towards the water. "I definitely don't want to stay here today if it's *this* windy."

"Me neither. Knowing Holly, she'll probably want to go wind-surfing."

"No," Dana said, ducking her head to protect herself from the blowing sand and debris. "This wind is too intense for windsurfing. It's too intense for *anything!*"

"This is awful! Let's just forget the fishermen and head back to camp." Barb peeked out from between her pinched-together eyelids. Holly and Camille were running up the malecón towards them, shouting and gesturing. "Hey, Dana," she said, pointing, "I don't think we need to worry about convincing Holly to leave. Here she comes to get *us....*"

CHAPTER TWENTY   **Ciudad Constitución to La Paz,**
                           Baja California Sur
                           October 29, 1997

Within an hour they were on the road again, even though the wind had stopped as abruptly as it had started. The road paralleled the ocean until the southern tip of Isla de Carmen disappeared. Then the highway turned to the west and wound up into the moutains and onto a flat plane, where it turned again to the south. Dana drove across the spine of the peninsula.

"Exactly how far south have you driven?" Holly asked Dana.

"Oh. Concepción," she said. "I've been in virgin territory ever since then. Why do we have to go all the way to the Pacific today? Why doesn't the road just go straight on down the Sea of Cortez side?"

"Because Mex 1 was built for commerce," Holly explained. "Not tourism. We're almost to Ciudad Insurgentes and Ciudad Constitución. The population of the two cities is over 50,000, which makes it the second-largest population center in Baja California Sur. It's a major agricultural region. Look," she pointed as the fields of corn began to appear on both sides of the highway.

"What do they grow here?" Barb asked from the back.

She looked in one of her guidebooks. "Wheat, garbanzos, cotton, sorghum, alfalfa and citrus for the most part. They raise cattle too. Most of what's produced is shipped to mainland Mexico from the port of San Carlos, 36 miles to the west of here on Magdalena Bay."

"But this is *desert,*" Camille said. "Where do they get the water to irrigate?"

"Artesian wells. There's tons of water under the surface."

"We need ice, remember?" Barb called out as they turned left at Ciudad Insurgentes and drove down a wide boulevard into Constitución. "And gas too."

There were four lanes here, instead of the two they were used to. Concrete dividers separated the lanes. Varying-sized palms had been planted at regular intervals in the dividers. The bottom five or six feet of their trunks had been painted white. Holly pulled into a partly remodeled Pemex station. "We're gonna be dry camping for the next few days, so anyone who has to use the restroom should go here. It may be a little iffy, though."

The other three got out while Holly made sure the attendant rolled the pump back to zero. She hated being ripped off. A few years back she'd caught a young assistant filling her gas tank—at this very station—without clearing the previous customer's charges. She'd ended up paying nearly double. Never again. Two minutes later Camille and Barb walked up to her, arms swinging, as she stood stretching in the shade of the Pemex overhang. They looked upset, to say the least.

"God bless Mexico," Camille said. "That is *the* most disgusting bathroom I've ever seen. It looks like someone just backed their butt up to the toilet and let her rip! There's piss and shit everywhere—and flies. Plus there's cockroaches on the wall and ceiling! Dana's tough. She said we should just tough it out and ignore them! Right! She's in there *singing* to the damned cockroaches. Singing! I swear to God on a stack of Bibles. She's out of her fucking mind! There's *no way* I can take a pee in there!"

"Neither can I," said Barb.

Holly shook her head. These two were trying her patience more every day. "Oh-kay," she drawled. "Use the toilet in here. You're the ones who dump the holding tank. I don't care...."

Dana came back as Holly was paying. She was laughing. "I wigged 'em out big time, Hol," she said. "Let me tell you. When I started singing, everyone bolted. Camille and Barb first. Then the roaches scurried off like I'd sprayed 'em with Raid or something. I couldn't scare the flies away, but I sure did a number on those nasty little cucarachas!"

"Help me guide this thing over there." Holly pointed to a building across way that had the word, *Hielo Purificada*—Purified Ice imprinted in huge letters across its front. "I need your help." The two women got into the motor home and maneuvered it across the four lanes of traffic.

They got out and went into the ice house. A middle-aged man

with a huge paunch got up from behind the counter. A black and white TV set with a fuzzy picture blared at them from the corner. A boy of four or five came out and asked them if they wanted to buy gum.

Holly ordered a block and two bags of ice. *"¿Tiene una copita de tequila, señorita*—Do you have a little cup of tequila, lady?" the fat man asked her.

"Sí, cómo no—Sure, why not," she answered. "Dana, go get him a plastic cup with a little tequila in it, will you?"

Dana returned a minute later with the cup. She handed it to the man. He took a long sip, grimaced, wiped his face with the back of his hand and rubbed his belly, smiling broadly. *"Ah, Mi Panza. ¡Qué sabroso! Gracias*—Oh, my Panza. How delicious! Thank you," he said.

"Papá, Papá, quiero probarlo—Papa, Papa, I want to try it," the little boy begged. His father handed the cup to him and he took a sip. "Mmmm." he grinned a toothless grin up at Holly and Dana and rubbed his tummy. *"Ah, Mi Panza. Muy sabroso,"* he said, mimicking his dad.

"It's a long straight stretch from here 'til we start to descend into La Paz," Holly explained when they were back on the road again. "If you see a good place to stop for lunch in the next hour or so, just pull of the road, okay?"

Dana nodded. "How far from Loreto to La Paz?"

"Two hundred and twenty-three miles. Once we get there I want to stop at CCC. That's the most shopped-at place in all of Southern Baja. It's so huge it makes Calimax look like a mini mercado. From there we'll drive along the malecón and head out toward Pichilingue, Puerto Balandra and Playa Tecolote."

"Would you repeat that?" Camille asked.

She did. "Those names are all blasts from my distant past," said Dana. "La Paz was the first place my dad took us when we were kids. Did I ever tell you that David and I had our picture taken with John Wayne in the La Paz airport when I was eight or nine?"

Holly looked over at Dana. Anger flared up inside her and she had to struggle to keep from blasting her sideways with a cutting remark. She was sick to death of listening to her brag about her exploits in Baja as a kid. She wondered, for probably the fiftieth time, whether she was gonna be able to make it through this trip. They still had another 13 days to spend together and already she'd been taxed to the end of her patience and beyond. The things they talked about! The things they complained about! Dana—who she'd hoped would make the trip bearable for her—had gotten to be even more annoying than the others.

Holly bit down on her frustration and smiled. "Wow," she said. "That's cool. Look, there's the Pacific Ocean. Hey, you guys," she called toward the back of the RV, "keep a lookout for the Sea of Cortez, will you? There's a point up ahead where we should be able to see both oceans at once." She glanced at the map. "Of course, that won't be for awhile, so disregard that remark for now." She tapped Dana on the shoulder. "Up ahead. By those crosses. That looks like a good place for lunch."

Dana pulled off the road and parked, remarking that the vegetation was noticeably greener now. The rains in Southern Baja came in late summer and early fall, she explained to Barb and Camille.

Ignoring them, Holly wandered over to look at the road crosses. There were two of them about two feet high, planted side by side in a pile of rocks. On each cross hung a perfectly scaled model of Jesus Christ. Above the twin heads were halos that looked like rising suns. Above them were pieces of paper that read, "INRI." She knelt down. A black and white photograph of a smiling couple beamed up at her. A wedding photograph probably. She tried to reconstruct their lives and deaths in her mind. Obviously, since the crosses were on the west side of the road, they'd been killed here, near this spot while driving between Ciudad Constitución and La Paz. A head-on probably, with a truck that blew a tire and swerved out of control. Or maybe they'd been trying to pass a motor home like theirs and gotten sandwiched between it and another vehicle....

She looked closer at the photo and guessed them to be in their early twenties. She wondered how long they'd been married and if they'd had kids. A sadness welled up from within her. "Life can be so cruel and unfair," she mumbled out loud. She straightened up and walked back to the motor home. "How long 'til lunch?" she called. Dana was inside making quesadillas and fruit salad. "Where'd Barb and Camille go?" Holly asked.

"They wanted to explore a little. They're stunned by the greenery all of a sudden. And the wildflowers. They wanted to take pictures." Just then they both turned as they heard squealing and bellowing laughter in the distance. They went outside to look.

Not too far away they saw Barb and Camille prancing through the undergrowth. They were both singing at the top of their lungs. Dana laughed out loud. "They're copying me. I sang to the roaches. Look at them!" She pointed. "Do you see what I see?"

Holly nodded.

"They're singing to caterpillars!" Dana ran off toward the others and Holly followed, slowly. Sure enough, there were three-inch to four-inch-long fat black caterpillars all over the place. Hundreds of them. Their front and rear ends were bright orange and they were speckled all over with orange dots. It was the weirdest thing she'd ever seen. When they heard the singing, they reared up on their tails and waved their bodies in time with the music. She watched them for a while, then turned and went back to the motor home. It was hot and she was anxious to get to La Paz.

Before they knew it, the road began a rapid descent toward the city and bay of La Paz. Holly heard a series of gasps as Dana, Camille and Barb each caught their first glimpse of what was, in her opinion, the most magical, unspoiled city on the peninsula. "It reminds me of the entry into Ensenada," Camille said.

"No way," said Dana. "This is much prettier. Look how dramatic the mountains are against the aquamarine of the gulf. This time of year is the *best*. I always came here in the springtime. It was the dry season then. It's luscious-looking now. A tropical desert. I feel like I'm on a south sea island. This place just oozes history! It's been frequented by Spanish galleons and pirates. Nowadays, if what I've heard is true, beautiful, sophisticated, long-legged señoritas dance in high heels at sidewalk cafes into the wee hours of the morning. This place is as exotic and European as I imagine Río to be. Or Buenos Aires. Watch out, ladies. It gets under your skin. Once you've been to La Paz, you will never be the same."

"Out here? In this bay? Galleons? Pirates? Sir Francis Drake and all that?" asked Barb.

Dana nodded.

"What a trippy place," Camille said.

"You betcha," Dana agreed. "La Paz is a trippy place, all right. There's no doubt about it. Its name means 'the peace.' But its history has not been peaceful. I was reading up on it last night. It was founded in 1535 by Hernán Cortez, but the Spaniards weren't successful in making it a permanent colony until 1811. It was a notorious pirate haven back in the early days. Its rich oyster beds lured fortune seekers and of course, the pirates weren't far behind. The Spanish galleons, en route from Manila to Málaga, would stop in at La Paz for water and supplies. We all studied Sir Frances Drake in school. Well, he hung out here. From what I understood, the smaller pirate ships attacked the galleons when the Coromuel winds blew from the north into La Paz Bay. They'd sail in with the wind and catch 'em off guard. The galleons were too big and too clumsy to escape. At night the winds would reverse and the pirates would sneak off to their hiding places, aided by the friendly south wind!"

"I can just see it now," Barb said from behind Dana.

"The city's nickname is the *Puerto del Illusión*—Port of Illusion. My dad always said it was called that because when you enter the port by sea, you have to go *behind* the breakers. It looks like you're gonna run aground until you get into the channel." She sighed. "And then there are the sunsets. Wait 'til you see the sunsets. They're unbelievable. The city faces west, so we'll see the sun go down over the mountains. It's worth writing home about!"

"Don't forget to tell them about the war," said Holly.

"Oh yeah. The Mexican-American War. Our navy blockaded the harbor and our troops occupied La Paz from 1845 to 1847. You can be sure that plenty of battles were fought in the streets. You want to know the trippiest thing of all, ladies?"

"Lay it on us," said Camille.

"When the war ended, the good old U.S.A. ended up winning Baja, along with a sizeable chunk of mainland Mexico."

"What?! What happened?!"

"What happened is we gave it back. We gringos figured it was worthless real estate."

"No way!" called out Barb, echoed by Camille.

Holly interrupted. "Remember that song about how they paved paradise and put up a parking lot?" Everyone nodded. "Well, that's what would've happened if we'd hung onto Baja. I, for one, am infinitely grateful that we gringos were too blind to see the value in this peninsula." She turned her head and looked at Dana. "That was a first-rate history lesson. I want to add a couple things though."

"Por favor."

"First interesting tidbit of trivia. La Paz has flourished as a seaport, a state capital and an agricultural community. I read recently that it has the highest standard of living in all of Mexico."

"I'll buy that," said Camille. "It's beautiful. Clean. Definitely prosperous-looking. How many people live here?"

"I've heard conflicting reports. Some sources say 250,000. Others say 175,000. Either way—it's a booming metropolis that does not rely on gringo dollars. It hasn't lost touch with its colonial roots and you'll notice, I think, that it has an understated elegance that feels more European than Mexican. It reminds Dana of Río. It reminds me of New Orleans. I'm not sure why. It's partly the pirate heritage, I think. But La Paz puts on an amazing Carnaval at the same time Mardi Gras is going on in New Orleans."

"Like Dana said, the people here are attractive, well-dressed and they hang out at the outdoor cafes all along the waterfront in the evenings. They go out late though. Much later than we're used to going out. So I'd suggest taking a nap or preparing yourselves for a long night tonight."

Barb clapped. "My God. I *like* this place. It's a real city. Look!" She pointed. A grocery store. CCC. Bigger than the Calimax even. "Are we going there?"

"You bet we are," said Holly. "Pull in," she instructed Dana.

Later, after they'd shopped, Holly took the wheel. She drove along the waterfront malecón that led them through town and out past the harbor, ferry landing and the buildings and beach of Pichilingue. The city receded from view as they followed the road as it wound north along alternately developed and pristine stretches of coastline. "I want to camp at either Puerto Balandra or Tecolote Beach tonight," Holly announced from the driver's seat.

"Can we go back into town?"

"Some friends of mine are supposed to be camped at one of those beaches. I'm hoping to find them today. Keep your eyes peeled for a silver Airstream trailer with one of those Ford Expeditions. It's dark green, I think. If we find them they'll be able to drive us into town and we won't have to keep making and breaking camp while we're here.

"It's remote out here," said Dana, sighing as they came upon an estuary populated only by birds, plants and sea life. "This is where my dad would take us fishing. There was no road out here in those days. The only way to get to these beaches was by boat. He conned me and my mom into going fishing with him and David by taking us to a new beach every day. They were all deserted back then. Just shells, shells and more shells. We must've collected hundreds every day. We'd stop and have a picnic and hunt for shells. Then we'd snorkel out through the green water to where the reefs are." She pointed. "See, out there."

Camille came forward and sat between the front seats. "What's that uninhabited island you told me about with the dozen beaches?"

Dana looked back at her with misty eyes. *Isla Espiritú Santo*—Holy Spirit Island. My dad made a point of taking us to every single west-facing beach on that island."

"Hey!" Barb called out. "There's a silver trailer on that beach with a big green sport utility vehicle next to it. Is that your friends, Holly?"

Holly couldn't look. She was rounding a precarious curve and her eyes were glued to the road. She turned off the highway and onto the side road to Puerto Balandra. "Let me see," she said. Pulling into the parking lot, she saw the rig. "It's them all right." Thank God the beach wasn't crowded. She maneuvered Boris into a spot close to them, next to some tent campers driving a maroon Toyota pickup with a camper shell. She parked behind a palapa, got out and ran over to the Airstream.

Three middle-aged men and a woman came from around the other side. The couple hugged Holly. She brought them all over and introduced them around.

"Larry and Bev, this is Dana, Camille, Barb," she said. "And these are their buddies, Jim and Doug. Let's make camp."

They now had the use of four kayaks, two of which were doubles. Six of them paddled out through the shallow pale green water of the bay, around the rocky point and out into the clear waters of La Paz Bay. Holly could hardly wait to tell the story of the rock at La Balandra. She heard Dana's rapid intake of breath behind her as she saw the extraordinary formation for the first time. A giant spiral of volcanic rock, it rose up out of the sea on a thin neck the size of a man's thigh and spread to a mushroom-shaped crown over eight feet high and seven feet in diameter.

"The most amazing thing about La Balandra," Holly said, "is that it was vandalized a few years back. Once the road was paved, people came out here to picnic and party. Somehow, somebody snapped it at its most slender spot and shoved it into the water. Recently, some engineers got together and brought a crane out here to hoist it back up again. How they managed to fasten it back on its perch, I have no idea, but I'm so glad it's back where it belongs—hovering happily above the bay."

The boat tipped sharply to the left as Dana slipped overboard. She swam underwater toward the mushroom. Surfacing next to it, she pulled herself up onto the lower section of rock and draped herself across it. She leaned forward and rested her head on her arms. Her legs were submerged. Holly squinted into the sun. With her wet hair flowing down her back and her shimmering green swimsuit, Dana was a mermaid at rest on La Balandra.

"You paddle back without me," she called to Holly. "I want to hang out here for a while and soak up the view. I'll swim back in."

"Want your mask?" Holly asked as she moved in closer to Dana. When Dana answered affirmatively, she handed off a mask and snorkel and paddled back toward the beach.

After saltwater baths, the eight of them snacked and got ready to go into La Paz. Just before sunset, they piled into Larry's Expedition and drove back to town. They stopped at the marina and watched the sunset. The sky had a savage look to it—the kind of look that foretold of a storm brewing. The air was noticeably cooler. Tall thunderheads rose in columns above the bay, multiplying as they grew closer and closer together. Their colors changed from purple and white to flaming orange and magenta as the leftover light of the sun played its evening games.

Then it was off to do the town. Larry parked on a side street near the Hotel Los Arcos. The group got out and walked the malecón in the fading light. The clouds gathered strength and darkened to a near black against the sky. The street lights came on, illuminating everything in a ghostly off-white light. Pangas of every color bobbed at anchor in the shallow water, while further out, they could see yachts, commercial crafts and Mexican Navy frigates. Whole flocks of pelicans splashed down in unison as they dove for their nightly meal. The air show they put on exceeded anything they'd seen thus far on the trip. Children played on the sandy beach that separated the walkway and the water.

The sidewalk cafes on the other side of the street were beginning to fill up with smartly attired Mexican women in high heels and their equally well-dressed men. The darker it got, the more people materialized. Music began to play. In one alleyway there was a bazaar with dancers, singers and a craft fair. They browsed a while.

"Let's eat here," Larry suggested as they stopped at an open air restaurant with a sign above it that read Bacho's. Under the name were these words: *"Zona Dorado por el sol. Cerrado en caso de huracán o chubasco*—Dorado in the sun zone. Closed in case of hurricane or chubasco."

"What's it say?" Barb asked Holly. She translated.

"Are we having a chubasco?"

The wind had picked up. There was no doubt about it. Holly laughed. "I doubt it. But I would put some serious dinero on there being a storm tonight. It should be fun."

They sat down and ordered a round of jumbo Margaritas. Barb and Dana ordered Bajaburgers. Holly ordered Tacos Bacho's, corn tortillas stuffed with shrimp and garnished with bacon and cheese. Camille and the three guys ordered Mexican combo plates. Bev hit pay dirt with the Poblano Tacos: carne asada, cheese, *rajas*—cooked chile strips and grilled onions. They ordered another round of drinks, and then another. Their waiters, handsome young guys named Sergio and Luis, couldn't stay away from the party.

Sergio was coming onto Holly. She knew it and she liked it. No one but her neighbors back in Mulegé were aware of this, but since the fiasco at the Chili Cook-Off, she and Rick had done precious little but fight the rest of the time they were together. It was obvious that Rick resented her success because he'd made way too many sarcastic, nasty remarks about her "big, important literary career." She didn't get it. Why did he have to be so *competitive* with her all of a sudden? They'd been perfectly happy living parallel lives. Why would he choose now to complain and insinuate that he wanted her to *stay home?!* Puh-lease! She hadn't stayed home in nearly 30 years and she wasn't about to start now!

The tunes cranked up. American Oldies. "Little Red Riding Hood," followed by "Wild Thing" and suddenly she was on her feet being whirled around and in between tables by Sergio. They danced through "Blue Suede Shoes" and "Surfin' USA." Then "Unchained Melody" came on. Larry and Bev were slow-dancing next to them. So were Jim and Camille and Dana and Doug. Barb was dancing with— of all people—that delectable-looking young hunk, Luís. Holly closed her eyes and eased into Sergio's embrace. He pulled her closer and began to spin again. She loved this song. The centrifugal force of their non-stop whirling and twirling motion welded her body to his and she felt in herself a rising excitement that exceeded anything she'd felt with Rick in a long time.

Just then the skies flashed pink and white with lightning. A long, low rumble of thunder followed. The clouds opened wide and it began to pour. She threw back her head and laughed, loving the feel of the rain against her skin. The music changed to "Rock Around the Clock." Holly took off her shoes and tossed them under her chair. She drained her drink. Sergio was back at work, cleaning the dishes off their table. She leaned over and gave him a lingering kiss on the mouth. Then she turned, grabbed Doug's hand and spun off with him. Her hair was soaked. Her dress clung to her body and she knew it revealed every curve of her 46-year-old body. Wishing for half a second that she was 20 years younger, she held in her stomach, raised her arms above her head and gave herself over to the dance.

CHAPTER TWENTY-ONE

**La Paz to Los Barriles,
Baja California Sur
October 30, 1997**

"What time did she come in last night?" Camille asked Dana as they walked along the shoreline, sipping coffee.

Dana shrugged. "Somewhere close to dawn, I think. You know what bugged me?"

Camille nodded. She sure enough did. It was payback time. Holly had purposefully paid Dana back for stealing Rick's attention that day in Mulegé. She'd swooped in on Doug the second she'd noticed his interest in Dana. She'd challenged the group to a tequila drinking contest. Only Doug lasted through four shots with her. When the storm ended and everyone else wanted to go home, Holly convinced him to stay out and party with her at La Paz Lapa's—the only bona fide tourist bar on the malecón. "She's a loose cannon, that Holly," Camille said. "The way she was kissing him on the dance floor, right after she'd hung that lipper on Sergio. Man, she makes me feel like a born-again virgin. Me!"

Dana made a face. "I liked him. He was fun. Not hard on the eyes, either. He's the first guy I've felt like flirting with in a long, long time. But he and Jim are heading back up north to Vancouver—where they're from—today, so it's probably for the best that Holly shoved me out of harm's way and snagged him for herself. I'm not looking for a one-night stand anyway."

"She's married...."

Dana picked up a pebble and skipped it across the water. "No duh. But you'd never know by watching her. I'd hazard a guess that she and Rick didn't quite make up after all. So," she shot Camille a hard look, "do you consider yourself married anymore, girlfriend?"

Camille looked Dana square in the face, crossed her eyes, faked a trip and fell sideways into the water. Her coffee cup went flying. She came up laughing and dripping and knelt in the water. "No!" she screamed to the heavens. "No! Would the real Camille Fleming please rise up from the depths of the sea and show the world that she can do it alone?! I am brilliant, world! Do you hear me?! I need no man to confine and define me! I am finished hiding behind a husband! *It's my turn to shine!"*

She jumped up, grabbed Dana by the hands and swung her around in the knee-deep water. "I got songs inside of me that are just beggin' to be sung, world!" she yelled. "Everywhere I go I hear music in my head. My notebook is full of new songs. *I need a piano!"* She swung Dana out as far as she could and then let go of her hands. She laughed 'til her sides ached as her friend fell ass first into the sea. Dana got up and, using her hands as a second set of legs, back-walked, crab style through the shallow surf.

Camille turned to see Barb, Bev, Larry, Jim and Doug lined up next to the Airstream, watching them. She fell to her knees, raised her arms and began to sing at the top of her lungs:

I heard the words you said,
they later jumble in my head
until I know you haven't changed.
I guess I'll have to rearrange my life
to suit myself....[2]

She bowed as they applauded. "Thank you ladies and gentlemen," she said in her deejay voice as she spoke into an imaginary mike. "This song is a Cinnamon Girl original, sung for you today by the artist herself. It's called 'Tall Tales' and it celebrates my impending freedom from my imperious soon-to-be-ex-husband, Drew. We're broadcasting live today from La Paz, BCS, known by many as the Port of Illusion. I for one, want to tell you that I'm sick to death of illusions. My eyes have been opened. I see clearly now and I am ready to stand up tall for the truth I see."

She raised her eyebrow and motioned to Dana with her eyes. The two got up, took each other's hands and skipped together back up the beach to their campsite.

Barb motioned them aside. "Nice show," she said. "Larry and Bev are heading to Todos Santos today. The guys are leaving too. Holly's hung over again. She says she'd planned to have us spend tonight at Tecolote Beach, but if we're game, she'd rather just head down to Los Barriles as soon as possible. What do you think, Dana? It's your stepmom's house we'll be staying at. I think it should be your call."

Dana pointed to the beach. "Let's go for a little walk," she said. They followed her down to the water's edge and sat down in the sand. No one spoke for a while. Camille watched Dana as she drew pictures in the sand. "I think I vote for Los Barriles," she finally said. "You have to do another call-in tomorrow, Camille. It'll be easier from there. I don't think there are any phones at Tecolote. I was hoping to take a boat out to see the sea lion colony at the north end of Espiritú Santo, but we can do all kinds of exploring in the Yellow Bird, my dad's panga. I wanted to eat at the Palapa Azul. It's the coolest restaurant—built around and in an old fishing boat, and it's right on the beach too. It has the best and freshest seafood there. But, hey." She looked up. "We have to drive all the way back to San Diego, right?" The other two nodded. "Well, we can stay at Tecolote on the way north. What do you say?"

"Sounds okay to me," Barb said. Camille nodded in agreement.

"Anyway," Dana went on, "We'll have quads to ride in Los Barriles. Showers. Separate bedrooms! I've been sorta kinda weirded out about going back there, especially since tomorrow's Halloween and right after that is *Día de los Muertos*—Day of the Dead. But, hey, what a better place to spend *that* most Mexican of holidays than at my dad's house...."

"What's Day of the Dead?" asked Barb.

"It's an ancient Indian celebration that somehow survived the Catholic invasion from Spain. My dad taught me about it. He loved it. The Indians believe that the souls of the dead return every year to visit their living relatives. They come back to party—to eat, drink and be merry just as though they were still alive. The *angelitos*—little angels [children] who died are honored on November first, All Saints Day. The Mexicans put toys, balloons and candies around their graves. The next day, All Souls Day, is the day the adults are remembered. Their graves are decorated with the food and drink they loved most, along with some of their treasured possessions. Of course there are tons of flowers, especially marigolds, which are supposed to help guide the spirits back to earth to visit their loved ones."

"How bizarre," Camille said.

"Oh. There's more. The people throw huge fiestas in the grave-yards. They decorate with piñatas in the shapes of skeletons and skulls. They put on these spreads of incredible food. For dessert they eat skull-shaped candies and cookies. All the women make *pan de muerto*—that's death bread, ladies. In reality it's coffee cake with white frosting that looks like bones. Didn't you see those cookies in the bakeries back in San Ignacio and Santa Rosalía?"

"Now that you mention it, yeah. I saw 'em. I thought they were for Halloween," said Camille.

Dana began drawing in the sand again. "Nope."

"What's the underlying point of it all? asked Barb.

Dana chuckled. "Good question. My dad said it's 'cause the Mexicans believe in the circle of life—we're born, we die, we move on to another plane of existence. They laugh in the face of death and remember their departed loved ones with joy. They're very different from us Norteamericanos, who hate death and go to great lengths to cheat it. The Mexicans are more philosophical. They see it as an inte-gral part of life. They miss their loved ones, so they invite them back to Earth every year and throw them a big fiesta. I think it's very cool."

"Do you think he'll come back for the holiday?"

"My dad?" She smiled. "Of course he will."

"But you scattered his ashes. How will we honor him if we can't do the graveyard gig?" asked Camille.

"We can take his boat out to where we scattered his ashes. It's out by Cabo Pulmo. It's a long boat ride, but I wanted to go there anyway. I figure that Jorge and María Pilar—they're Dad's and Ellen's helpers and close friends—will help us figure out a way to do proper honor to my daddy."

"You're right, Dana," said Barb. "This is a very cool holiday...."

Dana drove south and east out of La Paz and through the foothills of La Sierra de la Laguna. It had been an unusually wet year. The cardón cacti looked like they were about to burst after gorging them-selves on the abundant rain water. The red California bougainvillaea Dana remembered from her trip down in August were still blooming even more profusely than then—if that was possible. Everything was overwhelmingly green. Vines and bushes flaunting red, white, yellow, purple and pink flowers wove themselves in between the cardóns and

and decorated the giants with their luxurious blossoms. Every vado was a running brook. Dana had never seen these hillsides so beautiful.

The motor home emerged from the mountainous terrain at Los Barriles. Dana turned left just past the Pemex station and headed down a sandy road toward the beach. She felt a lump rising up in her throat as she saw the rooftops of the familiar homes of her dad and Ellen's neighbors. As the house came into view, she found her heart racing in anticipation. She envisioned herself rounding the corner and turning onto his street. The open garage door would reveal him inside, tinkering at his workbench.

It didn't happen of course. The garage door was closed and all the windows were shuttered tight. It was the first time she'd seen her dad's house closed up. She pulled Boris into the driveway, searched in her purse for the key and found it. She walked to the front door, unlocked it and walked inside. She inhaled deeply, searching for a lingering hint of her dad's scent inside. All she got was a musty, mildewy smell. She walked mechanically from door to window to window, pulling back the wooden shutters and opening everything up to the clean, salty breeze.

"Oh Dana," Camille said from behind her. "This place is spectacular. I can't believe we get to really stay here, instead of camping out in the driveway and using the patio!"

"Come out here," Dana said as she slid the floor-to-ceiling shutters out of the way and opened the French doors wide. The patio ended on a white sand beach. The Sea of Cortez spread out before them in varying shades of green and blue and decorated with flashing diamonds as the breeze and the midday sun frolicked together across its surface.

"I could stay here *forever.*" Barb said.

"Let's bring the patio furniture out and we can check the fridge and see what Ellen left us. I'd bet anything there's good supply of Diet Cokes and Pacificos."

They unpacked their essentials and put Holly to bed in the back bedroom. She'd slept all the way from La Paz and her condition showed no sign of improving anytime soon. "I'm going to look for Jorge and María Pilar," Dana announced. "Boris has been making a weird rattle the last coupla days. I want Jorge to give him the old once-over. I don't see the Yellow Bird out front. They weren't expecting us 'til tomorrow, but I feel a great need to take that boat out on the water. ASAP. Anyone wanna come with me?"

"Ten-four, Eleanor," Camille said.

"I hate to be a wimp," Barb added, "but last night took a toll on me too. I need a nap."

They came back a few minutes later and found Barb dozing on the front patio. They sat down. "Jorge'll be over in a while to check out the motor home," Dana said. "He's having some work done on the boat's motor and will bring it by first thing *en la mañana*—in the morning."

"You sure about that? What was it you told us about the mañana syndrome, Dana?" Barb asked, yawning.

Camille beat Dana to a response. "Mañana doesn't mean *tomorrow* at all to a Mexican. What does it mean, ladies?"

Barb answered. "It means *not today!*"

Dana shook her head. "Yeah, yeah, yeah. Well. Jorge's a little different than most. He knows time is of the essence with us. He'll be here. Besides, he wants to take us snorkeling at Cabo Pulmo tomorrow. It's been recently designated as a national marine park and there's all kinds of controversy going on with it."

"Controversy? In a marine park? Like underwater? How come?" Camille asked, sitting up straight.

Dana got up and paced. "I dunno. Every time I come down here I kick myself for not ever taking the time to get certified. The reef at Cabo Pulmo—about an hour and a half to two hour panga ride from here—is the biggest living coral reef on the west coast of North America. Most of it's about 40 to 45 feet down, so there isn't much we can see without tanks. But a few of the fingers reach all the way to the shallow water and we can snorkel there."

"I wish we could go now," said Camille.

"Nope. Mañana. We're a day early, remember? I'm gonna go over to Tío's and see if I can't sit in on Ellen's daily mah-jongg game. That way I'll have the skinny on everything that's going on in the entire East Cape region within the hour. Make yourselves at home. As they say in these parts, *Mi casa es su casa*—My house is your house."

"Could you show us how to work the four-wheelers before you go, Dana?" Barb asked. "I would *love* to take a drive down the beach. Wouldn't you, Camille?"

Camille jumped to her feet. "You bet I would."

Dana led them out to the garage where she gave them a 15-minute lesson on how to start the quads, shift gears and balance their bodies when they turned in the soft sand. She showed them where to keep their feet so they wouldn't be burned by the exhaust pipes. Then she watched them for a few more minutes as they roared up and down the beach—tentatively at first—and then with increasing confidence and enthusiasm. Grinning, she skipped off down the road.

The new moon hung like a silver sliver in the southern Baja sky. There were as many stars as Dana ever remembered seeing. She, Barb and Camille sat on the patio, watching the pangas and larger cruisers bob quietly at anchor.

"I really did love your performance this morning, by the way," Barb said. "Did you just make that song up on the spot or what?"

Camille chuckled. "Yup. I already had the title in mind, but I went berserk and the words, the music—they exploded out of me. I've been working on the rest of the song in my head ever since. It was my own insecurity that led me to unhealthy men. Enslaved me to 'em."

"Ah ha," said Barb.

"Ah-ha yourself. Take a look at my most recent marriage. I put my music on hold and played with Drew. We played *his* songs—not mine. I bought into his belief system and twisted myself into a Christian pretzel to please him. I've always lost myself in men. Hooked into their dreams to avoid the risk of living my own. Yet, my rebellious nature would always kick in and save me. Without fail, I'd do something dramatic to sabotage the relationship—and thus save myself from vanishing into nothingness." She got up and bowed. "Ladies. Reality slapped me upside the head yesterday. I see Drew's tall tales for what they are. I'm ready to live my own life now. Somehow I think I may be more likely to die *with* a man than *without* one at this point!"

"But how are you gonna live without sex?" Dana asked her. "You've spent the last year telling me you can't bear the thought of going without it...."

Camille laughed and reached for a cigarette. She lit it and inhaled deeply. Blew out the smoke. "Damn. I haven't smoked in *days*. But you nailed me good with that one. I don't know. I'm an addict, right? I have to take it one day at a time. I see so clearly, though, how my sexuality has gotten me into trouble over and over again. I had sex for the first time when I was 14. Right after my youngest brother's motor-cycle accident. My folks spent all their time at the hospital with him. He was 16. My two other brothers were already gone. I was home alone with no one to keep an eye on me. I went wild, to say the least. I've never gone longer than a couple of months without a guy since then."

Dana looked at her, confused. "What about those two or so years between Craig and Drew?"

Camille made a tortured face. "Uh oh. Me and my big mouth. Um—well—okay—I might as well speak the truth here. I was doing someone on the sly."

Dana and Barb said together, "Who?!"

"Mark."

"Mark?! Hendricks?! The Wise Guy?! Wasn't he living with Catherine back then?" asked Dana.

"Yes ma'am. He was. I told you we were doing it on the sly. I'm not exactly proud of it, believe me. And while I'm confessing—I've done him again since Drew. A bunch of times." She ground out her cigarette and threw the butt off the edge of the patio. "I *really* hate to admit this, but when I'm having sex with someone, I get lost in it and before you know it, I've convinced myself I'm in love. I'm a love junkie! All a guy has to do is send me over the edge and I fall at his feet. Yuck."

"Even Mark?"

She nodded. "Even Mark. The only way I get over him is to do Drew." She paused. "Okay. I'm a slut. I admit it. I'm not gonna be the only one sharing my deepest darkest secrets here, however. Barb, what about you? How old were you when you first got laid?"

"Nineteen. I got pregnant. My first time. Had an abortion. Dana knows about it...."

Dana spoke up. "I was 20. A late bloomer. I haven't had many lovers in my life. I kinda hate to admit it, but I've always been a little bit afraid of sex. You know that, Camille."

Camille nodded. "I'd say your worst fear is that the vulnerability, transparency and surrender required to have 'kick ass and take names' sex will destroy you. You, Dana Wallace, believe that sex equals love equals annihilation. Am I correct?"

Dana nodded mutely. Boy, did that dart ever hit the bull's-eye. "Ouch. But, yeah. I'm afraid that if I open myself all the way up and let myself *really* love someone, he'll destroy me all right. My mom did a number on me, I think. So did Brad. And Peter too, I guess."

"How so?"

"From the time I was tiny, my mom told me how repulsive sex was—how it was something a woman had to put up with in order to have children—who were a gift from God. She started accusing me of *doing that repulsive thing* when I was 12 or 13. *It was so demeaning and so confusing...."*

"You never talk about your mom, Dana. Why?" asked Barb.

Dana took a deep breath. "We were never close. When I was little, she ragged on me for being too fat. Then when I got older, she found other, meaner names to call me. She pretty much walked out of my life when I was 14."

All of a sudden it was as though Ellen was sitting next to her on the deck. She remembered their talk the night Ellen arrived from Baja. Had it only been two and a half weeks ago? It seemed like a conversation from another lifetime. Ellen's words came back to her and she repeated them aloud. "Find out what pushes your buttons and makes you crazy-fighting-mad or scares you so badly you want to run for the hills. Bring those things into the light of day. Examine them. *Don't judge them.* Just feel them, think about them and learn from them."

"What?" Camille asked.

Dana shook her head, startled. "That's what Ellen told me right before we left."

"Whoa," said Barb. "That's pretty powerful. What else did she say?"

Dana closed her eyes and willed herself back to the couch in her home in Encinitas. "She said that every time someone hurts us—even accidentally—we lose a piece of our innocence—our souls. We get scared and block ourselves off from being able to give and receive love. But with every act of forgiveness, we regain some of that lost innocence. And some love can back get in. And out."

"How are we supposed to forgive? How can you forgive your mom? Or Brad? How am I supposed to forgive myself for killing my only child?" Barb asked.

"How am I supposed to forgive Drew for being such a phony tight-ass? And myself for being such a man-hungry slut?" asked Camille.

Dana opened her eyes and looked up at the stars. "I asked her that. She said we have to call what wounded us up to the surface. We have to feel it again, however awful that might be. We feel it, we grieve it and somehow—I think—in the process, we let it go and it ceases to have power over us."

"I'm not following you."

Dana got up and began to pace. "Give me a minute. She didn't take it all the way with me. I think she knew I had to figure it out for myself. I'm starting to see though. Listen. What if the people who betrayed us—like Brad and my mom—were operating blindly? You know, totally unaware of anything but their own needs and enslaved by their own fears? What then?"

"I think you're onto something," Barb said.

Camille spoke in a dry voice. "'Father, forgive them; for they know not what they do.'"

"Huh?"

"Jesus. On the cross. Forgiving the Pharisees and the Romans who killed him."

"He rose again, didn't he?" said Dana. "Don't you see? He rose above the evil that was inflicted on him out of ignorance and fear! If he can do it—so can we!"

"You're comparing us to Jesus?" Camille asked, shocked.

Dana ignored her. "Camille. If Jesus forgave them, won't he forgive you too? And you, Barb? If he forgives you—doesn't it follow logically that you should forgive yourself? You acted out of ignorance and fear when you aborted that baby. How could you have *ever* known that would be your only shot at having a child of your own? You've been punishing yourself ever since. For how many years?"

Barb looked at her. There were tears in her eyes. "Twenty."

"How about you, Camille? How many years have you been beating yourself up for being a 'man-hungry slut?'"

"Nearly 33." Camille turned and touched Barb's hand. "I had two abortions," she said in a whisper-voice. Barb got up out of her chair. So did Camille. The two of them were all of a sudden together—hugging one another in a spontaneous, mutually comforting embrace—sharing and releasing their individual regrets to the past—where they belonged.

Dana walked to the edge of the patio and sat down on the wall, facing the sea. A sense of peace came over her and she whispered to the setting moon. "God, I know I don't talk to you all that often. I didn't even know I believed that until the words came out of my mouth. So—thanks. Thanks for the words. Thanks for believing in me, even when I wasn't sure I believed in you anymore. Thanks for showing me, tonight, what forgiveness really is. Ellen was right. I don't have to trust Brad again. Or my mom. But I don't have to hate them anymore either." She stopped and took a deep breath. "God. I can't stop thinking about Todd. I'm scared, but I think I might be ready to give him a chance this time around, if he's up for it. I know I need to find the courage to open that door to my heart and let some love in. And out." She closed her eyes as her heart expanded and contracted with a warmth and tenderness she'd never known before. Her entire being rejoiced as a cleansing flood of tears began to flow unchecked down her cheeks.

CHAPTER TWENTY-TWO   **Los Barriles, Baja California Sur**
October 31, 1998

The Yellow Bird sped across the glassy surface of the sea with Jorge at the helm. He reached into the half-submerged bait tank and pulled out a sardine, baited his hook and slipped the line with the wiggling fish on it overboard. Barb watched, fascinated, as it unraveled and disappeared in the boat's foamy wake. Grinning, he fastened a leather contraption called a belly buster around her waist and handed her the pole. A VHF radio crackled as someone from another boat spoke. Jorge listened, picked up the mike and answered. *"Mucho pescado hoy*—Lots of fish today," he said to her.

"What do I do, Dana?" she asked.

"Hold it. Just hold it. If you feel something tug really hard, yank back to set the hook, then shove the pole into the slot in your belly buster to anchor it. If the fish is too much for you, holler and Jorge or I will take the pole."

For a few long minutes nothing happened. Barb's eyes were glued to the coastline. Dana pointed out the large, palm-studded resorts in Buena Vista and the more remote lodgings in La Ribera, Punta Colorado and Punta Arena. "That," she said as she motioned toward a chunk of land jutting out to sea, "is Punta Arena. It extends furthest to the east of any part of the entire peninsula. You would never believe that right here—a mile offshore—the water's already 1,000 feet deep. My dad told me that all the game fish that migrate into the Sea of Cortez swim right by here."

"Where's the marine reserve?"

Before Dana could answer, Barb's shoulder was almost jerked out of its socket. Her reel howled as a fish took off with her line.

Something rose up at least four feet into the air and splashed back down before she could see what it was. She yelped and threw herself backward, bracing her feet against the side of the panga. "Help!" she wailed.

Jorge and Dana exchanged places. Jorge grabbed the pole from Barb and jammed it into his belly buster. "¡Dorado, dorado!" he called out.

"Best fighting fish in all of Baja," Dana explained as he began to crank the reel. Jorge spoke in rapid-fire Spanish to her and she bent down, strapped on a belt herself. Then she picked up a two foot length of pipe and held it, her eyes on the water. The fish broke the surface. It flashed a neon yellow body flecked with blue dots. Its fins were a brilliant shade of turquoise and its back was a sparkling, fluorescent green.

A few minutes later, Jorge handed the pole to Dana and she began to crank. Beads of sweat popped out on her forehead as she fought the fish. Finally, she eased the dorado up alongside the boat. Jorge gaffed it and flipped it on board. He picked up the pipe and slammed it against the fish's head. Blood spurted from its mouth and covered the deck. "Oh my God!" cried Barb as she scurried backwards, away from the sight of the bloody, dying fish. "How awful!"

Jorge flung a bucket overboard and filled it with saltwater. He rinsed the floor and moved the fish to the bin in the back. He baited another line and began to troll again. Barb was stunned by the brutality of the fish's death. "Why didn't you let him go?" she asked Dana. "He was the most *beautiful* fish I've ever seen. I thought you said you were into the 'catch and release' thing."

"Not with dorado. They're the best fighting *and* eating fish in the entire Sea of Cortez. Wait 'til you taste this guy," she said. "Pan-fried *al mojo de ajo*—in butter and garlic. Oh Barb, it's to-die-for."

"Oh he died all right," she grumbled under her breath, praying that they wouldn't catch any more fish before they got to Cabo Pulmo. She changed the subject as her mind darted back to Camille. "That was the most peculiar call-in this morning I've ever heard in all my years in radio," she said. "It reminded me of something that'd happen on one of sleazy talk-shows on TV."

"You mean like Jerry Springer?"

"No. Not kinky enough, thank God. More like Jenny Jones or Sally Jessy Raphael...."

"Ah." She nodded. "Yes. Holly bails on doing her segment—for the second week in a row by sneaking out at daybreak to catch a dive boat. Then dear old Wise Guy Mark Hendricks—closet-lover of

Camille Fleming—drops the big bomb on her—on the air. She handled it pretty well, I think."

"Honey, she's used to thinking on her feet. That's what they pay her to do. She only missed one or two beats. But we saw her. She went as white as a ghost. I was glad she handed the phone off to me right after that."

"Yeah. You saved the day by giving them the rundown on Día de los Muertos to the tune of Jimmy Buffett singing about Halloween in Tijuana. That was smooth."

"So do you think she'll stick to her guns when Drew shows up today?"

Jorge yelled "¡Marlín!" as another fish struck his line. He motioned to Barb and Dana, asking if either wanted to take the fish. They both shook their heads—no—as a huge marlin broke the surface, flung itself skyward and then slammed back down onto the water about 100 yards behind their boat. Jorge's line disappeared with a high-pitched scream as the fish took off. It jumped again. And again. Dana and Barb watched in silence.

"So this is what all the gringos come here for, huh?" Barb asked.

"Don't worry," Dana said. "This looks to be a striped marlin. We won't bring this one in. It's not real good eating and the sport-fishing industry is into protecting it from ever landing on the Endangered Species List. We're in conservation mode here. We'll release this beauty to fight another day. About Camille. I know it wigged her out. Big time. After all, it's flattering as hell to have your estranged husband fly all the way to Southern Baja to attempt a reconciliation. Now it's not just their church that's involved. RockSteady's entire radio audience knows about it too, thanks to dear old Mark Hendricks. God, I don't envy her!"

Barb sighed. "Me neither. I hate to see her suffer—she's been hurt too much already. But she's a big girl and it's her life, not mine. As much as I'd love to step in and save her from more pain, it's not my responsibility." She looked at her watch. "I guess we'll know when we get back—since his plane's due in Los Cabos in a little over an hour."

Dana shook her head. "I've known Drew almost as long as I've known Camille. He's basically a good guy. He means well. He really does. But, in my opinion, he uses religion as an excuse for not thinking things through for himself. He may be over 50, but I would not consider him to be emotionally mature. To me, he acts about 13—the same age as my girls, or Camille's son, Matt. He plays the same kind of games they do. And he talks out of both sides of his mouth."

"What do you mean?"

She thought for a moment. "Well, he wants Camille back now—bad enough to make a major scene. He didn't for the last year—no matter how much she begged, pleaded and promised to be the perfect wife. *Now* he wants her back, but she has to take full responsibility for their breakup and near-divorce. I don't ever see him being accountable for his own screwups. He's always got to put it off on someone else. To me, that's not maturity."

"No. It certainly is not. But when you're emotionally entangled—like Camille is with Drew—that can be mighty confusing."

"Ten-four."

Barb turned to watch Jorge battle the mighty marlin. "Look! There's a bunch of boats up ahead!" she said. "What's going on?"

Dana fired off some questions in Spanish to Jorge, who answered back in, to Barb, a stream of unintelligible gibberish. "Those are dive and snorkel boats off Pulmo. We can't go in any closer because it's illegal to fish there." Jorge turned the boat slowly away from the reserve. He spoke into the radio and listened carefully to the response. He talked to Dana again.

"As soon as we finish with our marlin, we're gonna head over to the inside of Pulmo Bay. The coral reefs there extend from right off the beach out about a mile and a half to sea. The tide's about at the midpoint right now, so there won't be too many pieces of the reef breaking the surface like there is at low tide, but we should see a lot of fish. Jorge says the viz is 60 to 70 feet today. That's awesome!" She jumped as the fish broke water and arced its magnificent body through the air again about six feet from the boat. "He's here! Look!"

The striped marlin was hauled up next to the boat. His long skinny bill poked up out of the water and his eyes met Barb's. "Oh my God," she said. "Please don't hit him. He's so cute...."

"Cute?!" Dana answered. "A marlin?! This sucker weighs at least 100 pounds! And anyway, I told you we're not taking him in."

Jorge leaned across the boat, slipped the hook out of the marlin's mouth and inserted a tag in its place. *"¡Suéltame*—Release me!" he called out and the fish's head slid under the surface. For a tenth of a second, Barb saw a ray of sunlight catch and reflect off his muscular body as he swam off into the depths—free again.

He added a marlin flag to the dorado one on the mast, turned the boat around and headed back toward Pulmo Bay. Jorge asked Dana another question. "Do you want to snorkel from the shore, Barb, or are you comfortable jumping overboard out a little deeper? The sights are better."

Barb's heart leapt in her chest. She wanted to see as much of this reef as possible. She didn't want to disappoint Dana. But the truth of the matter was, she *hated* deep water. She never liked to go out beyond where she could touch. The next words that came out of her mouth caught her completely by surprise, however. "Let's push the envelope, Dana. Take me somewhere that'll scare the living shit outta me!"

Dana gave her a funny look. "You sure? Are you Camille all of a sudden, or what?"

Barb laughed. "Must be. Since she isn't here, I have to be both of us. So let's do it, babe! Take me to the reef!"

Jorge cut the motor at a spot midway between a dive boat and a snorkel boat, about 300 yards offshore. *"Aquí, mira*—Here, look" he said to Barb and Dana as he gestured toward the crystal-clear water. Barb leaned over. She saw a school of needlefish glide by, right below the surface. She looked deeper and saw the brownish formations of the coral. A flash of gold sped by, followed by a school of white speckled fish. She put on her fins, grabbed her mask and snorkel and followed Dana into the water.

They kicked along, side by side. Dana pointed, surfaced and named the fish for her. They swam on, skimming over the tops of yellow, green and rust-colored coral outcroppings that looked to her like huge heads of cauliflower. They were spaced in uneven lines along the white sandy bottom. Graceful sea plants rose up from their nooks and crannies and waved back and forth in the underwater breeze. Barb swam through a school of multicolored angelfish, navy blue damselfish and lots of those skinny needlefish she'd seen from the boat. She laughed out loud at a tiny polka-dotted, spiny puffer that blew itself up into a ridiculous-looking ball when Dana reached toward it. Dana tapped her on the shoulder. "Parrotfish," she mouthed through her snorkel. Barb looked and gaped at the two-foot long pastel-colored fish. Its body was a rainbow of pale turquoise, lavender, green and pink. She followed it as it swam off to her left. Suddenly, she squealed and backpaddled as she saw the sinister eyes and darting head of a moray eel right in front of her, its body slithering out of a crevice in a huge coral head. At the high-pitched sound, it spun around and disappeared into its cave.

Barb saw so many fish she knew she'd never be able to remember them all. There were silvery triggerfish, tiny little fluorescent blue and turquoise fish that darted in and out of tiny tunnels within the coral. Dana showed her a poisonous puffer and a pair of *huachinango*—red snapper. She even caught a momentary glimpse of some roosterfish passing by.

Forty-five minutes later they climbed back into the boat and headed for shore. Jorge ran the Yellow Bird up on shore next to two big, high-powered super pangas. They hauled an umbrella, beach chairs, towels and their cooler onto the beach and sat down to eat. As they were finishing up their lunch, an attractive, tan and fit-looking couple walked up the beach toward them. "Dana! Is that you?!" the guy called out.

She jumped to her feet and ran to them. She hugged them both and brought them over to Barb. "Barb, this is Ben and his girlfriend, Marie. They run one of the biggest dive business in the East Cape. I've known you guys—how long?"

Marie smiled. "We've been here nearly five years," she said.

Barb lay down in the shade on her towel and listened to them talk.

"What's the latest with the gill net fishermen?" Dana asked.

"It's getting better. Your dad would be pleased. You know, when the park was established in '95, fishing was outlawed in this whole area. The park is 10 miles long and three miles wide. But the gill netters didn't care."

"Were they Mexicans or foreigners?" Dana asked.

"Mexicans mostly. From Sinaloa. They used shrimp boats as their mother ships and pangas to set the nets. I will *never* forget that time I saw two pangas filled all the way to the gunwales with 40-to 50-pound roosterfish," Ben said, shaking his head. "You wouldn't have believed it. Their gill net was overflowing too. They were catching six to eight tons of fish a *day!* Illegally! Sharks, rays, grunts, jacks, sea turtles, snapper and—of course—roosterfish. They'd leave three to four tons of guts rotting in the sun on the beach after they processed their fish, "

Barb opened her eyes and leaned up on her elbow. "How appalling. What's a gill net?"

"It's a drop-weighted net made of monofilament mesh. The nets are invisible underwater and trap anything swimming by, usually by the gills. The Japanese were the first to use them. If the Mexican government hadn't gotten a handle on them, they would have literally fished the richest sea in the world dry."

"How were they finally stopped?"

"Dana's father was one of the leaders of the movement, actually. He and I, Pepe Murietta, who's since been made the park director, and of course, Bobby Van Wormer, whose family owns the Las Palmas, the Playa del Sol and the Punta Colorado."

"Are those hotels?"

Ben nodded. "Yup. Two in Los Barriles and one out in the boonies."

"My dad never told me this story. How'd they catch the fishermen?" Dana asked.

"We all banded together with some officials from PESCA in La Paz [the Mexican fisheries agency] and formed the Patronatos del Este. Just a few months ago, we blew the whistle on two large boats and a dozen pangas. The boats were confiscated, the fishermen arrested and fined. Heavily. It was bitchin'. Seems to have slowed them down—although we won't know for sure until Lent rolls around again."

"Why Lent?"

"Because lots of Mexicans give up eating meat during Lent. The market for fish, especially on the mainland, increases dramatically then. And so, of course, does the poaching."

Marie spoke up. "Pepe said he turned away two shrimpers and a fleet of pangas just last week."

Dana smiled. "Bud would be pleased, wouldn't he?"

Ben and Marie nodded and grinned back at her. "Why don't you bring your friends over to our place for cocktails later? You remember where it is, don't you?" Marie asked.

Dana nodded. "We were planning to visit Chuy and Imelda at the Spa—oh, excuse me—I mean the Buena Vista Beach Resort, eat some dinner, listen to some mariachi music and watch the Ballet Folklórico show tonight. But we'll stop by beforehand for sure. Sound good to you, Barb?"

"Absolutely."

"Tomorrow can we come back here and hang out at the swim-up bar?" Camille asked as they finished the last of their flan and sipped coffee under the stars in Buena Vista. "I've always wanted to sip a Piña Colada while sitting on a submerged bar stool in some lush tropical resort with palm trees and hibiscus, plumeria and bougainvillaea blossoms all around me."

"Yes, dear," said Dana. "We can stop by here on our way back from Pulmo tomorrow." She looked at Drew and then at Holly. "You will come with us, won't you? It would mean a lot to me...."

"Of course," said Drew.

"All Saints Day isn't until the second of November, Dana," Holly said. "Why are you rushing it? We have to stay here another day any-way while the motor home gets worked on. Can't you wait? I was hoping to go windsurfing with some friends of mine tomorrow."

"What's this about?" Drew asked, flipping his long hair over his right shoulder.

Dana explained about Día de los Muertos and as she did, Barb felt the skin on her arms begin to prickle. She couldn't help herself. She disliked him intensely. He talked like a sincere-enough guy, but she found herself holding her breath whenever she listened to him—expecting him to launch into a hellfire and brimstone sermon at any moment. She hated the way he looked at Camille. It was so *conde-scending*. He talked to her like she was an idiot. It made Barb want to scream. She kept wanting to place her body in between them and to shout into Camille's face, "No! Don't revisit your hell! Don't go there!" But she kept quiet.

Dana finished her explanation of the Mexican holiday. "I want to do it tomorrow because the next day is Sunday and it isn't right to ask Jorge to be away from his family on Sunday. And I want Jorge to be with us. He was my dad's closest friend in a lot of ways."

"What time will we be going?" Holly asked.

"Early. The wind doesn't come up until the afternoon anyway," Dana said.

"Okay. I'll go."

"Count me in," said Camille.

Everyone turned to look at Drew whose eyes were on his coffee cup. "No. I've changed my mind. This Day of the Dead is a pagan holiday," he said.

"No! It's not!" Camille said. "It's sanctioned by the Catholic Church!"

He shook his head and rolled his eyes in disgust. "Catholics. There you have it...." He got up. "Let's go for a walk on the beach, Camille." He strode off.

Barb reached for her friend with her eyes. "Come with," Camille whispered as she got up and followed her husband.

"Stay out of it," Holly said. "Can't you see it's a bad scene?"

Barb stood. "Holly. I know it's hard for you to get close to peo-ple. I care about you and I care about what you think. What you feel. I want to be your friend. We all do. But you keep us at arm's length. Minimum. Please understand that I will go because she asked me to and because I care about her. I would do the same for you. No ques-tions asked." She turned and walked away as the mariachi band began to play "Cuando Caliente el Sol."

Her heart pounding, Barb looked for the silhouettes of Camille and Drew's bodies. She saw them a ways ahead, walking along the shore. As she watched, Camille stepped back from the water, lifted her dress over her head, removed her bra and panties and dropped them in a pile in the sand. She ran into the water and dove in. "It's hot!" she cried out into the night. "Come in, Drew! There are hot springs in here!"

To Barb's amazement, Drew took off his shirt and shorts and ran into the water after her. She turned away in embarrassment as the two of them came together and began to kiss passionately in the waist-deep water.

She went back to the table and sat down. Holly was gone. "Where'd she go?"

"Bathroom."

Barb told Dana what she'd seen. "I felt like a voyeur and a freak and a fool," she said.

Dana nodded. "We're in the tropics. Put on a little music. Light the sky up with stars and a new moon. Bring on the testosterone in the form of her horny husband, and there goes Camille. Frolicking naked and doing her best to get laid!"

"Oh, I'm sure she won't have a problem there...."

Thirty minutes later—when they presumed that the show would be over—Barb, Holly and Dana headed down toward the beach. "Which direction did they go?" Dana asked. "Tell me so we can make sure we go in the opposite direction."

Barb gestured to the north. "That way." They turned to the south. Before they'd gone 50 yards, they heard two voices arguing somewhere in the darkness. In English. A man and a woman. They looked at each other. "I'd recognize that voice anywhere. It carries well, doesn't it?" Barb said.

Dana nodded. "Shhh. Let's hang for a minute."

They dropped down and sat in the soft, still-warm sand. Drew's voice was impossible to hear. But Camille's came at them again—bold, loud and strong.

"This is how it is with me, Drew! I'm still so fucking attracted to you that it's all I can do not to rip your clothes off whenever I'm around you! But I'm sick and tired of leading with my pussy! Let's talk reality here, buddy. It takes two to make a marriage. It takes two to break a marriage. I owned my part of what went wrong. I was willing to give my all to make this work. But *you wouldn't have me!* Now you've completely switched channels and you *want me!* But you want to make all the rules! You're not into healing this relationship! All you give a rat's ass about is winning—and looking good in other people's eyes!"

She stopped talking. Drew's voice droned on inaudibly for a while.

Then she was back, burning up the airways. "You hurt me, dammit! Just seeing you hurts me! I want your love so desperately, but I can't trust you not to hurt me! You fucking hurt me every time I go near you! Why did you come here?! What do you want from me?! Why would you expect me to go back to the source of so much pain?! I'm not naive enough to expect things to be different between us— because—*nothing has changed!"*

Silence. Drew.

Camille. Louder now. "You are incapable of loving me the way I deserve to be loved—don't you get it?! You can't even begin to hope to take me where I want to go! And so you know what?! At this point, Drew Sheridan, I choose to walk alone!"

From out of the darkness two shadows emerged and parted. Barb bent down, tucked her head into her lap and curled herself into a tiny ball. Out of the corner of her eye, she looked at Holly and Dana. They, amazingly enough, had done the same thing—tried to become invisible.

"Peek-a-boo. I see you. Enjoy the floor show?" Camille asked, walking up and plopping herself down beside them. "What's that Who song?" she asked Barb. She jumped up. "From *Tommy?* Oh. Yeah. 'I'm Free.' That's it folks." She began to move her hips to some internal, ancient Mexican-Indian-Caribbean rhythm. She swung herself about in a circle, waving her arms and chanting in a singsong voice: "I. Am. Free. I'm free! And yes, dear ones. Freedom does tend to taste a whole lot like reality." She stopped, hands on hips. "All right. Off with your clothes, you nosy, snooping bitches! We're goin' swimmin'!"

For the second time that night, she tore off her clothes and raced into the warm surf. This time Holly, Dana and Barb followed her— naked, hooting, hollering and splashing each other gleefully with water.

CHAPTER TWENTY-THREE   Cabo San Lucas,
Baja California Sur
November 2, 1997

"Oh my God. There it is. Land's End. We're here. We made it. We arrived. Without killing each other—or ourselves," Camille said from her place up front next to Holly.

Holly looked at her and smirked. "Oh yeah. We didn't wipe out any innocent bystanders or interlopers either, did we?" They laughed. Then she lowered her voice. "Let me tell you a secret, Camille. I called a friend of mine in Cabo and he's having t-shirts made for each of us that have one of those big black-edged circles on them. Inside the circle will be the words, MEX 1 VIRGINS in all caps. There will be, of course a red slash through the circle—showing the world that every one of you is a Mex 1 Virgin no more!"

"All right! Way cool! But don't worry. I won't tell," Camille said. "So," she pointed. "On the other side of those rock outcroppings is the Pacific Ocean—right?"

"Correct. See that arch on the third-to-last rock?" Camille nodded. "Every time I come here, I dare somebody to shoot through it with me in a kayak or a wave runner. It's a private ritual of mine. You up for it?"

"I dunno." Camille looked at placid surface of the water. It was jam-packed with boats. A cruise ship and three yachts were anchored in the bay, just out from the marina. Jet skis, wave runners, kayaks and two pangas towing parasailers wove in and out between them. The marina looked *huge*. The hotel complex around it was *huge*. Developed. The whole place was developed—beach front, hillsides, flat lands, water. Ever since San Jose del Cabo, a *real* Mexican town that doubled as a resort less than 20 miles away, the road had been four lanes wide with a center divider. This stretch was known world-wide as *Los Cabos*—The Capes—and all of it was a gringo tourist Mecca. There were monstrous, extravagant four- and five-star hotels all along the coast. And *golf courses.* She'd seen five jets landing and taking off already—just in the last half hour! This was like waking up in Waikiki Beach after being on a semi-deserted island for nearly three weeks. Way too weird for words.

It was as if Holly was reading her mind. "There's a Planet Hollywood here. And a Hard Rock Cafe. You can dine on the beach with your toes in the Sea of Cortez at The Office or eat at the Finisterra or Solmar over there." She pointed to the white and stone buildings terraced up the hillside and spilling over onto the beach on the Pacific side. "Both are right on the tip of the peninsula. At the Finisterra you can see both oceans at once. The Solmar is right on the sand. On the Pacific. In Cabo you can watch the sun rise over the Sea of Cortez and set over the Pacific—without going anywhere. It's truly amazing."

They pulled up at a stop light, indicating that Highway 19 to Todos Santos was to the right and downtown Cabo to the left. Holly turned left. The traffic was intense all of a sudden. There were taxis, rental cars, motor homes, four-by-fours covered in 20 layers of dust and clean, normal-looking cars that must've belonged to the locals. "Doesn't it bother you—all this *chaos* after being in such *tranquil* places?"

Holly looked at her. "Oh no. I love Cabo. I love the water sports, the excitement, the nightlife, the restaurants. Barb will love the shopping. It's the best. The right way to do Cabo isn't in an RV, though, let me tell you. The way to do it is to fly in and stay at a place like the Pueblo Bonito, the Finisterra, Solmar. Or The Breakfast Bungalows if you're into a more cost-effective, but totally delightful, bed and breakfast. If you're into a more remote location, one of the hotels on the way in from San Jose would do. You know, like the Hotel Cabo San Lucas, Palmilla, the Westin Regina or the Melía Cabo Real. There are so many choices!"

"So basically this is a place to come with lotsa dinero in your wallet."

"Yes, ma'am."

"Where are we staying?"

"Since I had a phone at my disposal in Los Barriles, I made a reservation at the Club Cabo RV Park." She pointed to the sign by the Club Cascadas and turned left onto a sandy road that ran along the beach. She bypassed the Vagabundos del Mar RV Park and stopped just to the east of it. "This one's smaller, but it has beach access through the fence over there, which is why I like it. We have hookups too."

They pulled in, set up camp and dragged the kayaks down to the beach. "Who wants to go with me to shoot the arch in a kayak?" Holly asked.

Dana raised her hand. "Me! Take me!"

"Fine with me," said Barb. "I'll wimp out on that one, thank you very much."

"I wanna go parasailing," Camille said. "Flying behind a boat in a parachute sounds perfect. I could use a good safe rush, if you get my drift."

She and Barb watched as the other two paddled off into the crowded bay. "I think we had a break-through with Holly yesterday, don't you?" she said to Barb.

"Maybe. My bet is that she started to thaw out some when you blew Drew off in front of the rest of us. I'm so glad she did Day of the Dead with us yesterday."

Camille nodded. Drew had left abruptly in a taxi the night before—thank God. She didn't even want to think about him right now. Instead she went back to the previous morning. The women had all gotten up before dawn. María Pilar had helped them make pan de muerto and skull cookies, which they took out in the panga with Jorge when the water was still slightly pink with the leftover effects of the sunrise. Both he and Dana had talked to Bud in Spanish and sprinkled pieces of bread in the boat's wake. The crumbs were promptly gobbled up by ravenous sea gulls. They'd snorkeled, picnicked and returned home in time to get ready for the fiesta in the graveyard.

Dana and María Pilar packed another basket of food and they all piled into Ellen and Bud's old VW van. They drove a half mile inland from Los Barriles and arrived at a small cemetery on top of a knoll about 4:00 p.m. There were colorful decorations on every grave, there were tons of people, a mariachi band and, as Dana had forewarned them, an astonishing amount of food and drink.

Even though they had no graves to decorate, they all had loved ones to remember. Camille and Barb went off by themselves and made a tiny altar a ways away from the graveyard in memory of their aborted babies. Later Barb went off alone with Holly. Camille didn't know what they'd done together, but her intuition told her that whatever it was, it had been a very good thing for Holly.

She decided to ask. "What did you and Holly do at that graveyard anyway?"

"I promised her I wouldn't tell. She's had more than her share of tragedy too, though. I can guarantee you that. She just can't bring herself to talk about it...."

Camille picked up a pebble and threw it into the ocean. Just then a pair of beach vendors approached them. One was carrying a large black satchel and the other had blankets and dresses draped over his arms and a stack of *sombreros*—hats piled high on his head. "Beach dresses, amigas?" he asked. They shook their heads, no.

"You want to buy some jewelry, señoritas?" the other vendor asked, flipping open his case to reveal row after row after row of sterling silver rings, bracelets, earrings and necklaces. Barb and Camille ogled the goods. They tried on countless pieces of jewelry before each settled on a pair of silver earrings. They bargained with the man and he knocked a few dollars off each pair.

"Let's walk over there," Camille pointed after the vendor wandered off. "I think that's where the parasailing boat takes off. You wanna go too?"

Barb shook her head. "No gracias. I don't feel like being adventurous today. I just want to hang out and relax. I don't want to go near a boat!"

A half hour later and $30 later, Camille was airborne behind a red and white panga, circling Bahía Cabo San Lucas. The only noise she could hear was her heart pounding in her chest. Ah, this is the payoff for everything I've gone through, she said to herself. This is better than sex! It's fucking nirvana! She chuckled as she looked down at all the water craft in the bay. They looked like Tonka toys—even the cruise ship. She had a birds-eye view of the Finisterra and Solmar Hotels, along with the luxurious gringo houses that were terraced down the Pacific side of the hill in the Pedregal district. She could see the whole city, but all the hustle and bustle had been diminished and dismissed to another dimension, where the superfluous was naturally segregated from the vital—the essential.

The panga turned to the north and her parachute swung around.

Now she could see the hotels and golf courses lining the Los Cabos corridor. As she completed her sweep of the bay, she looked down again and tried to find Dana and Holly's yellow kayaks in the mass of miniature boats. She couldn't see them. Before she knew it, she was being reeled back in toward the panga. She landed dead-center on the platform behind the boat and was helped out of her harness by the deckhand. They launched the next tourist, and then another and finally they brought her back to Barb.

She jumped out of the boat and landed in knee-deep water. She sprinted over to where Barb sat, at The Office, drinking a huge Piña Colada. "Finish your drink," she said. "I want to take you on a quest to find the best swim-up bar in all of Cabo San Lucas. Are you game?"

Barb laughed. "Now that challenge I can meet. Help me drink this."

"I have a surprise for you guys tonight. Especially you, Dana. You're gonna love it," Holly said as they walked up Hidalgo Street from the marina in their matching MEX 1 VIRGIN No Más t-shirts. She turned into a festive, colorful restaurant, open to the sky. It was crowded with happily chattering, sunburned tourists. There were mariachis playing. The tables were covered in multicolored, checkered tablecloths. The napkins were colorful. The glassware was hand-blown. There were fresh flower arrangements everywhere and murals on the walls depicting life in Mexico. Camille read the sign out loud: "Restaurant Pancho's." The logo was a big sombrero with a moustache. Obviously named after Pancho Villa, she thought to herself. Hero of the Mexican Revolution. She mentally patted herself on the back. Hey! I'm learning something!

They were greeted with *abrazos*—hugs by the owners, Mary and John Bragg. "We've been looking forward to meeting you since Holly e-mailed us back in August," Mary said as she seated them. "Dana. Come with me. I'm taking you into the kitchen to meet my staff. I want you to come back some other time and be a guest chef at the restaurant—Christmas vacation would be perfect. I'll do an event with the Cabo Tomatoes—the women who are *the* movers and shakers in Cabo. We'll advertise in the *Gringo Gazette* and we'll have you teach a cooking class. How would you like that?"

Dana laughed. "I would like it exceedingly. I can't think of anything much more fun than a business trip to Cabo!" Mary put her arm around Dana and led her off toward the kitchen. Before the door swung closed behind them, she turned and called over her shoulder. "We'll both be joining you in a bit here. We have a special treat for you tonight. John's doing a tequila tasting for you after dinner." Their waiter came up and answered their questions about the menu. He recommended the tortilla soup, chiles rellenos, their carne asada, any of their seafood dishes or their pozole.

The meal was spectacular. Dana went nuts over the tortilla soup and Mary promised her the recipe. By the time they finished eating, the crowd had thinned out considerably. John took his place at the head of their table, surrounded by an array of bottles. He began to speak. "Mexicans are Latins. Like the French, Italians and Spanish, they consider the consumption of alcohol to be a natural part of life. When they drink, it's to celebrate life—but there's a sacredness to the way they drink. Rarely does one see a drunken Mexican—more often, sadly—it's the gringos who overindulge and get out of hand.

"Mary, I have no doubt, has already told you I have the largest collection of tequila in the world. I started collecting the bottles nearly seven years ago, right after we opened this restaurant. As of today, my count is 321 different types of tequila, pulque and mescal."

Barb raised her hand. "Yes?" he asked.

"Is tequila made anywhere else in the world, or just in Mexico?"

"Tequila is only made in Mexico, in the state of Jalisco. Mescal and pulque are made all over the country. Let me set you straight. *Tequila is the essence of Mexico.* It's *not* for lightweights—it's for Mexicans—and for those of us who are passionate, strong and warm-hearted—people who live life *con mucho gusto*—with much enthusiasm. While most of us think of tequila as something to be tossed back with a dash of salt and a lime, or put in a Margarita, serious tequila drinkers are thoughtful, slow sippers."

He went on to explain that the Mayans had started it all, way before the Spaniards showed up. Their fermented beverage of choice was pulque, which they made from the Agave Mezcalero and used primarily for medicinal and religious purposes. In those days, drunkenness was a crime punishable by death and only old people and nursing mothers got free access to pulque. "Why?" he asked. "Because of its high nutritional value and its tranquilizing effects. To this day, Indians still mix homemade pulque into their herbal medicines to treat diseases. There are still *pulquerías*—pulque bars in various parts of Mexico." He chuckled. "I've been to several in Guadalajara.

Women are not allowed in them."

"Why?" Dana asked.

He smiled and shook his head. Pulquerías don't have restrooms—just troughs on the floor in the back of the room."

"Oh...."

"When the conquistadors and missionaries arrived in Mexico, they tried pulque, but at 30 per cent alcohol, it wasn't strong enough for their liking. So they did some experimenting and came up with Mescal. Then they did some more experimenting with different varieties of agave and eventually came up with tequila, which is made from is the blue agave, or the Agave Tequilana Weber. It's considered the most exceptional of all agaves because it produces the most full-bodied, clean-tasting liquor. And it's all—every ounce of it—produced within 100 miles of Guadalajara. Today, over 90,000 acres of blue agave are being cultivated in this region, with the greatest number of fields near the town of Tequila. About 45 miles northeast of Guadalajara, it's home to 20 distilleries—*fábricas* in Spanish—that produce over 55 million liters of tequila per year."

"Phew!" said Camille, half out loud. "That's a lot!"

"Most top-of-the-line tequilas are made from 100 per cent pure blue agave. Okay, so what does an agave look like, you ask? Well, let me tell you. It resembles a large gray-green thistle with broad, flat, serrated leaves that come to a point on the end. When a plant is mature, at say, seven to 10 years old, it shoots a flower-bearing stalk as high as 15 feet in the air. The dramatic yellow bloom will last a month or so, but it signals the agave's impending demise, because it dies soon after. Right before the stalk emerges is harvest time. Field workers remove the agave's core, called the piña, carry it to the fábrica where it's split in half and cooked in a large oven—*horno* for about 24 hours.

"After cooling another 24 hours, the piñas are crushed, strained, mixed with water and put in large vats to ferment. They're allowed to ferment for 72 to 150 hours. Then the liquid's filtered and put into stills. The distillation process is carried out twice, and the final product emerges at 100 to 120 proof. It's then diluted with distilled water until it reaches the proper range of 76 to 90 proof."

He paused for a moment to let the information sink in. Then he picked up a bottle of clear liquid. The label on it read "Don Julio."

"There are three types of tequila. The first is a *blanco* or *joven*. *Blanco* means white and *joven* means young. A joven is only aged one or two additional months." He stopped. A waiter came up next to him and poured white tequila into shot glasses. John passed them around the table. Everyone took a sip.

"Remember. Slow, thoughtful sipping. This is *not* a chugging contest. Okay. The second type of tequila is a *reposado,* which means rested. It's aged in wood for three to 12 more months. Let me give you a hint here. A really good reposado grabs you by the throat and gently lets go." To prove this, he asked the waiter to pour a round of Hornitos Reposado for everyone. Camille took a sip of hers and grimaced. He was right. It did grab her by the throat. She shook her head. She liked the first one better. It was smoother.

"The third type of tequila is an *añejo* which means elderly or vintage. It has to be aged at least a year. Tequila ages quickly, so one that's five or six years old is considered, *muy añejo* or very old. I'm giving you each a shot of Patrón Añejo. This is seriously good stuff."

When he finished with his lecture on tequila, he gave them samples of pulque and mescal as well. John finished the tasting off with a shot of homemade brew from a big plastic jug and then offered anyone who dared it a shot of his very own rattlesnake tequila. They moved to the bar and stared at the huge, coiled snake that had been pickled in a huge glass jar. None of them opted to try it.

As they were thanking John and Mary and getting ready for the long walk back to camp, John hit them with one last thing. "Hey," he said. "If any of you ever show up here at Pancho's with a bottle of unopened tequila, and it's one I don't have in my collection, I'll buy the bottle from you and your dinner will be on the house."

"Does that happen?" Camille said.

"Oh absolutely. Mary and I've traveled all over Mexico looking for new tequilas. But there are people who come through here who've been to places we haven't."

"How many kinds do you think you could come up with altogether?" she asked.

He shrugged. "Three or four hundred easy. Maybe five. ¿Quién sabe?"

"Whoa Nelly Bell," she said.

Walking the streets of Cabo at night was almost like being in Las Vegas where the action never stopped. The bars overflowed with tanned, partying gringos. Music blared from everywhere. The streets were packed with bodies. One bar had dry ice in its planter beds, making the partyers inside look like they were dancing in a smoke den. The stores were all open, even though it was past 10:00 p.m. They went into one that advertised Huichol art—finely beaded, brilliantly

colored masks and figures of jaguars, wolves and other wild creatures, done by Indians in the mountains of Jalisco, behind Puerto
Vallarta. Inside a handsome young Mexican man named Ernesto
began chatting them up.

"Very good price today. Almost free," he said, winking.

The women laughed. "No, really. These Indians have only recently begun to sell this magnificent art," he explained to Barb as she fin-
gered a half-sun, half-moon mask.

"How much is it?" she asked

"$120 U.S. But, if you will go with me to a free breakfast tomor-
row morning at 9:30 at the Westin Regina, I can give this to you for a
much better price." His melt-in-your-mouth brown eyes sought out
Dana's and looked at her beseechingly.

"Is this a time-share presentation?" Holly asked, interrupting.

"Oh yes. It is. But there is no obligation to buy anything. For free,
you get a delicious breakfast buffet and a tour of the most beautiful
resort in all of Los Cabos. Even cab fare back to your hotel. Have you
seen it yet?" he asked.

Holly nodded. Camille and the others shook their heads, no.

"But you must come. It's free. And I want my brother, who works
there, to see me with four *muy guapas gringas*—very beautiful
American women."

Holly spoke up. "I've been there. It's lovely. But we're not interested. We're just passing through Cabo." She turned away and began
fingering some t-shirts. Then she went outside.

"I don't think so either," Barb said as Ernesto turned his ques-
tioning gaze to her.

He looked at Dana again. "You are from California?" he asked
her. She nodded. "What part?" She told him. "Where are you staying?" he asked, and to Camille's surprise, she gave him a rundown on
their trip.

"You are four very remarkable women. You must be famous back
in the States." He touched Dana's arm. "You? A chef? Of Mexican
cuisine? Ah, my grandmother, she is the best *cocinera*—chef in all of
the Baja. You *must* have her mole recipe. It is the very best recipe you
will ever find for mole. The ingredients are secret, but I am sure I
could persuade her to give them to you."

"You could?" It was obvious that Dana was interested.

"Oh yes. You are probably aware that mole is a very special meal
in Mexico, one that is served with great tenderness and pride to our
most cherished loved ones. I will convince my grandmother to give

you her recipe if you will join me for breakfast tomorrow morning at the Regina. Will you come? I will be by early to wake you up. Say 8:00."

Camille began to laugh. This guy was too smooth.

"What about the sun-and-moon mask my friend here is interested in? If I go with you, can I have the recipe and can she have the mask for $60?"

Ernesto's face lit up. "Of course," he said. "Of course. You come by afterward and I will give you the mask for $70." He shook Barb and Camille's hands, then he took Dana's. I will see you in the morning," he said.

They stopped in at Carlos and Charlie's for a beer, watched a bit of the show at the Giggling Marlin and voted to pass on Planet Hollywood and the Hard Rock Cafe. When they'd seen enough nightlife, they walked down by the marina and oohed and aahed at the yachts. Then they hiked up a small hill to the Hotel Hacienda, walked through its fragrant, beautifully manicured gardens and headed down to the beach.

"Are you really gonna go to that time-share presentation tomorrow?" Camille asked Dana as they turned left from the beach and entered through the chain link gate that surrounded the campground.

"To get Barb the sun-and-moon mask at half price, to get Ernesto's grandmother Conchita's mole recipe and to get a free breakfast to boot? You're darn right I am! Even if I do have to go by myself."

"I'll go with you," said Barb. "I want to check out the Westin. It looked absolutely beautiful from the highway."

"Oh it is," said Holly.

"I can't wait to see it. I've decided I'm definitely bringing Bob to Cabo for our next vacation."

"Well," said Camille thoughtfully, "maybe I'll go too. It sounds kinda fun. And I love watching Ernesto put the moves on you, Dana." She smiled and turned to Holly. "Sure you won't come with us?"

"Nah," she said. "I've been there before and I have no desire to subject myself to a boring time-share presentation. But you'll enjoy it. It's well worth seeing. Just don't buy anything. I'll use the downtime to catch up on my book."

CHAPTER TWENTY-FOUR   **Todos Santos,**
                                     Baja California Sur
                                     November 4, 1997

"This is the first time I've had a chance to spend more than a couple of hours in Todos Santos," Dana said to Holly as she drove north on Highway 19 on Tuesday morning.

"I spent four months here during the summer of '95, right before I met Rick," Holly answered.

"You did?! How'd you pull that off?"

"My downtime work-wise is June through October. I usually go back to Colorado or Utah or Idaho. One of my Rocky Mountain hangouts. I can always land a summer job up there leading white water rafting tours, backpacking tours—things like that. The summer of '95 however, I was offered a free place to stay in Todos Santos, house-sitting for Bill and Lois Reeves, a couple who've been regular customers of Shirley's and mine at Baja Explorer Tours for years. They have this incredible villa near the ocean and a farm where they grow countless varieties of tropical fruits and berries, plus around 10 types of bananas."

"You're kidding?! You got to stay there by yourself?"

"Yup. For four months, free of charge. I had plenty of visitors from up north though. Did I tell you I called Bill and Lois during my phone marathon in Los Barriles?"

"No. You didn't."

"I must've told Barb. Anyway, they're here and they don't have room to put us up in their house, but Bill said we can camp on their property. They have two RV pads—with hookups even—because they have so many snowbird friends who come to visit."

"Amazing. How close to the beach are they?"

"A five minute walk away. And another 15 or 20 minute walk into town. It's ideal, trust me."

"What'd you do when you were here?"

Holly sighed. "I hung out at the Caffé Todos Santos in the mornings. That's the local espresso bar. I started writing the stories of some of my travels in Baja and in the Rockies. I did some painting. Took sculpting lessons from a local lady. Partied with friends. Swam. Tried to learn to surf. It was heaven on earth. Sometimes I wish I'd never left...."

Dana sighed too. "I bet." She looked across Holly at the surf crashing on mile after mile of deserted beach. The desert was still a tropical thorn forest here on the west coast of southern Baja. The vegetation was nearly identical to what they'd seen on the eastern side of Baja, yet somehow, it seemed oddly out of place next to the Pacific Ocean. It must be, she figured, because she'd grown up next to the Pacific and was used to seeing it against a backdrop of familiar landmarks.

"Todos Santos is considered the Taos or Santa Fe of Baja, you know," Holly said. "It's got a gringo population of around 350 in a town of less than 3,500. It's still a Mexican town. And, as far as I'm concerned, it's the hippest place on the peninsula. It doesn't have a single fancy hotel—probably because it has no natural harbor. Nowhere for the cruise ships or yachts to dock, although as you can see from the traffic on this road, there are plenty of day-trippers who come up here from Cabo."

"Why do they come?"

She chuckled. "They come to check out the beaches with their so-called secret surf spots. They come to eat lunch at the Cafe Santa Fe. They come to see real live artists at work. And, of course, they come to see the Hotel California—hoping, I'm sure to catch a glimpse of one of the Eagles—or at least to see if there are really are mirrors on its ceilings and ice buckets jammed full of pink champagne!"

"But they don't spend the night?" said Dana.

"Nope."

"Well, thank God for that. Hey, Camille. Barb. What are you doing back there?"

Barb came forward and squatted down between the two front seats. "She's working on another song. I was reading. Why?"

"Get that article Holly wrote for Discover Baja Travel Club on Todos Santos and read it out loud, would you por favor? I need a refresher course."

"That's what I was reading." She went back, got the newsletter and sat down cross-legged. "Here we go: Todos Santos is located 45 miles northwest of Cabo San Lucas and 50 miles south of La Paz, on the Pacific coast of Baja. Founded in 1724, it pretty much crept along as a remote, inaccessible outpost until the late 1800s when its vast aquifer was discovered. Sugarcane farmers rushed in and it became a booming agricultural community overnight. Today, all kinds of tropical fruits and vegetables are grown in and around Todos Santos. Cattle ranching flourishes. It's an oasis—a tropical paradise that doesn't have a single fancy American hotel. The most expensive rooms in town are found at the Todos Santos Inn, an exquisite bed and breakfast that's located in the heart of the historic district, within walking distance of all the galleries, shops and restaurants in town. There are three more modest hotels too, starting at about $20 a night.

"Highway 19 runs from La Paz to Cabo and passes through Todos Santos. It was built in 1986—the year everything began to change. About that time, a pair of well-known artists from New Mexico, Charles Stewart and Ezio Columbo, moved to town. This duo has played an integral part in perpetuating the artist migration to the area. The permanent population of American and Canadian artsy types [painters, sculptors, poets, musicians, chefs, dancers and writers] currently numbers about 350. It fluctuates however, with much higher numbers of gringos during the cooler months.

"In addition to being an artist, Ezio Columbo is the executive chef at Cafe Santa Fe, a much-celebrated Italian restaurant in town that he owns with his wife, Paula. They helped found the five-year-old Todos Santos Festival of the Arts, which will be held in 1998 during the first week of February. Gabo, a local Mexican artist, has been given the responsibility of revamping the upcoming festival. He will be using a combination of art, theater, dance and music to raise the seven-day event to new heights of excellence. Nearly every business in town will be transformed into a gallery, showcasing works of Mexican and American artists. Every night there will be dancing, music and cultural revelry in the old theater at the plaza. 'For that week,' says Todd Hayward, owner of Cafe Todos Artes, 'we plan to really live up to our reputation as an artist colony.'"

Barb put down the newsletter. "Hey. Wait a minute. Isn't that the same Todd who used to be the executive chef at Hacienda Gaviota, Dana? Isn't that the guy we heard about on the second call-in?"

Dana nodded mutely. Her heart began pounding so loud she was almost certain everyone could hear it. Damn, but she was nervous about seeing him. She did *not* want to share that information with the others, however.

"What a small planet!" Barb exclaimed.

Holly gave Dana a strange look. "You know him?"

Dana nodded again. "I trained under him for over three years. He was my mentor. If it wasn't for Todd, I'm sure I'd still be stuck in sous chef mode. He was relentless about teaching me to stand on my own two feet as a chef. I haven't heard boo from him since he sailed off on a cruise boat in—I guess it was—the fall of '94."

"Did you date him?" Holly asked.

"No." Determined to avert any suspicion Holly or anyone else might have regarding her newly kindled interest in Todd, she went on. "I was seeing Peter most of the time I worked for him. He had a girl-friend too. He's younger than me. He was my boss. I never considered dating him. Did you?"

Holly shot her another, even stranger look.

"Get real," she snapped. "So go on, Barb."

"Why all the artists, you ask? I wondered the same thing myself when I first got town. I was told to go to the Tecolote Libros—the best bookstore within 100 miles. I did. I picked up a copy of the *Spirit of Todos Santos,* the local paper. It talked about meetings where artists shared their lives and processes. Poetry readings. A monthly writer's series. Historical house tours. Events featuring folkloric dancers and gourmet food prepared by local chefs. Medicine Women offering physical and spiritual healing. Concerts, sing-along campfires, medi-tation, massage. Organic food baskets. Authentic Mexican home fur-nishings imported from Guadalajara and San Miguel de Allende.

"Why Todos Santos? I wondered. What was the big deal? According to local painter and gallery owner, Michael Cope, it's because the light has the same vortex energy as Santa Fe or the Bermuda Triangle. He claims that people who live in the desert and watch what the light creates begin to see in Technicolor.

"Another local, author Jeanne Córdoba, claims it's the air, which supposedly melts in your mouth like a fine Parisian pastry. The native Mexicans claim it's in *la corazón de la gente*—the heart of the people. A close friend of mine always claimed that the erotic whisper of its tropical breezes attracts those who are more curious about than afraid of nature's harsh challenges and sensual pleasures. I agree with him."

"Who was that?" Barb asked, interrupting herself.

Holly shrugged and looked out the side window. "I don't remember. Probably some itinerant artist I had mad, passionate sex with. I was single that summer, if you recall. We're almost here. You want to stop for an espresso before we head out to Bill and Lois'?"

They did. Holly parked Boris in front of the Caffé Todos Santos. It was housed in what looked to Dana to be a colonial Mexican home. The door and window frames were painted bright, tropical colors. There was a tangle of multi-hued bougainvillaea covering and dripping down from its roof. They walked inside. The front room was, as Holly said, an espresso bar. It was also a juice bar and a bakery. She inhaled deeply and realized that she was starving. All she'd had for breakfast was a banana and a quick cup of coffee before they'd blown out of Cabo. Each chair and table in the restaurant was painted in funky, dazzling colors. The walls were covered with original works of art. It was crowded. There were no empty tables out on the sidewalk and none inside either.

"Let's order here and we'll go sit out back in the patio," Holly said. Dana ordered a double cappuccino, a croissant and a bowl of fresh tropical fruit. Then she followed Holly through the kitchen, down some stairs and out onto the patio.

"This patio used to be the courtyard of a nineteenth-century hacienda," she explained. Dana looked it over. The floor was weathered tile. The tables were hand-hewn marble. The doors to the restrooms were made of grape sticks. The entire patio was sheltered from the sun by a canopy of lush greenery and flowers. She could see why Holly chose to hang out here in the mornings.

As they were eating, they heard a new voice in the kitchen. From a window above their heads they could hear a gringo cursing under his breath. In English. Holly finished chewing her bite of food and called out. "Hey. Marcos. *¿Eres tú? ¡Si es la verdad, tengo que decirte que eres una boca de gusano malnacido cretino!"* Then she got up and made a beeline for the kitchen.

"What the hell did she say?" Camille whispered to Dana.

"As far as I can tell, called him a cretin and an ill-bred maggotmouth."

"Whoa."

"He cussed in English. She got him back in Spanish. I guess she must know him pretty well."

"I hope so," Barb said. "We're supposed to stay here three days. I don't want to be tarred, feathered and shipped out of town on a rail the first morning."

Marc Spahr came out of the kitchen with his arm around Holly. "Guess we're safe," Camille said under her breath. Holly introduced him around the table. He sat down and chatted with them a while. As a welcome gift he gave them two slices of his original Citrus Flan. It was the best flan Dana had ever tasted in her life—bar none.

She walked into the kitchen when Holly was in the restroom and thanked Marc for the flan. "I'm a chef," she said. "I would love to come hang out with you for a few hours while we're in town and share secrets—if you're game."

He smiled a big teddy bear smile at her. "You betcha. You should also try my good buddy Todd over at the Cafe Todos Artes. He's from San Diego just like you are. What?" he asked, obviously taken aback by the look on her face.

"I know him. I used to work with him...."

"Oh!" He knocked himself on the temple with his right hand. *"You're the one!* How could I have been so dense as not to make the connection?! He told me a week or so ago that you were coming. He said his sister talked to you live, on the radio when you called in from somewhere down here—right?" Dana nodded. "I remember hearing you were traveling with a disc jockey and some other women. I did not connect you and Holly—somehow. What a dork I am." He stepped back, looked her over carefully and then winked at her. "Todd has an APB out on you," he said very slowly. "Did you know that?"

Dana felt herself blushing from the top of her head down to the tips of her hot pink toenails. Oh shit, she thought to herself. Here we go. Too many coincidences again. This is starting to make me nervous...."

"I promised him I'd alert him immediately if you showed up here before he found you." He turned and pointed to the phone protruding from the wall. "I better call him right now. His restaurant is closed on Tuesdays. It's usually the slowest day around here. We hang out a lot together during the week, Todd and I. My wife's a lawyer in La Paz, you see. I go up there to see her on Wednesdays and Sundays. The rest of the time I'm here on my own—working mostly. Todd and I, we surf together and play basketball. He's a great guy."

He moved toward the sink and began to wash his hands. As he was drying them on his apron, Holly and Camille came up the stairs and walked into the kitchen. "We paid the cuenta, Marc," Holly said. "Your food is even better than I remembered. We're off to check out the bookstore and art galleries as soon as Barb gets out of the baño. You ready to go, Dana?"

She shook her head. "No. Marc here says I can hang with him for a while. He's gonna teach me how to make that flan we all said was to-die-for. Right, Marc?" she asked him, winking and imploring him with her eyes to say no more. She needed to see Todd privately— without any of the rest of them around, or even knowing about it— including Camille.

"Right. We're gonna do a little schmoozing and trade some of our best-kept secrets, Dana and I."

Twenty minutes later, Todd walked in, his hair wet and slicked back from the shower. He was dressed in shorts, a t-shirt and flip-flops, and he looked better than she remembered. Way better. He was about six feet tall, but his dark hair was streaked with gray. His skin was almost as dark as a Mexican's, making his hazel eyes stand out dramatically in his face. He smiled at her and his white teeth gleamed. Then he gave her a hug. She closed her eyes as she breathed in his male scent. Oh my God, she thought, as a warm, sweet ache welled up from deep inside her. Ladies and gentlemen, I am in major league trouble here.

"You look wonderful," he said and reached around to pull her hair loose from the knot she'd put it in. "Wow. It grew. I like you much better with long hair. What did Margo say they call you on the radio? A 'bodacious Baja babe?' Well, it fits."

"Gee thanks," she said.

"You eat?" he asked. She nodded.

"Me too. I was about to go surfing. Waves are kicking butt today. I have a boogie board for you to use if you want. I seem to remember you're quite adept with one." He looked away from her and toward Marc. "You go out this morning?"

Marc nodded. "Real early. Right after sunrise. There's no breeze to speak of though, so the waves should still be cranking. Why don't you take her down to Las Palmas Beach? I'll tell her friends to meet you guys about—when?"

"Sunset sounds good to me. I'm abducting this lady. Tell them to meet us at the Hotel California. No offense, bro, but you know we gotta spread the business around."

"Get outta here. Everyone knows the Hotel California is *the* place to go for sunset."

"On Tuesdays maybe." He gave Dana long look. "The rest of the time it's my place that's the place to go for sunset."

"He's lying."

Todd grabbed Dana's hand. "Get a life, Marc. We're leaving. Right now. Dana and I have *lots* to catch up on."

Dana felt like she was sleepwalking as she followed Todd out into the hot afternoon sun and got into his ancient pickup truck. "This is my around-town vehicle," he explained. "An honest-to-God Baja troque." He drove off down the street toward the ocean, turned onto a dirt road and rumbled on, past modest and elegant homes alike. "I live south of town a little bit, near Las Palmas Beach. I'll take you there tomorrow maybe. How long are you here for?"

"Three days."

"Cool. Today, I want to take you to the *big* beach. It'll blow you away. So, Dana. You're uncharacteristically quiet. Tell me what you've been up to these last three years. How's Hector? How's business? How did you get here and why are you here? I want to know everything!"

She began to talk then—about the restaurant, her kids, her dad's death, the motor home, the trip. When she finished, he filled her in on the major events in his life. By the time they'd caught up, they were at the beach and had hauled his cooler, surf board, boogie board, an umbrella and a grass mat down to the sand, under a sand cliff. They sat down, popped open two Pacificos and kept on talking. It was utterly deserted. There wasn't another soul in sight.

Dana barely noticed the expanse of turquoise ocean looming in front of her. She barely saw the waves as they swelled up, crested and broke in perfectly choreographed sets. She hardly noticed them pounding toward the sand in explosions of frosty white foam. Her eyes were on Todd.

"Let's go in the water," he said when they'd momentarily run out of things to say. "Follow me!"

He grabbed his surf board and ran for the waves. All of a sudden Dana noticed everything. The breeze was light, the ocean glassy and clear. Sunlight skipped across its surface, its rays glittering like a million diamonds wherever they touched down on the water. She squinted and shaded her eyes to keep the brilliance from blinding her as she watched him.

He paddled out toward what looked to be a three-foot wave. At exactly the right moment, he spun around and faced the shore, paddling in an every-other-arm motion as he worked to catch it. He caught it. He stood on his board and zoomed down the wave's face, cutting expertly to the right and then to the left, hooting and hollering the whole way. He rode the wave into the soup, jumped off, blew her a kiss, jumped back on and turned to paddle back out again. His exhilaration uprooted her and she picked up the boogie board.

Twenty minutes later she was lying on the grass mat under the umbrella, letting the warm air dry her skin. Her back was to the sand. She was toasty. So toasty. Her eyes closed and she dozed.

She was jolted awake as her bare stomach was sprinkled with sea water. "Get lost, Casey," she mumbled from inside her dream. In it her dog had just come out of the ocean and showered her with salt-water and sand.

Wait a second. Casey was tickling her under her arms. Since when did dogs tickle people? Dana opened her right eye. Todd's face was inches from hers. Tiny drops of water fell from his hair onto her skin. He was the one who was tickling her.

"Come on. Wake up. Let's go for a swim."

Dana nodded, shaking her head to clear it. Todd grabbed her hands and pulled her to her feet. Then he pulled her toward him. He hugged her. A distinctly different hug than the one he'd given her in front of Marc. Molding himself to her, he folded her up in a salty, slick embrace. He pulled away and yanked at her arm. "Come on! Let's go!"

"Wait," she said. Without even thinking, she dug her feet into the blistering sand, reaching down for a cooler footing. "My turn." She drew him back to her, wrapped his arms back around her. She hugged him, leaned into him, nuzzled his neck and stroked his back. "Todd," she whispered, "I think I've been needing to do this for as long as I've known you."

He hugged her back. "My lady, you feel good. Real good." He paused and smiled into her eyes. "I don't think we're quite ready to go swimming yet." He cradled her face in his left hand and kissed the tip of her nose. His right hand moved from her waist to her lower back, massaging. "I've always needed to do this too," he added. "But then I think you know that."

"Mmmmm." She snuggled against him. She could *not* remember the last time anything had felt this good. Oh my God, a voice in her head screamed out to her. Slow down! You're on your way to bed with this man, Dana Wallace. At least make him wait a day! Shut up, she told it.

He leaned his upper body away from hers. From the waist down they were still fused. "Dana. Dana. Dana. Shit. I feel like I'm 15 again. I want to kiss you. All I've thought of since Margo called me week before last is kissing you. Can you believe that? I always regret-ted not doing it when we worked together. I always wanted to, you know." He laughed.

She traced the outline of his jaw with her fingers, then eased his face down to hers. She stopped when their mouths were less than an inch apart. "So kiss me," she whispered.

He did. Like no one had ever kissed her before. Ever. She felt like she was melting into him in a kaleidoscope of swirling colors. Everything in his heart was revealed to her somehow and she *knew* that everything in hers was revealed to him. She felt his loneliness, his longing. She felt his desire for her most of all and it lit her up. Her every nerve ending was on fire. Her heart swelled and convulsed with a joy she'd never dreamed possible. Her mind and body reeled together in ecstasy. For the first time in her life, she felt truly loved. Complete. Cherished. Perfect. This was better than sex. Better than the best love songs, the best love stories. Better than anything.

Eventually, they tore their mouths apart. Their bodies were still locked together. They were panting.

Todd looked at her, his eyes soft and gentle. He laid her down on the mat and unfastened her bathing suit top. His hands moved to her breasts and he began to massage her nipples. His was the most exquisite, tender—yet insistent touch she'd ever felt. She moaned and shivered uncontrollably. "I don't think I've ever been so excited in my life," he said.

She opened her eyes. "Oh my God," she whispered. She wanted him so bad. "Me too. I haven't had sex in over a year. I haven't had *good sex* in so long I can't remember. Oh, Todd...."

"Shhh." He touched her lips with his index finger. "I love you, you know," he whispered. "I've loved you for *years."* He stopped talking and touched the sensitive skin inside her left ear ever-so-lightly with his tongue. She shuddered against him. "I didn't want to be a rebound after your marriage or after your relationship with that dee-jay guy ended." He rocked back on his heels. His fingers danced up and down her body. Smiling wickedly at her, he leaned down and ran his tongue up the calf of her right leg, all the way up her thigh. It was all she could do not to scream.

"Todd..." she whispered back. "Take my pants off. Please. Now...."

"You better love me," he whispered to her left ear as he slid her bathing suit bottoms off. "You better."

"I do. I do. I do. I think I always loved you too. I just wasn't ready to see it."

"Are you ready now?"

She helped him remove his trunks. "Oh yes," she moaned. "Yes. Please. Yes...."

EPILOGUE   **Todos Santos,**
                               Baja California Sur
                               November 6, 1997

"Camille? Barb?"

"Yeah?"

"Yeah?"

"Come with me down to the water. I wanna go boogie boarding. I wanna make a drip castle. I wanna chase waves and hunt for sand crabs like a little kid. But I don't wanna go alone. Will you come?"

"You betcha," Camille said. "Let's do it." They lathered themselves up with sunscreen, grabbed boogie boards and headed down the dirt road toward the ocean.

"There is something enchanted about this place," Holly said as she kicked up little dust bunnies with her bare feet. "Do you feel it too?"

"I do," said Camille. "It revs up my creative engine. I played the piano for two hours straight at Todd's restaurant yesterday, remember?"

"I can't get that song you made up out of my head. Sing it again for me, will you?" asked Barb.

"Why certainly," Camille said with a grin. "It's called 'The Water's Edge,' by the way." She began to sing:

I went down to the water's edge
to see what the people do.

They take a chance
they make romance.
They remember how to care
They want to stay
forever there.

I went down to the water's edge
to see what the people do.
I went down to the water's edge
to see what the people do.

They move real slow
and they don't know
what the next moment brings.
They play maracas and sing.
They have a burning desire
and a soul full of fire.

I went down to the water's edge
to see what the people do.
I went down to the water's edge
to see what the people do.

They smile at me
as if they understand
my need to be free.
They accept me
for who I am
we proceed cautiously. [3]

As she finished with the chorus, Holly and Barb were already clapping. "I love it," said Holly. "You've got to record it."

"I want to record it here. At the same studio where Chris Isaak recorded 'Baja Sessions.' Todd's offered to set me up with some of his musician friends. A rhythm guitar and some conga drums. That's all I need. But we'd have to stay an extra day."

"Dana won't mind," said Barb. "That's for sure."

Holly touched her on the shoulder. "I think you'd be a fool not to go for it," she said.

"You mean we can stay?!"

"You betcha."

Camille let out a whoop of joy and rushed ahead of them to the beach.

"I'm glad we're staying. I keep walking around, checking out the light, trying to *feel* what all those artists are talking about," said Barb to Holly as they followed her. "I don't quite get it...."

"Follow me," Holly said. "I think I can help you there." For the first time since they'd left San Diego she felt at peace with herself. She no longer felt resentful or left out. She didn't feel either superior or inferior to anyone. She was Holly Malone—ecotour guide and author-to-be. Confused, cheating wife of Rick Nichols. Would this fourth marriage of hers survive? she asked herself. She had to admit that although she hoped so, she honestly didn't know—and she was okay with not knowing. For now. She'd seen Camille end an unhealthy marriage after *months* of agonizing, and she'd watched Dana and Todd fall head over heels in love. They were amazing. Never in her life had she seen two people who were so in love or so well-suited to one another. Yet both had been alone awhile—Todd almost as long as Dana. She knew this, because she'd been his last lover, back in the summer of '95.

If she was really honest with herself, Holly had to admit she'd intended to reclaim Todd for a fling while she was here in town. She'd come really close to throwing a fit when she saw him and Dana waltz into the bar of the Hotel California—draped all over each other and reeking of sex—just after sunset two days ago. But what she saw in Dana's eyes was mirrored in Todd's. It was real and it stopped her dead in her tracks.

They were at the beach. Holly took off her shorts and top and walked toward the water. A lone pelican drifted over the top of a cresting wave, heading south. She spun around. The mountains behind her rose up like pale purple monoliths. The ocean in front of her rushed out to claim her as its own child. She stood in the knee-deep surf and waited for a set of smaller waves. Barb was right next to her. Camille was already out there. She jumped on her board and paddled for all she was worth to the smoother water beyond the breakers. She caught wave after wave with them and rode each one all the way into shore.

On the upstairs patio of the Cafe Todos Artes, Holly and Dana stood together. They looked out over the rooftops and treetops toward the ocean and watched as the sun dropped into the sea. They could see the mission church and plaza in the golden light and hear the ringing of the church bells as it mingled with the chanting of evening mass.

"We leave day after tomorrow. Can you handle it? Or are you tempted to bail on us and fly home in a week?"

Dana gave her a long, hard look. "I'm not bailing, as much as my heart is begging me to. I signed on for this trip just like the rest of you did and I'm in for the duration. I've enjoyed every minute of it, although I do have to admit that the last three days have been the happiest of my entire life." She stopped and smiled. "He told me about you guys. Thanks for being so cool about it...."

Holly smiled. "It's obvious that you two aren't anything even resembling a fling. So how in the world will you manage to spend time together?"

Just then Todd came upstairs, balancing a tray laden with guacamole, chips, a pitcher of Margaritas and three salt-rimmed glasses. "There you are," he said and kissed Dana on the tip of her nose. "I heard the question, Hol. We're still working that part out. Go ahead and tell her what you told me, Dana."

He filled Dana's glass. She took a sip and began to speak. "This is how I see it. I've raised my daughters by myself for the past seven years—since they were six years old. I have five more years to go until they're out of the house. It gets harder, not easier, as our kids age to bring a new man into the fold. I know this for a fact. I saw what Camille went through trying to do the whole blended family thing. Even if Todd lived in Encinitas, I'm not so sure I'd want to go that route. A husband deserves to be number one in his wife's life. When he marries a woman with kids, he finds himself in competition with the kids for their mom's affection—whether he wants to be or not. The kids were there first and—nine out of 10 times—they feel threatened. The woman, like Camille, ends up being torn in half. Unless the man and kids bond at the heart and soul level, and he loves them as though they were his own—everyone's in for a rough ride."

Todd looked at Holly. "Help me out here, Hol. That goes along with what I've seen, for the most part. I've dated too many women with kids over the years not to know that it can be tricky, but I keep telling Dana that I've known her kids since they were in first grade. I refuse to believe it will be a problem for us."

Dana looked out over the tree tops to the ocean. "The night before we left on this trip, I lay in bed awake for the longest time. My brain was in overdrive. I kept wondering why Baja draws me to itself like a magnet. I kept wondering what lessons were in store for me on this trip. I wondered if I'd always be alone because I was too scared and too broken to trust any man enough to let him near me. I wondered why my dad had died so suddenly and whether I'd ever be okay with that. I am okay, and I have the answers to most of those questions now. The only thing I don't get is why I feel more at home here, in Mexico, than I do in my own country. But you know what?" Her eyes teared up and she put her glass down. She put a hand on each of their arms. "I realize, finally, that I don't have to know exactly why I love it here so much. I just *do* and that's enough. I love you, Todd—more than I've ever loved anyone in my whole life—and that's enough too. For now."

"How can you say that? Won't you miss each other terribly?"

Dana nodded. "Of course. Don't you miss Rick?"

Holly shrugged. "To tell the truth—most of the time I don't."

"Well. I've been telling myself for *years* that I'm not in the market for a husband at this point in my life. I can't move down here because I wouldn't send my girls to live with Brad. I'd never ask Todd to leave his restaurant and move back to the States." She stopped talking, leaned over and kissed Todd on the mouth. "I'm not a bit afraid of having a long-distance relationship. We'll see each other over Christmas vacation for sure, 'cause the Braggs have already invited me to Cabo. We can e-mail each other every day. It'll work out, right Todd?"

He looked at her with adoring, twinkling eyes. "I have family stateside too. I can come up for summers...."

"I'll miss him, Holly. No doubt about that. But my life is incredibly busy up north. I won't have an ounce of trouble being faithful. I've spent the better part of the last seven years without sex. I've been cheated on too many times in my life not to know how badly it hurts. I would *never* do that to Todd."

"I'd never cheat on you either, Dana," Todd said. He looked back at Holly. His eyes were still twinkling. "Not only do I love this lady with my whole heart, but I'm a monogamous kinda guy. You were the last woman I was with, Hol, and that was over two years ago. It hurt like hell when you left. Especially when you married Rick less than six months later."

"I'm sorry I hurt you," she whispered, as she felt her fight-or-flight reflex kick in. She gripped onto the thick plaster wall to keep herself from running downstairs and disappearing into the gathering darkness. Then she flashed on what Camille had said to Drew that night on the beach and felt herself relaxing. She took a deep breath. "Where men are concerned, I think I've always put my brain on ice and led with my libido. That and my fears. I haven't made the most intelligent choices in that arena."

"Boy can I relate," said Camille as she and Barb came up the stairs.

"Me too, actually," said Dana. "Except that for the last few years—since my divorce—I've put my libido on ice because I didn't trust it anymore! It's all a variation on the same theme—ya know?"

A waiter came upstairs and told Todd in Spanish that there were people below ordering food.

He winked at Dana and grinned. "You ready to get to work, my lady?" he asked.

She winked and grinned back. "Oh yes, mi capitán, I am."

"Well, you know the drill. We're ready. *Mise en plac*—everything's in its place. Let's roll."

APPENDIX I   *Recipes from COOKING WITH BAJA MAGIC—*
                   Mouth-Watering Meals from the Enchanted
                   Kitchens and Campfires of Baja—by Ann Hazard

AUTHENTIC BAJA MARGARITAS

These Margaritas are the real thing. No mix. Serve them on the rocks
or blended, whichever way you prefer. One blender serves four.

4 ounces tequila
4 ounces Mexican Controy (Cointreau or Triple Sec may be substi-
tuted)
juice from 10 - 12 Mexican limes, freshly squeezed
crushed ice to top of blender
Margarita salt (optional)

Place tequila, Controy, lime juice in blender. Fill until almost full with
crushed ice. Shake well or blend until very slushy. Wet rim of marti-
ni or Margarita glass with water and swirl in small dish of salt. Pour
Margarita into the glass. ¡Olé!

STUFFED CLAMS ON THE GRILL

This recipe comes from the Palapa Azul—one of the must-try restaurants at the end of the paved road on Tecolote Beach just outside of La Paz. Serves four.

16 Pismo, chocolate or queen clams in their shells
4 tbsp butter
6 - 12 fresh jalapeños, finely diced
2 cups Cheddar cheese, cut into small cubes
2 large white onions, finely diced
2 large tomatoes, finely diced
1 tsp garlic powder
2 Mexican limes, quartered
1 cup ham, finely diced
salt and pepper to taste

Remove the clams from their shells and dice into small pieces. Mix together in bowl with jalapeños, cheese, onion, tomatoes, garlic powder, lime juice and ham. Add salt and pepper to taste and scoop back into each of the 16 clam shells. Wrap each shell in aluminum foil and place over hot coals on the grill. Cook four minutes on each side.

CEVICHE

Ceviche originated in places where seafood was plentiful but refrigeration rare. This appetizer is light, low in calories and has become popular all over California, Baja and mainland Mexico because of its subtle but spicy taste. Serves six to eight, depending on their appetites.

2 pounds cubed white fish or bay scallops, raw
5 - 10 fresh serrano or jalapeño chiles (very hot), diced
1 red bell pepper, diced
1 green bell pepper, diced
1 onion, diced
3 ripe tomatoes, diced
1 - 2 cloves garlic, minced
2 avocados, peeled and diced
1 bunch cilantro, with stems removed and diced
1 tsp brown sugar

salt and pepper to taste
2 cups lime juice
1/2 cup lemon juice
tortilla chips or saltine crackers

In a large bowl combine all ingredients. Toss gently but thoroughly, making sure all fish is coated with lemon-lime mixture.

Cover and refrigerate a minimum of two hours, stirring occasionally. Fish should become quite white and scallops will lose translucent appearance. (Once this happens, you will know that the lemon juice has "cooked" them and they are okay to eat.) Serve in a bowl with chips or saltines.

PACIFIC RIM FLAUTAS

This recipe is Marc Spahr's—real-life owner of the Caffé Todos Santos. He marinates them in coconut milk with a hint of curry and are they ever good! Serves four.

4 boneless, skinless chicken breasts
12 flour small flour tortillas
2 cups fresh (if possible) coconut milk
1/8 tsp curry powder
1 cup corn or canola oil
1 head Romaine lettuce, shredded
1 cup Cheddar cheese, shredded
1 cup tomatoes, chopped
1 cup guacamole (recipe on page 259)
1 cup sour cream
1/4 cup Parmesan cheese, grated
salt and pepper to taste
Mango Salsa Tropical (recipe follows)

Simmer chicken in coconut milk until cooked through. Set aside to cool and marinate for about an hour. Then shred chicken and place in bowl with curry and just enough coconut milk to wet. Mix well, adding salt and pepper to taste. Roll chicken in tortilla tightly and fasten shut with a toothpick. Fry in oil just until tortilla is golden brown. Drain on paper towels.

Place three flautas on each plate and cover each serving with shredded Romaine, tomatoes and cheese. Add guacamole and sour cream sauce. Sprinkle with Parmesan cheese and serve with Mango Salsa Tropical.

MANGO SALSA TROPICAL

This unusual, spicy-sweet salsa—also created by Marc Spahr—is best when made with all fresh ingredients. Serve with Pacific Rim Flautas or try it spooned over grilled chicken breasts, red snapper, or with carnitas.

1/2 cup mango, chopped
1/2 cup pineapple, chopped
1/4 cup papaya, chopped
2 tsp vinegar
2 tbsp water
1/4 tsp salt
2 cups tomatoes, chopped
1/2 cup white onion, chopped
1/2 cup cilantro, chopped
1/2 cup serrano chile, chopped

Mix all ingredients This should make about two jars of salsa. It's best if refrigerated at least eight to hours and will keep for several days in the refrigerator.

SALSA FRESCA

A construction laborer doubling as a chef shared this recipe several years ago in Spanish during a Christmas party. The ingredients may be varied, depending on how hot you like your salsa. If you're unsure, experiment. If your salsa turns out too spicy, add more tomatoes. If it's too mild, add more jalapeños or yellow guero chiles.

5 - 10 fresh jalapeño (small, green, very hot) chiles
5 - 10 fresh guero (small, yellow, very hot) chiles
2 - 5 fresh Anaheim chiles (long, green, mild)

10-12 medium-sized tomatoes
2 onions
4 garlic cloves
1 large bunch cilantro
1 1/2 tbsp beef bouillon powder
1 tsp lemon juice

Wash all chiles and tomatoes and remove stems. In a large Dutch oven, place chiles and tomatoes in about one inch water. Bring to boil and simmer for two to three minutes.

Remove from stove and cool for a few minutes. When you can handle the chile mixture, drain off about half the water and mince, by hand or in the food processor. Put all minced chiles and tomatoes in a large bowl. Dice onions and garlic in food processor and stir into chile mixture. Wash cilantro and cut off the longest portion of the stems. Dice remaining part of the plant in the food processor. Stir into salsa.

Add lemon juice and bouillon. Stir well. Place in quart size jars and refrigerate. Depending on quantities of chiles and tomatoes you use, this should make two to three jars of salsa. It's best if refrigerated at least 8-12 hours and will keep for several days in the refrigerator.

FIFTEEN BEAN CHILI

This is as hot as any Texas chili, especially if you go heavy on the New Mexico chile powder or chipotles. While its claim to fame is the 15 different kinds of beans, the chili's intense heat has raised more furor among dinner guests than its originality. There have been many whose foreheads have broken into a sweat over the years as they poured glass after glass of water down their blistered throats. (Well, maybe not quite that bad!)

Hint: If, like 99 per cent of the world, you prefer your chili milder than that, just leave out the New Mexico chiles. Or go light on the chipotles. Taste it as you go along, adding chiles very slowly.

A pot of this chili will last you a few days. If you serve it up for a crowd, as long as you keep it on the mellow side, you will be praised. Serves six to eight.

1 1/2 pounds lean ground beef
1 1/2 pounds smoked turkey sausage, ground
2 large onions, chopped
3 garlic cloves, minced
1 16 ounce bag "15 bean soup" (beans only)
1/4 cup American chili powder
New Mexico chile powder or chipotle chiles in adobo, pureed and to taste (optional)
1 tbsp salt
1 tsp pepper
2 1 pound 12 ounce can Italian tomatoes in puree
2 tbsp oregano

Garnish:
2 cups grated cheddar cheese and 1 chopped onion

Soak beans overnight according to directions on package. Drain and rinse thoroughly in collander. In Dutch oven, brown beef, pork, onion and garlic. Drain off excess fat. Add beans and all remaining ingredients and bring to boil over high heat. Reduce heat, cover and simmer for at least two hours or until beans are tender and all flavors well-blended. Serve in bowls and garnish with grated cheese and chopped onion. Add a dozen or so hot, buttered tortillas to round out the meal.

GUACAMOLE & CHIPS

Guac:
3 - 4 ripe avocados
2 tsp lemon juice
1 large tomato, diced
1/2 bunch green onions, chopped
1 tsp garlic powder or 2 garlic cloves, minced
1 tsp salt
1/2 tsp pepper
1 - 4 tbsp salsa verde (to desired spiciness)
1/4 cup grated Mexican queso cacique or feta cheese
1 large black olive

Chips:
1 dozen corn tortillas
1/2 cup corn or canola oil
salt to taste

To make the Guac: Slice avocados in half and remove seed. Scoop avocado pulp out of the skin using a spoon. Mash avocados in a medium-sized bowl. Add lemon juice, diced tomatoes, green onions, garlic, salt and pepper. Add salsa verde to taste. Stir well, but stop while it's still slightly lumpy. Refrigerate, covered until ready to use. Can be made up to three hours in advance.

To make Chips: Slice tortillas into eight pie-shaped wedges. Heat oil in frying pan until a drop of water sizzles when dropped into the oil. Cook tortilla wedges about one to two minutes, browning on both sides. Remove from pan and drain on paper towels. Lightly salt. These can be made up to three hours in advance.

To serve, place guacamole in a bowl in the center of a round serving dish. Garnish with shredded cheese and olive. Surround with chips. Feel free to substitute packaged tortilla chips, made from either yellow or blue corn. This Baja staple feeds four to six.

SWIM-UP BAR PIÑA COLADAS

This blender-made version is less heavy and calorie-laden than Mexican Piña Coladas, but it's just as delicious. Try these and you'll see yourself lounging under a palm tree next to the surf. Serves four.

6 ounces light rum
2 cups pineapple-coconut juice
Ice to top of blender
Pineapple slices for garnish
dash of nutmeg

Pour rum and juice in blender. Fill to top with ice. Blend until very slushy. Pour into tall glasses and garnish with pineapple slices.

ANITA-CONCHITA'S CHICKEN MOLE

There really was an Ernesto and his grandmother's mole recipe really was a gift given in exchange for attending a time-share breakfast in Los Cabos! Serves six.

12 filets of boneless, skinless chicken breasts
1/2 cup butter or margarine
1 onion, finely chopped
1/2 green pasilla, ancho or Anaheim chile, finely chopped
1/2 tsp pepper
4 cloves garlic, minced
1   17 1/2 ounce can tomato puree
1   1/2 cups beef bouillon
2 tbsp sugar
1 tsp American chili powder
1/4 tsp ground cinnamon
1/4 tsp ground nutmeg
1/4 tsp ground cloves
1 tsp sesame seeds
1 tbsp ground almonds
1 - 2 tsp hot pepper sauce
1 dark chocolate candy bar (about 4 ounces)
4 tbsp cold water with 2 tbsp corn starch

In large skillet, brown chicken slowly in butter. Remove chicken and add onion, bell pepper, pepper and garlic. Cook until tender. Add tomatoes, beef bouillon, sugar, chili powder, cinnamon, nutmeg, cloves, hot pepper sauce and chocolate. Add chicken, cover and reduce heat. Simmer until chicken is tender, about 50 minutes. Remove chicken to a serving platter and keep warm.

Slowly blend cold water into cornstarch. Pour into sauce and cook, stirring constantly until sauce is thickened. Spoon over chicken and serve.

SALSA RANCHERA—PANCHO VILLA STYLE

This recipe comes from the highly acclaimed Restaurant Pancho's in Cabo San Lucas. It's used in their Tortilla Soup recipe (following). You can also spoon it over fried eggs and tortillas to make Huevos Rancheros or serve it over omelettes, grilled chicken or turkey breasts.

4 whole green peppers, thinly sliced
8 large, ripe tomatoes, thinly sliced
2 large, white onions, thinly sliced

2 tbsp dried or fresh oregano, or to taste
6 bay leaves
6 tbsp powdered chicken bouillon (they use Knorr Suiza in Cabo)
4 tbsp olive oil
fresh ground black pepper to taste
salt to taste

Place peppers, onions and tomatoes in large skillet with the oil and saute until cooked. Add the seasonings and bouillon and cook about a half hour. Adjust seasonings and set aside. This recipe makes enough for 12 servings of soup.

PANCHO'S TORTILLA SOUP

This Mexican favorite comes to you from Restaurant Pancho's in Cabo San Lucas. When the owner, Mary Bragg, was asked what she was most famous for, she didn't hesitate one second before telling me, "Why our Tortilla Soup. Of course." She was right on. Serves six.

1/2 chicken
2 quarts water
salt, pepper and other seasonings to taste
12 corn tortillas, cut into strips about 1/2 inch wide
1/2 cup corn or canola oil
2 avocados, cut into chunks
1 1/2 cup Chihuahua or Jack cheese, grated
6 cups of Salsa Ranchera (see recipe preceding)
1 cup sour cream
 fresh cilantro, in sprigs

Cook half chicken well seasoned with water for one hour. Remove chicken and cut into chunks.
Deep fry the tortilla chips and drain on paper towels. Divide among six large soup bowls Place chunks of chicken, avocado and grated cheese in each bowl. Pour one cup of salsa ranchera and one cup of chicken broth into each bowl. Float a bit of sour cream on top and garnish with cilantro sprig. Serve immediately and prepare to gloat!

MARC'S CITRUS FLAN EXTRAORDINAIRE

If you ever are so fortunate as to find yourself in Todos Santos, make sure you stop in to see Marc Spahr at Caffé Todos Santos and order this dessert. It really is to-die-for. Serves eight.

Coffee Caramel:
1/2 cup sugar
1/4 cup Espresso

Flan:
2 cups milk
1 cup heavy cream
1 cinnamon stick (4 inches long)
1 tbsp citrus zest (lemon, Mexican lime and/or orange)
1 tbsp pure vanilla extract
1/4 tsp nutmeg (fresh, grated)
1 cup sugar
6 egg yolks
3 eggs
1/8 tsp salt

Coffee Caramel:
In a small copper saucepan, mix sugar and coffee. Cook over medium heat, stirring only until sugar is dissolved. Then cook until syrup forms a soft ball when dropped into ice water. (If you have a candy thermometer, this happens at about 238° F) Pour mixture into mold— a nine-inch round, two-inch deep cake pan works well. Let the syrup set up in refrigerator while making flan.

Flan:
Preheat oven to 325°. In medium saucepan, combine milk, cream, vanilla, nutmeg, cinnamon stick and zests. Cook until almost boiling on low heat, stirring, constantly. Pour mixture through fine sieve into a bowl. In another bowl, whisk together eggs, egg yolks, salt and sugar. Pour milk mixture slowly into egg mixture, whisking constantly.

Remove mold with caramel from refrigerator and pour flan into it. Set this mold inside a larger mold (a ten-inch round cake pan works) filled a quarter of the way up with water. Bake for one hour. Remove from oven and refrigerate for four hours.

To serve, loosen edges with a knife and invert onto a platter. Cut flan into eight wedges.

APPENDIX II: *WHERE TO GET INFORMATION*
on Baja California

BY PHONE: Call **Discover Baja Travel Club** at 1-800-727-BAJA
In San Diego call 619-275-4225

ON THE WEB: The following list of websites is offered in alphabetical order. Although the list is not all-inclusive, several sites have search engine capabilities. All sites offer hyperlinks to related Baja sites.

Amazon.com—www.amazon.com
World's largest bookseller stocks all Baja books mentioned in this novel, plus all Baja books currently in print.

Amigos de Baja's Baja Net—
www.geocities.com/TheTropics/4888/index.html
Road and fishing updates, bulletin board, recipe exchange and more.

Baja California Travel Resource Guide—www.escapist.com/baja
Research and book whale-watching, kayaking, scuba tours, etc.

Baja Destinations—www.BajaDestinations.com
New, interactive online magazine offers comprehensive information on Baja.

Baja Life Magazine—www.bajalife.com/maghome.htm
Online version of picturesque, informative Baja Life Magazine.

Bajalinks—www.bajalinks.com/index.html
Extensive index linking to Baja websites in wide array of categories.

Baja Quest—www.bajaquest.com/index.html
Online publication with up-to-date info on Baja, plus a large search engine.

Discover Baja Travel Club—www.discoverbaja.com
Lowest cost Mexican insurance, newsletter, member discounts, whale trips, ecotours and more—online.

MEXICO OnLINE—www.mexonline.com/websites.htm
Directory and search engine for business, travel, culture and real estate in Mexico.

San Diego Natural History Museum—www.sdnhm.org
Offers classes, lectures and articles about Baja, plus exciting ecotours.

APPENDIX III:
BAJA RESTAURANTS and HOTELS of Baja—
in Order of Appearance

Index	Page
Tío Pablo's Restaurante—Los Barriles, BCS	5
La Fonda Hotel and Restaurant —La Misión, BC	66
Hussong's Cantina—Ensenada, BC	69
Estero Beach Resort—Ensenada, BC	73
Hotel La Pinta—San Quintín, BC	86
Cielito Lindo Hotel and RV Park—San Quintín, BC	87, 95
Pete's Camp and Cantina—San Felipe, BC	89
Mama Espinosa's—El Rosario, BC	107
Hotel La Pinta—Cataviña, BC	110
Rancho Santa Ynez RV Park and Restaurant—Cataviña, BC	111
Guillermo's—Bahía de los Angeles, BC	126
Malarrimo Hotel, RV Park and Restaurant— Guerrero Negro, BCS	131
El Padrino Restaurant and RV Park—San Ignacio, BCS	132
Hotel La Pinta—San Ignacio, BCS	132
El Boleo Bakery—Santa Rosalía, BCS	161
Hotel Francés—Santa Rosalía, BCS	161
Las Palmas RV Park—Santa Rosalía, BCS	161
San Lucas Cove RV Park—Santa Rosalía, BCS	161
Villa María Isabel RV Park—Mulegé, BCS	173
Hotel Serenidad—Mulegé, BCS	181
Las Casitas Hotel and Restaurant—Mulegé, BCS	181
Jungle Jim's—Mulegé, BCS	181
Playa Santispac—Bahía Concepción, BCS	181
Posada Concepción—Bahía Concepción, BCS	181,182
Eco Mundo Center—Bahía Concepción, BCS	181,183
Playa Armenta—Bahía Concepción, BCS	182
Hotel La Pinta—Loreto, BCS	186
Hotel La Misión—Loreto, BCS	186
Diamond Eden Resort—Loreto, BCS	186
Plaza Loreto—Loreto, BCS	186
Villas de Loreto—Loreto, BCS	186
Loreto Shores and RV Park—Loreto, BCS	186
McLuLu's Fish Tacos—Loreto, BCS	186
Hotel Los Arcos—La Paz, BCS	203
Bacho's Restaurante—La Paz, BCS	203

Index   **Page**

La Paz Lapas—La Paz, BCS, ...205
La Palapa Azul—Playa Tecolote, La Paz, BCS 207,254
Tío Pablo's—Los Barriles, BCS 210
Hotel Palmas de Cortez—Los Barriles, BCS 220
Hotel Playa del Sol—Los Barriles, BCS 220
Hotel Punta Colorado—La Ribera, BCS 220
Hotel Buena Vista Beach Resort—Buena Vista, BCS 221
Planet Hollywood—Cabo San Lucas, BCS...........................226
Hard Rock Cafe—Cabo San Lucas, BCS 226
Hotel Finisterra—Cabo San Lucas, BCS 226
Hotel Solmar––Cabo San Lucas, BCS 226
Hotel Pueblo Bonito—Cabo San Lucas, BCS 226
Hotel Cabo San Lucas—Cabo San Lucas, BCS 226
Hotel Palmilla—Cabo San Lucas, BCS 226
Hotel Westin Regina—Los Cabos, BCS 226,233
Hotel Melía Cabo Real—Los Cabos, BCS 226
Club Cascadas de Baja—Cabo San Lucas, BCS 226
The Bungalows Breakfast Inn—Cabo San Lucas, BCS 226
Club Cabo RV Park—Cabo San Lucas, BCS 227
Vagabundos del Mar RV Park—Cabo San Lucas, BCS........227
The Office Restaurant—Cabo San Lucas, BCS 229
Restaurant Pancho's—Cabo San Lucas, BCS 229,260,261
Carlos and Charlie's—Cabo San Lucas, BCS 234
The Giggling Marlin—Cabo San Lucas, BCS 234
Hotel Hacienda—Cabo San Lucas, BCS 234
Caffé Todos Santos—Todos Santos, BCS 236,239-241,255,262
Cafe Santa Fe—Todos Santos, BCS 236
Hotel California—Todos Santos, BCS 236,241
Todos Santos Inn—Todos Santos, BCS 237
Tecolote Libros—Todos Santos, BCS 238

APPENDIX IV: *REAL PEOPLE of Baja*

Index	Page
Francisco Muñoz—San Diego, CA and Bahía de Los Angeles, BC	40,41,129
The León Family, La Bufadora, BC	76
Don Abel—San Ignacio, BCS	132
Francisco Mayoral—San Ignacio, BCS	135-138
Pepe Murietta—Cabo Pulmo, BCS	220
Bobby Van Wormer—Los Barriles and La Ribera, BCS	220
Chuy and Imelda Valdez—Buena Vista, BCS	221
John and Mary Bragg—Cabo San Lucas, BCS	229-232,260,261
Charles Stewart—Todos Santos, BCS	237
Ezio and Paula Columbo—Todos Santos, BCS	237
Gabo—Todos Santos, BCS	237
Michael Cope—Todos Santos, BCS	238
Jeanne Córdoba—Todos Santos, BCS	238
Marc Spahr—Todos Santos, BCS	239-241,255,256,262

APPENDIX V: *Baja Books Mentioned*

Index   **Page**

Automobile Club of Southern California: *Baja California*....... 61
Crosby, Harry: *The Cave Paintings of Baja*.................................. 114
Gardner, Erle Stanley: *Hovering over Baja*.................................. 42
              Off The Beaten Track in Baja.................. 41
              The Hidden Heart of Baja.......................
42,114   ....
Hazard, Ann: *Cooking With Baja Magic*..42
Jones, Fred and Gloria: *Baja Camping*   42
Kira, Gene and Kelly, Neil: *The Baja Catch*.................................. 42
Peterson, Walt: *The Baja Adventure Book*...42
Potter, Ginger: *The Baja Book IV*   42

ORDER FORM

Renegade Enterprises Order Form

Cartwheels in the Sand by Ann Hazard $14.95
Cooking with Baja Magic by Ann Hazard $21.95

Four easy ways to order:
1. Phone orders: 619-259-9122 (Pacific Time)
2. Fax orders: 619-259-9122
3. E-mail: cookbaja@aol.com
4. Mail: Renegade Enterprises
   P.O. Box 1505
   Solana Beach, CA 92075

	Quantity Each	Total Cost
Cooking with Baja Magic	_____	_____
Cartwheels in the Sand	_____	_____
Subtotal		_____
Shipping & Handling $3.95 per book (continental US)		_____
Add Sales Tax for delivery to CA: 7.75%		_____
TOTAL AMOUNT		_____

Enclosed is my check, money order or credit card information for the amount of: $ _____ payable to RENEGADE ENTERPRISES

_____Check/Money Order _____ Master Card _____Visa _____ Am/Ex

Account # _____Expiration Date _____

Signature _____

Send book(s) to:
Name _____
Street Address_____
City/State/Zip _____
Daytime phone_____
E-mail (optional)_____